Major Bible Doctrines

Sam A. Smith

Biblical Reader Communications

Major Bible Doctrines

First print edition: August 2010, updated January 2014

Published by
Biblical Reader Communications (www.biblicalreader.com)
Raleigh, N.C.

In cooperation with **CreateSpace**

Library of Congress Cataloging-in-Publication Data

Smith, Sam A.

   Major Bible Doctrines / Sam A. Smith

   Includes bibliographic references (p. 387-391).

   ISBN: 9781453720653
          1453720650

   1. Theology. 2. Doctrinal.

   BT75.3.S65 2010

A PDF edition is published online by Biblical Reader Communications (www.biblicalreader.com).

Contents

Preface

Many factors influence one's theology, and it would be impossible to document all of the influences in my own theological development over the past forty years. The thoughts of others have been folded into my own thoughts time and again. In writing this volume I briefly considered trying to trace the development of my theological notes so that proper credit could be given to whom it is due. However, the impracticality of that is readily apparent.

This is not a new academic work; if it were, it would be thoroughly documented and footnoted, with a great deal more development than the reader will find here. This is simply a compilation of my basic teaching notes on Bible doctrine that have developed by accretion over the past forty years. However, I would like to acknowledge some works that have proven to be useful to me, and important in my own theological development. As the one who takes the time to check will find, many of the ideas expressed in this volume have been adapted from these sources, and those authors are due all the credit for their ideas. The only credit that I will take for myself in this volume is for making this material more freely available for people, who like myself, long to understand the message of the Bible. The following works (listed alphabetically) have been depended upon heavily in the development of this material: *A Systematic Theology of the Christian Religion* by J. Oliver Buswell, *Basic Theology* by Charles Ryrie, *Christian Theology* by Millard Erickson, *Dogmatic Theology* by William G.T. Shedd, *Evangelical Dictionary of Theology* edited by Walter A. Elwell, *Evidence that Demands a Verdict* and *More Evidence that Demands a Verdict* by Josh McDowell, *Lectures in Systematic Theology* by Henry C. Thiessen, *Major Bible Themes* by Lewis S. Chafer and John F. Walvoord, *Practical Theology* by Floyd

H. Barackman, *Systematic Theology* by Lewis S. Chafer, *Systematic Theology* by Louis Berkhof, and *Things to Come* by J. Dwight Pentecost. In addition to these works, I would also like to acknowledge the contributions of my professors of Bible and theology in college and seminary, especially Dr. Raymond Gingrich and Dr. Kenneth McKinley at LeTourneau College, and Dr. John F. Walvoord and Dr. Robert Lightener at Dallas Theological Seminary.

Some aspects of a truth only become apparent when seen within the broader context. Regrettably, there seems to be a diminished emphasis today on the systematic study of Bible doctrine. As a result, many Christians embrace a collection of doctrines that they "feel good" about, but which are fundamentally incompatible.

There are probably no two theologians that agree on everything, but even in disagreement we can find the views of others to be food for thought in the pursuit of truth. Knowing why we disagree can be immensely helpful in giving definition to our own beliefs. In fact, in the history of theology many of the great truths only came into focus through sharp disagreements. With that in mind the reader is encouraged not only to look for what he or she agrees with in this volume, but for what they disagree with, since that will prove to be the most challenging. In the end, we may still disagree, but for the one who takes this challenge seriously, at least they will know why. This work is not intended to be a complete theology; it is, as the name indicates, a presentation of major Bible doctrines. The reader will need to consult the standard theologies for more detailed information on some subjects.

Finally, I would like to say that this volume would have never been written were it not for the insistence of my wife, Gail. She has for many years urged me to write a work of this sort, and I have resisted on the grounds that many fine surveys of Bible doctrine already exist, and there is little use in plowing the same ground again. Nevertheless, her persistence has prevailed. Gail also volunteered to spend many hours editing the manuscript and making helpful suggestions. This book is offered in the hope that it will serve as a foundation for those just getting started, as well as those taking a new look at systematic Bible doctrine.

Sam A. Smith

Theology

The Nature and Possibility
of Theology

The possibility of knowing

Is it really possible to know anything about God, what he is doing, and what he wants? According to the Bible, the answer is "Yes." In fact, the message of the Bible presupposes that man can obtain and comprehend at least some knowledge of God and his acts, purposes, and plans. While it is more detailed than our present study will allow us to develop, the possibility of knowing anything about God is built upon three foundational truths.

1. Theism — that God exists
2. Revelation — that God has spoken
3. Epistemology — that it is possible for man to know some things, and thus to discern truth

It is interesting that Satan has always attacked on these three fronts in his warfare against man. He seeks to deny that God is, that God has spoken, or that man can be certain of what God has said. It was in each of these three areas that Satan aimed his attack upon Eve in the Garden. He attacked first in the area of epistemology; he worked to create doubt in Eve's mind as to whether she actually understood what God had said about eating from the tree (Genesis 3:1). Failing in that attack, he turned to two other tactics: outright contradiction of what God had revealed (3:4), and disparagement of God's motives (3:5) by implying that God selfishly did not want Eve to know that she could become like him. These are still the principal means Satan uses today to foster rebellion against God.

It is important to know what you believe

There are many reasons for developing a systematic understanding of biblical truth. Here are just a few of those reasons.

1. We can deal with organized information far more efficiently than with disorganized information.

2. Organization in itself has informational content, in that it shows relationships, and thus imparts new capacities to bare facts. When it comes to knowledge, the whole is greater than the sum of its parts.

3. Certain truths are difficult to understand in isolation. For example, election only makes sense in light of total depravity; impeccability is incomprehensible apart from the hypostatic union of Christ's divine and human natures in one person; inerrancy is dependent upon inspiration, the doctrine of the rapture of the Church presumes premillennialism and an understanding of the uniqueness of the Church.

4. Organization (systemization) contributes to more effective memory, communication, application, and defense of biblical truth.

As we embark on our study of major Bible doctrines there are a few important things to keep in mind.

1. The revelation of truth from God to man was progressive. Understandably, God began with simple concepts and moved to the more complex truths as man was ready to receive them. Because of the progressive nature of the revelation of truth, it is often necessary to follow the development of a truth through the Bible in order to understand how all the pieces fit together. One of the biggest pitfalls in the study of biblical truth is trying to understand the more highly developed truths without first understanding the more basic concepts. Since the basic

concepts are usually taught first, it is important to understand Old Testament truths before tackling New Testament truths. The biggest reason so many people are confused about the meaning of the New Testament is because they have little understanding of the Old Testament. To illustrate: "The gospel" is "the good news" (that's literally what the word means), but it's hard to fully appreciate the good news if one hasn't first understood the bad news!

2. Our knowledge of truth is incomplete. While God has revealed many things to us, he hasn't revealed everything. In fact, not only has he not revealed everything about everything, he hasn't even revealed everything about anything! We could get very frustrated over the fragmentary nature of our knowledge, but doing so wouldn't help much. We have to be content with what is obvious (*i.e.*, self-evident), and what God has revealed, and what we can properly infer (logically figure out, or deduce) from what we already know. Our knowledge may not be complete, but even incomplete knowledge can be immensely helpful. We don't need to know everything about something in order to know something. For example, I'm not an engineer, and I don't know how a microprocessor works at the physical level, but I was able to use a computer to produce this text, and that was very useful! The fact is, not only do we not have complete knowledge of any theological truths, we don't have complete knowledge of anything at all. Nevertheless, everything we learn helps us to some degree or another, at some time or another, and God has given us all that we need to know for now — we just have to learn it!

3. Biblical theology makes use of both induction and deduction. Induction is information that is either self-evident or given (categorical statements of truth in the Bible are examples of truth that can be known by induction; for example: Christ is coming back some day). Deduction is new information that can be properly inferred from what is

self-evident or what is given; for example: Since Christ is coming back (a fact given in the Bible), we need to be ready (a reasonable inference from the information given). In theology, induction is what the Bible plainly says, and deduction is what that information reasonably (logically) implies. Both induction and deduction are equally valid forms of knowledge as long as the induction is factually true and the deduction is proper (logical).

To illustrate the use of induction and deduction let's look at a classic example. The doctrine of the Trinity (that God is one divine being comprised of three distinct persons) is a truth derived from a combination of induction and deduction. As you may already know, there is no single statement in the Bible that says God is a trinity (the word "trinity" doesn't even appear in the Bible), or that he is "three-in-one," or any such equivalent phrase. So, how do we know that God is a trinity? We know this truth from a combination of induction and deduction. Here's how it works: We know (because we are told in the Bible) that there are three distinct persons who are God (the Father, 2 Cor. 1:2; the Son, Jn. 1:1-2; and the Holy Spirit, Acts 5:2-3). We are also told that there is one God (Deut. 6:4; Isa. 43:10; 44:6,8). These two pieces of information are known inductively from the Bible (*i.e.,* they are given). From these two sets of facts we can then logically infer that the God of the Bible must be one God existing as three persons. While this leaves us with many unanswered questions, we know that the doctrine of the Trinity must be correct since the underlying facts (the two inductions) are beyond dispute, and the inference (the deduction) is logically sound. Does that mean we know everything about the Trinity? Absolutely not! But we do know something about God, and something is better than nothing!

While it may seem cumbersome to go through these steps to derive a truth, a doctrine like the Trinity can only be known by this process. There are many other doctrines that are derived in the same way. Without the use of deduction in theology our understanding of God and his works would be far more limited. Nevertheless, the process is not without pitfalls. It is possible for two people using this process to arrive at incongruent conclusions. In such cases it is possible that one is right and the other wrong, or that both are wrong, or that both are partially right and partially wrong. (Obviously, both cannot be completely right if their conclusions disagree.) It is therefore necessary to carefully check to make sure our conclusions are valid; this means making sure that the facts we used are really facts, and the logic we used is really logical.

There are several questions we can ask ourselves to help us stay on track with the truth.

    a. Do I have the correct interpretation of all the passages that the conclusion is based on?

    b. Have I missed some significant and related information located somewhere else in the Bible?

    c. Is all of the logic that was used really logical?

    d. Are there other legitimate conclusions that could be drawn from the same information?

4. It is important to recognize that biblical theology is more than simply truth, it is connected truth. Think of it this way: Would you rather have all the parts to your dream car in a box (or boxes), or would you rather have it sitting in your driveway, engine purring and ready to go? Connected, related truth is always more useful than bits and pieces of disconnected truth. In doctrine, as in other endeavors, the whole is greater than the sum of its parts.

Review Questions

1. The possibility of knowing anything about God and his plans and purposes is based on what three propositions?

2. Briefly state three reasons for developing a systematic understanding of biblical truth.

3. What is meant by "progressive revelation"?

4. Explain why even incomplete knowledge can be useful.

5. Explain the difference between "induction" and "deduction" as it relates to biblical truth.

6. Give an example of the use of induction and deduction in the development of a doctrine.

7. What four questions should we ask ourselves in order to make sure we don't stray from the truth?

8. Why is connected truth more useful than isolated truth?

God: His Existence and Nature

The Existence of God

Unless God exists there's not much point in talking about Bible doctrine. So, how do we know that God exists?

Reasons people give for believing in God

Here are a few often heard reasons for belief in God. *Reason #1:* "My grandmother told me there is a God." Granted, grandmothers are an unusually good source of information; but really, how does she know for sure? *Reason #2:* "I can feel his presence." Okay, that's not entirely bad, but have your feelings always been one hundred percent accurate? Can you really trust your feelings with something this important? *Reason #3:* "The Bible says God exists." That's right, but if there is no God, then the Bible isn't true. *Reason #4:* "I've seen prayers answered." But, you've probably seen some requests go unfulfilled too. I once saw a TV clip where people claimed that touching a fertility statue enabled them to conceive—honest, I'm not making this up! Some couples that had been trying to have children for years claimed that shortly after they touched one of these figurines, they were able to conceive. One scientist, when asked how this could be simply said, "You only hear about the ones who conceived shortly afterward, but there may have been hundreds or thousands who touched the statues and didn't conceive; you don't hear about those." Offering answered prayer as evidence of God's existence is subject to the same criticism. That's not to say that answered prayer isn't important or significant, just that it's not a convincing proof of God's existence.

Arguments offered by atheists

When looking for evidence that God exists, the best place to start is to look at the arguments atheists use in their attempt to prove that God doesn't exist. Although these arguments are stated in many different ways, there are essentially five arguments that are commonly used. We will start with the strongest arguments and work toward the weakest.

The problem of evil

Statement of the argument: The existence of evil seems incompatible with the existence of an all-good, all-powerful God.

Explanation: If God were all good, he would want to do something about evil and the suffering associated with it. If he were all powerful, he would be able to do whatever he wanted to do. So, according to this argument, the fact that there is evil in the world demonstrates that the concept of an all-good, all-powerful God is illogical.

Problems with this argument:

1. It's illogical. If there is no God, there is no standard for determining what is good or evil; there is only "what is." Actually one cannot talk about evil unless there is good, and if there is no God, there is no good, just better or worse depending upon one's perspective. Interestingly, this argument actually presumes God's existence! (The connection between God and good has long been recognized; in English the word "God" is actually a contraction of "good.")

2. How does one know that God isn't doing something about evil? Is the world as bad as it possibly could be? The Bible says that God has done something about evil, that he is now doing something about evil, and will do more about evil in the future. How can the atheist be certain that what the Bible says God has done, is doing, and will do, isn't true?

3. This argument is built on the false assumption that an all-good, all-powerful God would deal with evil immediately.

However, the atheist gives no rationale for that assumption. In fact, if God dealt with evil immediately when it happened, he would have had to destroy mankind rather than redeem it. Redemption requires time, so when God chose to redeem his creation he necessarily chose to tolerate the existence of evil for a time. The argument from the existence of evil assumes that it would be more in the character of divine goodness for God to have destroyed his creation rather than to redeem it, but this is clearly an illogical assumption.

There is a natural explanation for every phenomenon

Statement of the argument: Man developed the idea of God to explain things he did not understand; someday science will be able to explain everything in purely natural (*i.e.*, non-supernatural) terms, so there is no longer a need for God.

Problems with this argument:

1. First, this argument assumes a naturalistic origin of religion; thus the entire argument is merely built on a naturalistic (atheistic) assumption. In order for the assumption to be true (that all religion has a purely natural origin), the conclusion must be true (that there is no God). Thus, this argument is merely circular reasoning (*i.e.*, God does not exist because he does not exist).

2. The premise that science will one day be able to explain everything in purely natural terms is highly doubtful, at best. Science can't even answer the most basic question of all: Why is there a universe, and how did it come into being? The "big bang" theory doesn't help the atheist either, since there is no way to know what came before the bang.

3. How could an atheist know that science will someday discover a natural cause for every phenomenon unless he or she has already excluded all possibilities other than the

natural? When the atheist puts forth this argument, they unwittingly make naturalism unfalsifiable, and therefore unscientific.

"God" is a meaningless word

Statement of the argument: The word "God" cannot be defined, and undefined terms are meaningless, so we can't talk intelligently about God.

The problem with this argument:

While we may not be able to define God completely, that does not mean that we cannot talk about him at all. We don't have to know everything about something to know something about something, and that's fortunate because if we had to know everything about something in order to know anything about it, we would never know anything at all, since we don't know everything about anything.

The failure of positive arguments for the existence of God

Statement of the argument: It is impossible to prove the existence of God.

The problem with this argument:

Even if it were true that the existence of God cannot be proven, that would not prove that God does not exist. God could still exist even if every argument for his existence were proven to be false. At best, this argument leads only to agnosticism, which doesn't help the atheist much.

The failure of religion

Statement of the argument: Religious people, including Christians, are often immoral, dishonest, and cruel; therefore, the actions of religious people argue against the existence of God, especially an all-good God as Christianity claims exists.

Problems with this argument:

1. It isn't fair, nor is it reasonable to judge Christianity by religion in general. Even Christians believe that most religion is corrupt, including Christianity when it deviates from biblical principles.

2. To the extent that those who claim to be Christians do not live holy lives, they are living inconsistent with the principles of the Bible; thus, their behavior is an indictment of themselves and their claim to be a Christian, not of biblical religion. In all fairness, if atheists are going to point to the sinful lives of those who profess to be Christians as evidence against the existence of God, they ought to recognize the testimonies of the many people who have lived lives of great personal sacrifice in the service of God as evidence for his existence. We could point out that there have also been some pretty notorious atheists (Joseph Stalin for example). Christianity does not claim that men will be perfected in this life, but that they can be forgiven and live less sinful lives by the power of God's presence within, and there is ample historical evidence to support that this has been the case in the lives of those who are sincerely devoted to Christ. No religion in the history of the world has done more to foster the principles of truth, justice, the protection of the weak and helpless, and the status of women, children, and minorities, than biblical religion. For a moment, forget about the actions of individuals of all religions, then ask the question, "What set of religious principles is responsible for more good than any other?" and the answer, if one is historically literate, will be "biblical religion." Compare the freedoms and institutions of those nations founded (imperfectly, of course) upon the principles of the Bible with those founded upon the principles of any other religion (including atheism) and the Bible wins hands down. Compare the status of women in the Christian world with the status of women in countries founded upon other religions, and biblical religion wins hands

down. Make a historical comparison of the voluntary individual charitable giving of those holding to biblical religion as compared to any other religion, and biblical religion wins hands down. Compare the number of hospitals, orphanages, educational institutions, and other works of kindness and charity founded by those holding to biblical religion over the past two thousand years, and biblical religion wins hands down. Atheists are fond of pointing to the cruelty of some of the crusades, and slavery as examples of the product of belief in the Bible (and hence, God). But such examples are not products of belief, but of unbelief, by the fact that they are fundamentally at odds with the basic principles of biblical religion. Incidentally, it was not atheism, but the revival of Christianity in England and America that led to the eventual eradication of slavery both in Europe and America, and it is those nations least impacted by biblical religion that have longest tolerated slavery and class abuses.

The problem of the universal negative

Now you know the basic arguments atheists use in attempting to prove that God does not exist, and you know the flaws of those arguments There's one more huge problem that atheists face in seeking to disprove God's existence. It's called, the problem of the universal negative. Simply stated, the problem of the universal negative says this: It is impossible to prove a universal negative (*i.e.,* that something isn't) unless you know everything, or unless a logical contradiction is involved (like "square circles"). When atheists claim that there is no God, they are presuming to be omniscient (all knowing), because only someone who knows everything could know that there is no God! (Interestingly, the atheist that says there is no God is implying that he or she is God!) Because of the problem of proving a universal negative, many atheists simply claim to be agnostics or deists.

Can the existence of God be proven?

When it comes to proving the existence of God, there are two schools of thought among Christians. Some believe that the existence of God cannot be proven scientifically, that the knowledge of God is intuitive; this is called "fideism," signifying that belief in God is essentially a matter of faith. Others believe it is possible to empirically (scientifically) demonstrate the existence of God using observation and logic; this is called theological "empiricism." Which of these two views is correct? Both have an element of truth. It is certainly not unreasonable that man could know of God intuitively and without empirical proofs. On the other hand, there do seem to be some pretty good reasons to believe that God exists. Practically speaking, at best logical arguments seem to merely point to the probability, rather than certainty, that God exists. This is because all scientific proofs are expressed as probabilities. Having said that, a 1 in 10^{50} chance that life arose purely by random processes could be construed as reason to presume the existence of a Creator by most reasonable people. So, while it might be impossible to absolutely prove the existence of God, it may be possible to demonstrate that belief in the existence of God is far more reasonable than the alternative.

Whether we can prove the existence of God or not, there are two things we do know with a high degree of certainty.

1. There are no pure atheists. A pure atheist would be a person who genuinely has no reason to even suspect that God exists. According to Romans 1:16-18, all men know that God exists. Therefore, we conclude that those who claim to be atheists, inwardly know, or at least suspect, that God exists, but suppress that knowledge. They are "practical atheists," because they find atheism convenient or practical in view of prior choices they have made.

2. While it is probably true that logical arguments cannot absolutely prove the existence of God, they can and do demonstrate that belief in the existence of God is reasonable; in fact, far more reasonable than the alternative.

Understanding this gives us an advantage in the spiritual and intellectual warfare that surrounds us. Atheists already know there is a God, but have built barricades to suppress that knowledge from themselves and others. We don't have to prove God's existence; we merely have to confront people with what they already know intuitively.

Arguments theists have used in attempting to prove God's existence

Before we begin, let's step through a small mental exercise designed to give us some idea of the difficulty one faces in attempting to prove the existence of God. Imagine for a moment someone who lives inside a metal can. He or she cannot see out, and has no reason to believe that the physical laws inside the can apply outside. How could such a person prove that anything existed outside the can? Obviously the arguments are going to have to be philosophical in nature, since they can't take their science outside the can. The following are classical arguments that have been offered by theological empiricists for the proof of God's existence. While they may not prove the existence of God absolutely, they do demonstrate that belief in the existence of God is reasonable.

The cosmological argument

Statement of the argument: If something exists, unless something comes from nothing, something must be eternal.

God isn't mentioned directly in the argument. The argument simply seeks to demonstrate that something eternal must exist. The argument merely posits two alternatives: either something is eternal, or something must have come from nothing. "Nothing" as used here doesn't mean just empty space; it means absolutely nothing — no time, matter, energy, space, or physical law. Unless something could come from absolutely nothing (which is self-contradicting), we are left with three possibilities.

1. The first possibility: The natural world is eternal.

   It is generally acknowledged by physical scientists that the second law of thermodynamics precludes this possibility. Given enough time all of the potential energy in the universe would be used up. Of course if the universe is eternal, then there has already been a sufficient amount of time for that to happen. Owing to the second law of thermodynamics, there can be no doubt that the universe (as described by the laws of physics) has not always existed. The real question is, "Where did it come from?" Physicist Stephen Hawking suggested that there is an eternal "imaginary time" that is responsible for the physical universe as we know it. However, if such a principle were to exist, which could not be proven by the laws of physics, it would certainly be more akin to the idea of God than to anything in the natural realm. In fact, it would thoroughly redefine nature in the direction of pantheism. (Ultimately, either God is God, or nature is God.) So, if necessity is the cause of the universe, how do we explain the existence of the necessity? To claim that the universe emerges out of some sort of necessity and not explain the source and nature of such a necessity is no explanation at all. Isn't the idea of a Creator just as reasonable?

2. The second alternative: Impersonal unconscious intelligence produced the universe.

   This view has some affinity with pantheism, but isn't quite the same, since in pantheism there is divine consciousness. We ought to pay careful attention to this, since it is becoming a backstop position for many natural philosophers and cosmologists who have to acknowledge the complexity and design of the universe and biological systems, but who do not want to acknowledge a personal Creator. The following are problems with this alternative:

a. "Unconscious intelligence" seems to be a contradiction in terms.

b. If some sort of intelligence were the cause, then it would seem that a personal intelligence (God) would be a more reasonable alternative. It would at least account for where the personal and self-conscious came from. One of the problems with viewing unconscious intelligence as the source of complex biological systems is that it doesn't provide a pattern for the creation of personal beings, nor is there any explanation for where the unconscious intelligence came from. One might ask if the same isn't also true of Christian theism. The answer is "No" — because in Christian theism God is separate from creation (time, matter, energy, space, and physical laws); in the unconscious intelligence theory the unconscious intelligence is itself part of the natural order, and this offers no explanation of the ultimate origin of the universe. This is really an onion theory in disguise. (An "onion theory" doesn't answer the question of ultimate origin; it just pushes the question out to another layer and leaves us with another unanswered question.)

3. *The third possibility:* A personal eternal being (God) created the universe.

While the cosmological argument certainly doesn't prove God's existence, it does prove that belief in the existence of God is at least as reasonable as any of the other alternatives.

The teleological argument

The teleological argument is by far the best logical argument that has been put forward for God's existence. While the cosmological argument proves that something has to be eternal, it doesn't prove that the something had to be intelligent, personal, or transcendent. It is important to understand the teleological argument, since it is currently framing the debate between theism and naturalistic (atheistic) cosmology and evolutionary science. Up to this point in time naturalism has depended upon the Darwinian evolutionary model as an alternative to intelligent design; however, the inadequacy of the Darwinian model to account for biological complexity is becoming more apparent as we learn more about the complexity of life. In time, as Darwinism wanes, some atheists will simply look to another layer of nature for the answer to the complexity of the universe and of life (natural necessity, or unconscious intelligence, or what some natural philosophers call, "the anthropic principle"), but perhaps some will be open enough to consider the possibility that someone outside of creation designed both the universe and life.

Statement of the argument: The teleological argument is sometimes referred to as the design argument. Design implies intelligence and purpose in the originating cause. The universe evidences a high degree of design, and that design implies an intelligent originating cause.

The following are generally considered to be weaker arguments; however, they may still be helpful.

The anthropological argument

Statement of the argument: This is actually a variation of the teleological argument. It says: It doesn't seem possible that a chemical system could arrange itself to be self-directing and self-conscious, much less moral and religious.

The moral argument

Statement of the argument: People seem to recognize the existence of a supreme moral law (*i.e.,* a sense of right) to which all men are obligated, and to which all men appeal in matters of dispute. For example, men innately believe in justice, whether or not they practice or promote it, or agree upon its particulars. Such a law implies a lawgiver.

The ontological argument

This is essentially the argument of Leibnitz, and Decarte (though they proposed different forms); it is not considered to be logically valid and is given here only for historical interest.

Statement of the argument: We have the idea of an absolutely perfect being, but existence would have to be a quality of perfection, so an absolutely perfect being must exist.

Of course, if there is an absolutely perfect being, he must exist; however, merely conceiving of such a thing does not necessitate it any more than conceiving of the perfect spouse (or church) means that one must exists.

Summary of theism and atheism

Perhaps you've noticed from your reading that the Bible nowhere attempts to prove God's existence through rational arguments. There is probably a reason for that; deep down inside, everyone believes that God exists (cf. Rom. 1:18-20). That being the case, the person who claims there is no God isn't struggling with an intellectual problem, they're struggling with a rejection problem. They have a reason to exclude God from their knowledge. Perhaps for some, such a belief allows them to think that they are free to live according to their own rules (see again, Romans 1:18-32). By the way, that raises an interesting question. If everyone really knows that God exists, how do they know it, particularly in light of the inadequacy of logical arguments to absolutely prove God's existence? The answer is that the knowledge of God is intuitive, that is, everything points to God's existence. The denial of God's existence is just that: a denial of what man intuitively knows to be true.

Review Questions

1. What are the five key arguments used by atheists in their attempt to prove that God does not exist?

2. Explain how the existence of evil is used as an argument against the existence of an infinitely good and powerful God. How could you counter this argument?

3. Evaluate the statement: Science will some day be able to give a natural explanation for everything.

4. In light of the difficulty of defining the word "God," how is it possible to talk about God in a meaningful way?

5. Atheists claim they have valid objections to every argument for the existence of God. For the sake of argument, if we assume that to be correct, why would it not prove atheism?

6. How would you respond to the argument that it is better not to believe in God, since belief in God often results in evil (religious wars, the Spanish Inquisition, *etc.*).

7. Give four arguments for the existence of God.

8. State why you believe in God.

9. Explain the cosmological argument for the existence of God.

10. Explain the teleological argument for the existence of God.

11. Explain the anthropological argument for the existence of God.

12. Explain the moral argument for the existence of God.

13. What do you think would be a good plan for presenting the gospel to an atheist?

Conceptions of God

A few years ago in America, you could assume that your neighbors had basically the same idea of God as did you. At that time the religious diversity of most neighborhoods consisted of Baptists, Presbyterians, Lutherans, Catholics and other Christian denominations. That is no longer true. The chances are good that in your neighborhood there are people from a variety of cultures and religious backgrounds. Since we can no longer assume the people we come into contact with share the same basic conception of God as we have, it is important to understand how other people conceive of God.

Judaic and Christian theism

The Judaic and Christian conception of God (the view of God portrayed in the Bible) is that God is an eternal, transcendent spirit, infinite in all of his perfections, (moral, intellectual, *etc.*) and thus immutable, since he can neither be more nor less than what he is. The Christian theology differs from Judaic theology in that God is viewed as a tri-unity (trinity), consisting of three distinct and co-equal persons (Father, Son, and Holy Spirit) sharing a singular essence. In both the Judaic and Christian theologies God, though transcendent (separate from his creation), is nonetheless involved with his creation (immanent), exerting continual providential care and control over creation, working all things according to his purpose.

Non-Christian conceptions of God

Deism

Deists view God as eternal and transcendent, but they are not agreed as to his specific attributes. They believe that God cre-

ated the world, but left it to operate according to the laws he created. Generally, deists do not believe that God intervenes in the
natural order he created; thus, they do not believe in miracles,
which is why they are unclear as to God's qualities (some of
which could only be known through divine revelation).

Two obvious problems with deism are:

1. While rejecting the miracles of the Bible, deism accepts the
   biggest miracle of all—creation.

2. Deism's rejection of miracles is purely arbitrary. Why
   should one assume that miracles don't exist? Miracles are
   not an abrogation of physical law, but irregularities in
   God's regulation of nature. Thus the ordinary regulation of
   nature (expressed as physical law) and the extraordinary
   regulation of nature (expressed as miracles), proceed from
   the same source. Miracles can be viewed as simply deviations from the usual work of God as observed in nature.

Pantheism

Pantheism views the universe as God, and matter as an illusion. Reincarnation is viewed as bondage for misdeeds or for
lack of understanding reality. Some of the problems with pantheism are as follows.

1. Pantheists believe that there is one unchanging reality:
   God. They also believe that we can come to understand
   that we are God (or, at least a part of God). But, if God
   comes to understand that he is God, he (it) isn't an unchanging reality, is he?

2. If matter is only an illusion, why do pantheists eat, sleep,
   bathe, brush their teeth, and perform other bodily functions? The fact is that pantheism fails the test of reality.
   One simply cannot live consistent with pantheistic beliefs.

3. Pantheism is characterized by a lack of compassion toward those who are suffering. According to pantheism, people suffer to work off bad karma (negativity from past misdeeds or failings), so in helping a suffering person one is actually preventing them from working through their karma, which they eventually must do to escape the cycle of reincarnation.

Finite godism

Finite godism is the belief that god (or the gods) is part of the creation, and thus finite. There are several obvious problems with finite godism.

1. A finite god would require a cause since he or she could not be eternal; therefore, no finite god could be responsible for the ultimate origin of the universe. We would have to ask: Who made the finite god?

2. "Finite" and "god" are incongruent terms. How would such a god differ from any other created thing, except in the magnitude of his or her attributes?

3. In most finite god religions the god (as conceived by his worshipers) is beset with all of the weaknesses as mortals, and differs from them merely in the extent of his or her powers. Such a god-concept is inferior logically and morally to the transcendent God of the Bible.

Polytheism

Polytheism is similar to finite godism, but admits to many gods rather than just one. Usually these gods have dominion over only specific domains, such as the sea, or the mountains, etc., or over particular functions, such as fertility or war. Baal and Astarte, mentioned in the Old Testament, were heathen fertility gods, and their worship involved debased sexual practices. Most ancient religions were polytheistic. Because polytheism was prevalent in ancient times, the Bible has much to say about it (see:

Isa. 43:10-11; 44:6,8; 45:5-6,18-25; 46:9-10; Jer. 10:1-16; 1 Cor. 8:4; Rev. 9:20).

Open theism

Open theism is a post-evangelical theology (dating from the 1980s) arguing that God is not immutable. Open theists also have a fundamentally different concept of God's eternality than traditional Christian theists. Proponents conceive of God as growing; in other words, in some respects God is more today than he was yesterday and will be more tomorrow than he is today, especially in terms of his knowledge. Open theists see a logical contradiction between the idea of an omniscient God and free will. They argue that if God knew everything, then everything would be determined (since nothing could change), thus there could be no free will. The basic error in open theism is in the process by which its conclusions are derived; it is essentially a philosophical rather than biblical theology. In philosophical theology human reason takes precedence over divine revelation. Man is aware of four dimensions (three of space, and one of time), but most philosophical argumentation is one-dimensional since causality, not extension, is the basis of most philosophical arguments. How is it that a being like man whose causal thinking is limited to one dimension (what we might call, "flat thinking") presumes to know how God knows what he knows and what the implications of that knowledge might be? Natural philosophy is simply not in a position to do what the open theist presumes to do—to rationalize the nature of God from a unidimensional frame of reference. Only God can understand God. In trying to understand the nature of both reality and God we are completely dependent upon biblical revelation; and biblical revelation is clear that God is omniscient and immutable and that his creatures do make free choices (though we are not here arguing that fallen men have a completely free will). Open theism is an example of how theology goes wrong when philosophical rationalization is allowed to trump biblical revelation. We should ever keep Paul's warning in mind when we are tempted to philosophize what is contrary to revealed truth (Col. 2:8).

Review Questions

1. Describe the Christian conception of God.

2. What is pantheism?

3. What do you think might be a good plan for witnessing to a pantheist?

4. What is deism?

5. What do you think might be a good plan for witnessing to a deist?

6. Describe finite godism and polytheism. How are these views similar, and how do they differ?

7. What are the problems with finite godism and polytheism?

8. What do open theists believe?

The Attributes of God

Having discussed the existence of God, now we turn our attention to God's nature. In discussing the attributes of God, it is important to acknowledge that we don't fully understand any of them, and God undoubtedly has qualities of which we are completely unaware. (Heaven will be full of learning!) Of course, God would need to be finite in order for us to fully comprehend him. The attributes of God can be grouped according to various categorical schemes; one scheme is to arrange the attributes as moral or non-moral.

Non-moral attributes

God exists

God isn't just a concept, or an idea. It is common for theologians to say that God "self-exists"; however that implies the need for God to have a cause, even if that cause is within himself. It would be better to simply recognize that God needs no cause at all. God is, in fact, uncaused, owing to the fact that he is an eternal being.

God is holy (metaphysically)

The Bible describes two kinds of holiness: moral holiness, or God's separateness from evil, and metaphysical holiness, or God's separateness from creation. Most people are familiar with the concept of moral holiness, but few are familiar with the concept of metaphysical holiness. Metaphysical holiness means that God is not part of creation. The Bible declares that God made the creation out of nothing (Heb. 11:3). If you want an analogy (there really isn't a good one), think of it this way: All of creation can be likened to a bubble in nothing (not space, that would be something, but real nothing—no space, no time, no quantum mechanics, just nothing). Creation (matter, energy, time, space, physical law) exists only in that bubble, but God exists independent of the bubble. He made the bubble so that his creatures could exist.

The concept of metaphysical holiness is usually referred to as "transcendence." A complementary truth is that God is also "immanent." Immanence refers to the fact that God is not aloof, but engaged with his creation. The Old Testament saints seemed to have had a better grasp of metaphysical holiness than do we, perhaps that's because we don't spend a lot of time reading what they wrote! They understood that God is, well—GOD. Today, many people, including many Christians, fail to understand this. We've trivialized God into little more than a cosmic buddy, psychotherapist, or worse, a cosmic Santa Claus.

God is spirit (Jn. 4:24; Heb. 12:9)

God's essence isn't material, it's spirit. We don't really know what spirit is. Angels are also spirits, and the question comes up as to whether their spirit is like God's spirit. It seems safe to say that since God's spirit is eternal, and thus uncreated, it is fundamentally different from a created spirit, whether angelic or human.

God is eternal [timeless] (Ex. 3:14-15; Deut. 33:27; Isa. 40:28; 57:15; Mic. 5:2; Rev. 4:11).

Many people, when they think about eternity, think of God as very, very old. Actually, that's about as far from what eternal means as one can get. Eternal means "timeless." In other words, God is completely unaffected by time. He can see his creation moving through the stream of time, and he can interact with it, but his essence is not affected in any way by time. Now, are you ready for a really interesting idea? If God's essence is unaffected by time, he could never have aged, not even a second! So that idea we get of a very old God sitting on a throne with a long white beard is way off. We also need to keep in mind that only God is eternal, and that will never change. God's creation will always exist in time. Even those to whom God imparts eternal life will still be bound to the linear existence of time forever (actually, the term most commonly translated "eternal" in the New Testament means, "unto the ages"). There are four key ideas associated with God's eternality.

1. Since God is eternal, his attributes must be immutable.

2. Since God is eternal, he must be infinite, because only an infinite being could be eternal.

3. Since God is eternal, he must be uncaused.

4. Since God is eternal, he must be omniscient, because he can never learn anything he doesn't already know. Remember, he sees the end from the beginning.

God is immutable (Ex. 3:14; Mal. 3:6; Jam. 1:17; Psa. 102:24-27; Heb. 1:10-12)

If God is eternal (timeless), his eternal attributes cannot change. Time is a measure of change; no time, no change. Do you see how eternality and immutability are linked together? The fact that God is immutable doesn't mean that he cannot respond to things that do change; it simply means that his attributes never change. The Bible occasionally refers to God changing his mind (Gen. 6:6; Ex. 32:14); such references are figures that refer not to a change in any of God's attributes, but a response to changes in his creatures.

God is infinite in knowledge and wisdom (Psa. 147:4-5; Prov. 15:3-11; Jer. 23:23-24; Heb. 4:13)

Whereas knowledge is an awareness of facts, wisdom is insight and ability to use that knowledge rightly. God possesses all knowledge and wisdom; in other words, there is nothing that God does not know. He has all insight, and there is no knowledge that God does not know how to use wisely. God's knowledge of the future does not preclude free choices on the part of his creatures as some (the open theists) have suggested. God is capable of foreknowing the free choices of men and how he will respond to those choices in the exercise of his power. Thus there is no conflict between God's omniscience and omnipotence, and the free will of his creatures. Those who see a conflict do so because they have a defective view of God's eternality.

What does God know?

1. God knows all things that are (in actuality):

   a. In all places (Job 26:6; Ps. 33:13; 139:1-16; 1 Sam. 16:7; 1 Kings 8:39).

   b. In all times (past, present, and future) (Isa. 42:9; 44:6-8; 46:10; Acts 2:22-23; Heb. 4:13).

2. God knows all things that could be (potentially). This is referred to as "contingent knowledge" (1 Sam. 23:10-12; Mt. 11:21).

That God knows all things is usually referred to as "omniscience." God's omniscience is a great source of comfort to believers, but it should be a great cause of concern for his enemies.

God is infinite in his power   (Psa. 135:6; 148:1-5; Jer. 10:1-16; 32:17,27; Rom. 1:20; Heb. 1:3; Rev. 19:6)

How much power is infinite power? It's so much that even when some is used, there's just as much as there was before. The following are a few observations concerning God's omnipotence.

1. Omnipotence doesn't mean that God can do anything. It means that he has unlimited power to do whatever power can accomplish, and which is consistent with his own nature (Heb. 6:18; 2 Tim. 2:13). Even unlimited power cannot make square circles, because square circles by definition

can't exist. (The same is also true of "rocks so big that God cannot lift them" and other nonsense.)

2. God's power is inherent in his being. That is to say that he does not draw upon or leverage power outside of himself. In fact, all power is ultimately derived from him, even the power to do evil.

3. God's power is never diminished by its exercise.

God is personal

Some religions conceive of God as an unconscious force or merely the intelligence behind the universe; this is particularly true in pantheistic religions. However, the Bible presents a very different picture of God. Some of God's known personal qualities are:

1. He is living (Jer. 10:10 cf. vv 3-5).

2. He is intelligent (Prov. 3:19).

   a. He possesses knowledge (perception of facts/truth).
   b. He possesses understanding (insight into facts).
   c. He possesses wisdom (the ability to use knowledge to the best and highest purpose).

3. He has emotions (Jn. 3:16).

4. He has purpose (Eph. 3:8-11).

5. He is active (Dan. 6:25-27).

6. He is free (sovereign) (Dan. 4:34-35 {per Nebuchadnezzar}, Eph. 1:11 {per Paul}).

7. He is self-conscious (1 Cor. 2:10-11).

If God is personal, and he made us personal, doesn't it seem reasonable that he desires a personal relationship with us? If we look, we can find illustrations of this truth all the way through the Bible. Think of the Bible characters that had a personal relationship with God. Their relationship is a model for our relationship with him.

Personal beings communicate, and God wants his personal creatures to communicate with him. Communication is a two-way street. In this dispensation God usually speaks to us through his word, the Bible; we speak to him through prayer. Regrettably, prayer for many people is little more than presenting God with a petty, often selfish wish list, as if he were a cosmic Santa Claus. The person who wants his or her prayer life to be effective needs to discover what God wants, and then pray to that end. God loves to answer prayer that is offered in accordance with his will. Below are some biblical principles, which if applied can help us to pray more effectively. They come primarily from Matthew 6:8-13.

1. We should focus on God, not ourselves (Mt. 6:9).

2. We should pray for God's will to be accomplished (Mt. 6:10). Of course, we can be more effective at this if we read and study the Bible to discover God's will. But even if we're uncertain about God's will in a particular situation, we should still pray that his will be done.

3. We should focus on what we need, rather than frivolous desires (Mt. 6: 11, cf., Jam. 4:3).

4. We should confess our sin (Mt. 6:12). It's difficult to pray a sincere prayer when we're harboring sin.

5. We should pray for our life to reflect God's character (Mt. 6:12).

6. We should pray with an awareness of the spiritual warfare around us (Mt. 6:13).

7. We should examine our own motives. Remember, if we are praying in Christ's name (Jn. 14:13-14), we should ask for what Christ would ask.

8. We must be willing to accept God's answer, otherwise we aren't praying, we're demanding!

God is purposive

God has a purpose and plan for his creation. Do you think it might be important for us to know what that purpose is? Of course! How do we discover God's purpose (or "will")? The fact is, God has revealed his will to us in the Bible. That will is that everything should be made subject to Christ (1 Cor. 15:24-28).

God is a trinity

The Trinity refers to the fact that God is three distinct persons sharing one divine essence. Apart from understanding the triune nature of God it is impossible to fully appreciate either the ministry and sacrifice of Christ, or the present work of the Holy Spirit in our lives. The doctrine of the Trinity is central to Christianity, and that is evidenced by the fact that every so-called "Christian" cult denies this truth. The doctrine of the Trinity is not difficult to prove, even if it is difficult to understand. It is a deductive truth.

How the Trinity is deduced:

<u>Induction</u> (observations from the Bible)

1. The Bible says there are three distinct persons who are God:

   a. The Father is God (2 Cor. 1:2).
   b. The Son is God (Jn. 1:1-2).
   c. The Holy Spirit is God (Acts 5:2-4).

2. The Bible states in many places that there is only one God (Isa. 43:10; 44:6,8). This is referred to as the "unity" of God (see Deut. 6:4; Jn. 5:44).

Deduction (logical inference)

Since three distinct persons are said to be God, and there is only one God, God must exist as three persons sharing the same divine essence.

Additional support for the doctrine of the Trinity:

1. The three members are seen working co-extensively (meaning at the same level, *e.g.*, creating, *etc.*). See, Jn. 14:16 and 23; also see Isa. 43:10-11 cp. Jn. 4:42; and 1 Jn. 3:22-24.

2. The three members are referred to in ways only appropriate for equals (*e.g.*, Mt. 28:18-20 in the threefold baptism formula).

3. Various grammatical structures are used in the New Testament to affirm the connection between members of the Trinity. Note the following:

    a. *Titus 2:13*
        Here "God" and "Savior" both refer to Jesus Christ. These two words (connected by the copulative "and" —Gr. *kai*) share the same definite article. In Greek grammar that is only permissible when both words refer to the same thing. The one definite article indicates that there is only one object (*i.e.*, Christ is both God and Savior).

    b. *John 1:1-2*
        This passage emphatically asserts the absolute deity of Christ: "...the Word was God." This is the most definite statement on the deity of Christ to be found in the Bible. Why so? Writers of Greek didn't underline or italicize words to emphasize a point, instead

they moved the emphasized word closer to the beginning of the sentence. (That would wreck havoc in English, but they had a way of keeping things straight.) Here's the way the Greek reads (word for word).

"...and God [nominative case] was the Word [nominative case]"

To a Greek reader, it would be obvious that this sentence has been constructed to emphasize the deity of "the Word." Why? —Because "God" is clearly the predicate nominative of this clause, not the subject, indicating that it has been moved forward for sake of emphasis. We know this because the article ("the") is absent from the word "God," and you can't have a definite subject ("the Word) without a definite predicate nominative. So why did John drop the definite article from "God?" Simply to indicate that "God" was the predicate nominative, not the subject. A predicate nominative before a verb is both definite and emphatic. [Note that John wasn't saying that the Word was "a god" {as mistranslated in the Jehovah's Witness *New World Translation*}; he was saying the Word was GOD! {definite and emphatic}.]

4. The connection between various members of the Trinity is often stated.

John 10:30-33
In this passage Jesus asserts that he and the Father are "one." A common approach in denying Jesus' claim to deity in this passage is to say that he was merely claiming to be in harmony with God. However, the context is clear that this was intended as a claim of equality with the Father; notice how the Jews responded to this statement, they wanted to stone him for making himself out to be

God, cf. v.33. What Jesus was claiming was that he and the Father are "one and the same" essence.

5. Context often reveals a connection between various members of the Trinity.

   Hebrews 1:10
   This passage is quoted from Psalm 102:25 and applied to Christ. It says, "Thou, LORD, in the beginning didst lay the foundations of the earth...." Here the Father refers to the Son as the Creator of the world; the Son (the Creator) is also identified as Jehovah. (Hebrews 1:10 is a condensed quotation; the name "Jehovah" [Heb. YHWH] appears in Psalm 102:22.)

   (Details on the deity of Christ and the Holy Spirit will be presented under those topics.)

Incorrect views of the Trinity

It is important to understand some of the incorrect views on the Trinity so that we don't repeat the same mistakes that others have made. Many heresies from the past are being recycled because people don't know that some theology has already been found to be unbiblical. In fact, all of the cults are simply recycled heresies (mostly gnostic heresies). Recognizing false teaching can help one not to become a victim.

1. Modalism
   Modalism says that the persons of the Godhead are simply three modes of God's existence. According to this view, the Father, Son, and Holy Spirit are simply three manifestations of the one being of God, not three distinct persons. In other words, modalism claims that God sometimes appears as the Father, and at other times as the Son or the Holy Spirit. However, the Bible indicates that the three members of the Godhead are distinct persons. For example, at Jesus' baptism we see all three members distinctly

(the Son coming for baptism, the Father speaking from heaven, and the Spirit descending upon Christ, cf. Mt. 3:1-17, esp. vv. 13-17). Also Jesus prayed to the Father, and said that when he returned to Heaven he would send the Holy Spirit.

2. Arianism
    Arianism claims that the Father is the only eternal God, and that he created the world and the Son, and the Son created the Holy Spirit. According to Arianism neither the Son is God, nor the Holy Spirit; therefore, Arianism denies the doctrine of the Trinity. A related view called "Patripassianism" claims that the Father became flesh and died on the cross. (There are many variations of each of these views.) Arianism was a heresy that developed out of Christian gnosticism and was condemned by the early Church. Today, Jehovah's Witness is the largest Arian group in existence still claiming a connection to Christianity.

3. Adoptionism
    This view claims that Jesus was born a mere man and at some point, possibly at his baptism, he was adopted as God's Son. Naturally, adoptionism denies the eternality of the Son. (This view also has ties to early Christian gnosticism.)

Moral attributes

God is morally holy (Lev. 19:2; Deut. 32:4; Psa. 145:17; Ezek. 39:7; Jam. 1:13)

A number of qualities are associated with holiness, such as goodness, righteousness, truth, and justice. Each of these qualities expresses God's holiness in a particular way. It is important to realize that God doesn't just choose to do good — he is good. He doesn't just choose to act righteously — he is righteous. He doesn't just choose to be holy (separate from evil) — he is holy. God acts the way he does because he is what he is; that is to say, God's moral qualities are intrinsic, they are a function of who and what he is. Let's look at each of these expressions of God's holiness, beginning with some basic observations.

God's moral holiness refers to his complete separation from evil. Note the following.

1. God cannot be the source of evil, though he can be the source of the free will that allows one to choose evil.

2. God in no way necessitates (requires) evil in his creation. Sin is always a voluntary act (Jam. 1:13-18; 1 Cor. 10:13).

3. God's holiness is manifested in his original creation, his perfect moral laws, his pure teachings, his just judgment, and his ultimate restoration of both the sinner and the creation to perfection (Rom. 8:18-25).

4. The moral failure of one of God's creatures in no way blemishes God's holiness as long as God fully judges each sin. Although God created man with the capacity to choose good or evil, he did not create man sinful, nor was there any necessity for man to sin. Man freely chose to sin. [Although we will deal with the issue of free will later, we will just mention here that God originally created man with a free will; however, in falling into sin, man's will became enslaved to sin and is no longer capable of righteousness apart from special divine enablement (Rom. 8:5-13). Therefore, while man appears to make free choices in his fallen state, apart from divine enabling those choices are limited to the range of choices that a fallen creature is capable of, which is far less than what he was created for. Therefore, while man's will appears, from the human perspective, to be free, it is only free to choose those things that are consistent with a fallen nature. This can be seen from the fact that man, unaided by the Holy Spirit, cannot choose to live righteously; even with the aid of the Holy

Spirit believers cannot choose righteousness consistently, *i.e.,* they cannot in this life reach a state of sinless perfection, cf. Rom. 7:13-25.]

Goodness (Lk. 18:18-19; Rom. 2:4)

Not only is God separate from evil, he is positively good. Goodness is difficult to define, but the idea is that good is wholesome and constructive, what we might call "for the best." God's goodness speaks of his fostering whatever is consistent with his perfect will, which is man's highest and best end. Think about this for a moment: If God is good, as the Bible says, then whatever God desires is best for us, since he never desires what is not good. That means that we can never do better than to do God's will, even though it may not be what we want at the time (Rom.12:1-2).

If God is good, why would anyone not want to respond to him in faith, obeying his will? The answer is simple: Every time we refuse to respond to God in faith, we are, perhaps without thinking about it, denying his goodness, because we have allowed ourselves to believe that what he wants is less than the best for us. Paul touches on this in Romans 12:1-2 when he challenges believers to be transformed through the renewing of our minds that they might discover, in their own personal experience, that God's will is good, and perfect.

Righteousness (Psa. 89:14; 97:2; Jn. 17:25; 2 Tim. 4:8; Rev. 16:5)

Righteousness refers to obedience to a revealed standard (the Law for instance). Of course God is the epitome of every precept of moral law that he has ever given. Think of it this way: God doesn't conform to moral law; rather, moral laws are expressions of God's own character. When God says, "Don't lie," it reflects the fact that he would never lie. When God says, "Don't commit adultery," it is because he would never be unfaithful. Moral law wasn't intended to be an onerous burden that God put on man; it was intended to teach us about God's nature.

As far as God's moral standards are concerned, all men and women fall short (Rom. 3:23) and are deserving of death (Rom. 6:23). How does God solve this problem? Amazingly, when he washes away the sin of a person believing in Christ, he also conveys to them Christ's own righteousness (Rom. 3:21-24). That's right...in God's eyes a redeemed individual is as righteous as Christ, not by works, but by faith.

Truth

The most basic definition of truth is that truth conforms to reality. Anything that distorts the truth is an offense to God. Why is this so important? — Because the distortion of truth (reality) is to sin what fertilizer is to plants. Think about it, was Satan thinking in accordance with reality when he thought he could be like God? Was Eve thinking in accordance with reality when she thought she could be like God? Was Judas thinking in accordance with reality when he betrayed Jesus? Is anyone who rejects God to his own destruction thinking in accordance with reality? Twisted thinking is at the root of all sin, and the denial of truth is always the first step in committing any sin.

So when God says that he is the God of truth, what does that mean? It means we can depend on the fact that God will never misrepresent anything, and he will never lead us wrong in anything; it means we can trust him better than we can trust ourselves. Because God is true, he cannot lie (Heb. 6:18), he cannot be deceptive (*i.e.*, having some evil motive), and he cannot fail to keep his promises (1 Thess. 5:24; 2 Tim. 2:11-13; 1 Cor. 10:13; 1 Jn. 1:9).

Justice (Psa. 11:4-7; 19:9; Rom. 2:1-16)

God's justice refers to the expression of his holiness in dealing with the sins of his creatures. Sin is an assault against God's holiness, and condemnation of the sinner is essential in order for God to remain holy. It is impossible that God could allow any sin not to be judged. When God condemns a sinner he is doing what his holiness requires. There are many expressions of God's temporal (earthly) justice in the Bible; however, the final and eternal expression of God's justice will be in condemning sinners to Hell (the Lake of Fire) forever (Rev. 20:11-15), that is, those sinners who refuse to accept Christ's sacrifice in their place, by receiving him as Lord and Savior. God has only two options in dealing with man's sin.

1. Sin can be graciously forgiven in Christ, based on Christ's substitutionary sacrifice, accessed by faith (in which case God's holiness is satisfied by the infinite value of Christ's death for our sin).

2. Or, the penalty for sin must be paid in full by the sinner through eternal damnation. A question that sometimes comes up is this: "If man's sin is so brief, why must his punishment be forever?" The answer, as difficult as it may be to comprehend, would seem to be that any sin against an infinitely holy God, no matter how insignificant it may seem to us, is infinitely evil. None of us really understands the enormity of this problem, and that leads some people to accept theological errors like annihilationism, the denial of eternal punishment.

The will of God

In considering the will of God there are a number of questions to which we would like to have answers, such as: 1) What is "the will of God"? 2) If God is sovereign, and evil exists, must we conclude that evil is within God's will? If so, is God responsible for evil? 3) Are there aspects of God's will that are going to happen no matter what we do? 4) Does God have a "perfect will" and a "not-so-perfect will"?

So as not to become confused, it is important to understand that the will of God is comprised of three distinct aspects.

1. The decreed (or "determinant") will of God

The decreed aspect of God's will is that which must come to pass. It has been predetermined and God will infallibly bring it to pass (Deut. 29:29; Acts 2:22-23 cf. Lk. 22:22; Eph. 1:11). That Christ should come into the world to die for our sins was decreed by God; thus it could not fail to happen.

2. The expressed (or "revealed") will of God

   The expressed aspect of God's will is what God wants but does not necessitate (Mt. 6:10; Rom. 12:2; Eph. 5:17). In other words, we have the capacity to disobey God's expressed will, but when we do so, we incur serious consequences as a result of our sin. An example of God's revealed will is that he doesn't want us to steal from others (Ex. 20:15; Rom. 13:9); he will allow us the freedom to steal, if we choose to, but we will incur the consequences of our action, both temporal and eternal.

3. The sovereign will of God

   The sovereign aspect of God's will encompasses everything—past, present, and future—and includes what God decrees, desires, and what he neither decrees nor desires, but what he allows (Eph. 1:11). Of course God does not cause, nor does he desire evil, but he is sovereign over it, just as he is sovereign over everything else, and he does use the evil caused by his creatures to bring about his eternal purpose. For instance, God may use the terrible circumstances of war, ultimately created by the sinful actions of men, to cause people to turn to him.

The following are some basic principles for discovering God's will.

1. The expressed will of God as revealed in the Bible should be the foundation for all decision making for a Christian.

   a. We do not need to ask God for guidance regarding matters already addressed in the Bible. Asking when we already have the answer is usually nothing more than a pretext for rejecting God's revealed will.

b. God will never lead us in a path that is clearly inconsistent with his revealed will.

c. God wants his children to grow to spiritual maturity (Eph. 4:11-16). Mature people make better choices than immature people, so if we want to be a better decision maker, we need to concentrate on growing up spiritually. There are no shortcuts, so forget about finding some experience that's going to instantly transform you into a really spiritual person. Spiritual maturity is a challenging, lifelong process of opportunity, trials, learning, trusting, and growth (along with occasional failure); the sooner we get started, the better!

2. If God needs to position us into some place, situation, ministry, or whatever, that cannot be determined from following the general guidance of scripture, he has other means at his disposal. God can, and sometimes does intervene supernaturally on our behalf; such intervention often takes the following forms:

a. God can arrange events so as to engineer a particular outcome. This is a non-predisclosing form of guidance in that we don't find out what God is doing until after it happens; he simply works out the details without telling us what to do in advance.

b. God can convict, convince, and comfort us; he can also illuminate our understanding through his indwelling presence.

c. God can use any means necessary and consistent with his purpose, will, and nature, meaning that he could lead us through virtually any means or modality he chooses. God is not limited in how he can reveal himself and his will to us. Of course, some means are more normative than others.

Christians often worry needlessly about finding God's will, but if we are obeying his word, and seeking his will, we will find that it is impossible to miss!

Review Questions

1. List the non-moral attributes of God.

2. List the moral attributes of God.

3. What is the difference between moral holiness and metaphysical holiness?

4. What is another term for metaphysical holiness?

5. How old is God?

6. What does "eternal" mean?

7. What does "immutable" mean in relation to God?

8. Describe the proof for the doctrine of the Trinity.

9. What are three incorrect views of the Trinity?

10. Give four important observations based upon the fact that God is morally holy.

11. Define "goodness" as it relates to the character of God.

12. Define "righteousness" as it relates to the character of God.

13. What is meant when we say that God is true (or truth)? Why is truth important?

14. Define "justice" as it relates to the character of God.

15. What does "omniscience" mean? What kinds of knowledge does God possesses?

16. Does omnipotence mean that God can do anything? Explain.

17. What is meant when it is said that God is personal?

18. Define each of the three aspects of God's will.

19. Is everything that happens, including evil, part of God's will? Explain.

20. How should your answer to question 19 above affect your view of life?

21. What is a non-predisclosing form of guidance? Give an example.

22. Where is the correct place for any Christian to start in seeking to determine God's will?

The Bible

The Bible Among Books

The Bible is a unique book

The Bible is a totally unique book, even though it's not uncommon to find religious writers, even theologians, who minimize the uniqueness of the Bible, placing it on a par with the literature of other religions. So, is the Bible just another "holy book"?

Other than the Bible, there are five major groups of religious writings in use today: the Veda of Brahmanism, the Tripitaka of Buddhism, the Zend-Avesta of Zoroastrianism, the writings of Confucianism (actually a philosophy), and the Koran of Islam. While there are other ancient religious writings that date from before the writing of the Bible, the Bible claims to contain a comprehensive record of God's dealings with man from the creation, a record assumed to be passed down from one generation to the next in oral tradition, perhaps along with some written material long lost in antiquity. If the message of the Bible is taken at face value, though it may not be the oldest religious writing, its truth antedates all other religions, since its story begins with the creation of the world.

The question, "Is the Bible true?" is certainly the most important question anyone could ask. If the Bible is true, we are in the midst of a gigantic cosmic struggle between light and darkness, good and evil, and the outcome, both cosmic and personal, defines our eternal destiny. Could anything be more important than that? Many people dismiss the Bible as just another collection of religious myths, stories, quasi-history, and religious doctrine, most of which was written by well-meaning, but basically naive and ignorant people who didn't have the capacity, or means to see that their beliefs were merely superstition dressed up as "truth." After all, we have so many contradictory religious writings that most of them can't be true.

What makes the Bible different? To answer that question we have to look at the Bible from several angles. For instance, it is important to know whether or not the Bible is historically accurate. If the Bible isn't correct in basic historical facts and geography, there's not much reason to believe it's correct on religious truth. Second, we need to know if the Bible's message makes good common sense. Anything that violates common sense isn't likely to be taken seriously. Mythology violates basic common sense, and that's why thinking people don't take the truth claims of mythology seriously. Third, we need to know whether the supernatural element in the Bible is really believable, and whether it, or its effects, can be verified. Fourth, we need some means of determining whether or not the religious truths taught in the Bible are actually true. Of course, this is a tall order for one very simple reason: There is no way to verify the supernatural from within the natural realm, but God anticipated this problem. Although it is not possible to scientifically test the supernatural from within the natural realm, it is possible for the supernatural to manifest itself within the natural realm. As we begin, let's take a look at the uniqueness of the Bible.

1. The Bible is the only book that presents a comprehensive and connected history of man's spiritual condition and needs from the time of his creation all the way to the eternal future.

2. The Bible is the only book to present a comprehensive picture of the nature and purpose of God, and his plan for mankind and the physical universe.

3. The Bible is the only book that provides clear and consistent evidence of its supernatural origin through the record of accurately fulfilled, detailed prophecies. For example: Isaiah 53, written over seven hundred years before the birth of Christ, gives over thirty highly specific details of the life of Christ; and Daniel 9:24-27, written over five hundred years before the birth of Christ, prophesied that the Messiah was to die sometime after March 29 [Nisan 9],

A.D. 33; Jesus was crucified April 3 [Nisan 14], A.D. 33, just five days later. (For detailed information on this prophecy, see: "Daniel 9:24-27 — The Prophecy of Daniel's 70 Weeks," by the author, Biblical Reader Communications, 2009.) The modern media is busy trying to obscure the existence of fulfilled biblical prophecy by questioning whether the prophecies are legitimate and by pointing to non-biblical examples of prophecy, like Nostradamus and others. However, the Bible's prophecies aren't vague riddles into which almost anything can be read, rather they are clear and precise statements dealing with particular people, places, events, and times, and have been shown to be 100 percent accurate. (For a catalog of biblical prophecy and its fulfillment see: *The Prophecy Knowledge Handbook* by John F. Walvoord, Victor Books, 1990.)

4. The Bible is the only ancient book that consistently proves to be the product of a superior (supernormal) intelligence based on its statements about the physical universe. For example: The Bible states that the earth is round and suspended in space (Job 26:7; Isa. 40:22), a fact not confirmed by science until the late fifteenth century; the Bible says that the universe had a beginning and that it was created out of nothing (Gen 1:1-2, cf. Heb 11:3; Jn. 1:1-3), a fact not confirmed by science until the mid-twentieth century. The Bible also declares that the stars and the earth are in space (Gen. 1:1-31) [On his point see the NASB, which correctly translates the Hebrew term *rakia* as "expanse," not a solid as indicated by the KJV "firmament" (from the Septuagint). Also, contrary to the beliefs of the church of the middle ages, the Bible nowhere says or even implies that the earth is the center of the universe.]

5. The Bible, though written over fifteen centuries by more than forty different authors, exhibits a singularity of purpose, morality, message, and theology. Features like "types" (a sort of prophetic analogy) demonstrate the interconnectedness of the Bible's message across many cen-

turies. ("Types" are Old Testament people, events, or objects that were clearly intended to prefigure some New Testament person, event, or truth; for example: The Old Testament sacrifices and the Passover are typical prefigurements of Christ's work on the cross.)

The Bible's message is unique

Not only is the Bible unique, but its message is unique too. The following are some of the themes that permeate throughout the Bible.

1. There is one true God, though existing as three persons.

2. The universe is not eternal, God created it out of nothing. [It is interesting that modern science has just, within the last fifty years, discovered that the universe had a beginning. Up until the mid-1960s, most scientists assumed the universe was eternal (the "steady state" theory). We now know the universe is expanding at an incredible pace. If we could simply play this history in reverse, we would see the universe shrink into an infinitesimal point and then vanish, which confirms the Bible's statement that the universe indeed had a beginning.]

3. God is transcendent; he exists apart from creation (this is in sharp contrast to both pantheism and polytheism, which view God, or the gods, as being part of the creation). It is interesting that many present-day theoretical (scientific) cosmologists are forced to admit that only something (or someone) completely outside of the universe could be the ultimate cause of the creation. Most religions in history have overlooked the simple necessity of transcendent causality and thus proven themselves to be logically and factually deficient. No religion that is wrong about the universe's ultimate origin can be right about man's present spiritual need. While modern science has only recently admitted this transcendent causal necessity, it was the very

first fact recorded in the Bible (Genesis 1:1), and reaffirmed in the New Testament as the very cornerstone of belief concerning Christ's qualifications as Savior (Jn. 1:1-3). If man needs saving, only a transcendent Creator could save him (John 1:1-5; Colossian 1:16-17). While the Koran accepts the concept of a transcendent God, that idea was recorded in the Old Testament over two thousand years before the Koran was written.

4. God is perfect in every respect, and his creation was originally made perfect.

5. Man was originally given a free will to choose good or evil.

6. Man did evil by disobeying his Creator, and became sinful in both his nature and choices. In this state, man is "lost," separated from God and unable to remedy his fallen situation by his own power. In man's spiritually dead state, his will is in bondage to sin, and he cannot please God. [From the human perspective, man's will appears to be free, but it can only choose from a limited range of choices — those choices native to a fallen nature.]

7. Man's sin is passed down from one generation to the next, so that all who are born through natural generation are born in a ruined, fallen state.

8. God, from eternity, knowing of man's choice, set in motion a plan to redeem his creation.

9. For thousands of years God prepared man so his plan could be brought about. Through prophecies, types (prophetic analogies), and pronouncements, God prepared man for his saving work on the cross. During that time he revealed himself and his plan to man in many ways.

10. When the time was right, God sent his only, divine Son into the world to offer him as a sacrifice so that sinful men could be brought back to God. In fact, God's plan calls for

more than just reconciliation; it calls for adoption, by which the reconciled actually become members of God's family.

11. God will someday send his Son, Jesus Christ, to bring to a close the present era and reconcile all things to himself through the completion of redemption (for the saved), and judgment (for the rest).

How do we know the Bible's claims are true?

If the Bible isn't true it doesn't matter where it came from or what translation one uses or how much one gets from reading it. That means the question of truthfulness is fundamentally important. When we ask someone who believes the Bible to be true, how they know it's true, we get a variety of answers. For example, it's not uncommon to hear some of the following reasons.

"My Sunday school teacher (or pastor) told me the Bible is true."

Good for your Sunday school teacher or pastor, but did they tell you how they know the Bible is true, or did you simply accept their opinion?

"The Bible says it's true."

Okay, but unless you already knew it was true, you couldn't trust what it says about itself—right? So, how did you know it was true, so you knew you could trust it when it said it was true? Unfortunately, if we say the Bible is true simply because it says so, that's circular reasoning. Nevertheless, while the Bible's claim to be true isn't proof, it is important, in that it invites the reader to consider the possibility, something people would not be obliged to do were the claim not made.

"The Bible can be proven to be true historically."

It is true that archaeological and historical research confirms the accuracy of the Bible, but can we conclude that the Bible is accurate in spiritual matters because it is historically accurate? Don't you suppose that there are some secular books that are historically accurate, but which might not be reliable in spiritual matters?

"The Bible has been shown to be scientifically accurate."

This is true, and probably much more significant than historical accuracy, though both are important. The reason scientific accuracy is so significant is that it reveals a state of knowledge that could not have been obtained through any ordinary means of discovery available at the time the Bible was written. In other words, if the Bible was written with scientific accuracy thousands of years ago, that would imply that knowledge was communicated to the biblical writers by someone who knew the truth about the way the universe operates. So, couldn't that someone be God? "Yes," it could. But, a critic could claim that such knowledge could have come from advanced intelligent beings (extraterrestrials, for example), or they could claim that the information was gathered through time travel. While those are admittedly far-fetched objections, there are people who would make such objections, and it illustrates the problem of using scientific accuracy as a logical proof that the Bible is true.

"The Bible accurately predicts the future. Since only God knows the future, this attests to his authorship of the Bible."

If one is looking for proof, this is about as good as it gets. We can definitely prove that details about future events were revealed in scripture with remarkable (100 percent) accuracy. In order for this to have happened, the biblical writers had to obtain this information from somewhere. A common tactic of those who seek to discredit the Bible is to postdate as many biblical prophecies as possible. [Postdating of prophecy means to assign a date for a prophecy that is later than the date of the supposed event prophesied. For example, scholars that do not believe in predictive prophecy generally postdate the book of Daniel, claiming that the book was written after the prophesied events happened, but in such a way as to make it appear that the prophecies were written before the events happened. The problem is that many prophecies are impossible to postdate, because there is strong historical evidence that the books in which they are contained were written well before the prophesied events occurred. The Isaiah 53 predictions of the death of the Messiah are a good example. While skeptics have attempted to cast doubt on the validity of some prophecies, they have been unsuccessful in explaining away the bulk of biblical prophecy. Fulfilled prophecy remains the best proof we have that God has spoken through the Bible. Nevertheless, God provides an even better way for us to know with absolute certainty that the Bible is his message to us.

The Bible is a self-authenticating message

What does "self-authenticating" mean? It means that when God speaks, those to whom he is speaking innately recognize his voice. Think of it this way, Jesus said in John 10:27, "My sheep hear my voice, and I know them, and they follow me." In the Bible, whenever God spoke to people they seemed to recognize who was speaking. Since God's communication to man is self-authenticating, it doesn't require logical proofs. Those to whom God speaks, whether directly in Bible times, or indirectly through the reading of the Bible, will always know that God is speaking. However, evidences such as historical and scientific accuracy, and fulfilled prophecy can be useful in combating false allegations about the Bible, *i.e.*, that the Bible cannot be true because it isn't accurate. Because God authenticates his word to man directly, through the ministry of the convicting power of the Holy Spirit, we can spend less time defending the Bible and more time using it. Hebrews 4:12 says, "For the word of God is living and active and sharper than any two-edged sword, and piercing as far as the division of soul and spirit, of both joints and marrow, and able to judge the thoughts and intentions of the heart" (NASB). While it may be necessary at times for us to challenge the critic who charges that the Bible isn't accurate, or that it doesn't evidence supernatural character, our focus should be on using the Bible rather than defending it; God will do the rest.

Review Questions

1. Explain why the Bible is unique.

2. Why is the scientific accuracy of the Bible of even greater significance than historical accuracy?

3. Why are the Bible's accurate predictions of the future the best evidence of its supernatural origin?

4. How can we know that the Bible is true?

5. What does "self-authenticating" mean in reference to the Bible?

How We Got Our Bible

The question, "How can we know the Bible is true," is a theological question. "Where did the Bible come from?" is a historical question. Basically there are six steps in the delivery of God's communication to us. They are:

1) Revelation   *(God speaking)*
2) Inspiration   *(Man recording)*
3) Canonicity   *(The Church recognizing)*
4) Transmission *(Men copying)*
5) Translation   *(Men translating)*
6) Illumination *(The Holy Spirit giving understanding)*

Let's take a look at each of these six steps.

Revelation

There are two types of revelation referred to in theology: natural revelation and special revelation. Natural revelation is what is revealed about God and his work through nature, that is, through non-supernatural means. Special revelation refers to the direct supernatural disclosure of things that man could not know by natural means (for example: God's plans for man's future). Both kinds of revelation have limitations. Natural revelation is limited to what can be seen and inferred from the physical creation, but there is only so much that can be learned about God and his plans through nature. Natural revelation is also limited by the fact that creation has been marred by sin. Nevertheless, there are some important truths that can be learned about God from nature, such as, his existence and power (cf. Rom. 1:20). On the other hand, special revelation is limited by man's ability to comprehend the message. Special revelation also requires that man have access to the message. Some examples in the communication of special revelation occur in Genesis 20:1ff; Exodus 19:1ff; 1 Samuel 3:1-14; Daniel 7:1ff; Revelation 1:1ff.

An often-asked question is whether or not God continues to give special revelation today as he did in Bible times. Historically, conservative Christianity has taken the position that the scriptures are now complete, and therefore, there is no need for additional special revelation to the Church. However, such a position should be regarded only as a general observation of the normal work of God. God can speak anytime he pleases. Perhaps a more relevant question would be: "Are the revelatory gifts that existed in the first century church (tongues, prophecy, and word of knowledge) part of the normal experience of the church today?" To this question we can give a definitive answer: "No, they are not." However, this does not mean that God could not, or does not give special revelation to individuals today. It simply means that such does not appear to be the normative experience of the present-day church, in spite of what some claim. (This topic will be discussed further under the ministry of the Holy Spirit and spiritual gifts.)

Here are some of the ways God has revealed himself to man:

1.   In the material creation, Ps. 19:1-4

2.   In man's own nature, Acts 17:28-29

3.   In providence, Deut. 4:33-35

4.   In the experiences of God's people, 1 Pt. 2:9; Philp. 3:10

5.   Through direct (special) revelation (as in a voice, vision, dream, etc.), Gen. 6:13

6.   In and through Jesus Christ, Jn. 1:18; 14:8-9; Col. 2:9

Special revelation differs from natural revelation in that it comes directly from God or his agent. How does God communicate to man by special revelation? Revelation was given through the spoken word (Ex. 19:9; 1 Sam. 3:1-14; 2 Sam. 23:1-2), through dreams (Gen. 20:6; 37:5-9; Dan. 2:1-45; Joel 2:28-29), through visions (Gen. 15:1; 46:2; Isa. 1:1; 6:1; Ezek. 1:3), through God's Son, Jesus Christ (Mt. 12:30-32), mainly through the ministry of the Holy Spirit (Jn. 14:26; cf. Jn. 16:13-14). When we read the Bible, we get the impression that special revelation was fairly common in Bible times; however, that is not the case. Special revelation was quite rare even in Bible times. As far as the biblical record is concerned, revelations from God occurred over only a relatively short period of several hundred years out of about six thousand years of history covered by the Bible. These revelations almost always occurred at a time when there was a major transition in God's program for his people, usually at a dispensational transition; for instance, at the call of Abraham, at Mt. Sinai, and during the ministry of Christ. God's people sometimes went many hundreds of years with little or no new revelation.

Inspiration

Inspiration involves God guiding the human authors of scripture, so that using their own unique qualities, background, style, and vocabulary, they composed and recorded God's message without error. The content of the message they recorded may have been derived from special revelation, natural revelation, history, personal experience, or the experiences of others; but no matter how the informational content was derived, only what God wanted to be said was recorded, such that the original manuscript (the autograph) of each inspired document is God's word without error or omission. This view of inspiration is usually referred to as "verbal-plenary inspiration." The terms "verbal" and "plenary" are useful because they specify that the very words of the Bible, from Genesis to Revelation, are inspired. The word "inspiration" is translated from the Greek world *theopneustos*, which is found in 2 Timothy 3:16 (cf. 2 Pet. 1:20-21). *Theopneustos* literally means, "God (*theos*) breathed (*pneustos*)." The idea is not that God breathed on the scriptures, but that he breathed them out; thus each book of the Bible is "God breathed." Of course, if the Bible is inspired, it is also inerrant (without errors) in the original manuscripts, and authoritative (binding upon man).

Logical support for verbal-plenary inspiration

Assuming that God has communicated to man, verbal-plenary inspiration is the only reasonable method. Why? Because an intelligent God would certainly know that unless the communication was one hundred percent inerrant (*i.e.*, truth without error) there would be no way for man to ever sort out the truth from the non-truth. Therefore, it would have been completely illogical for God to allow his truth to be mixed with error in such a manner that the two could not be distinguished. If God has spoken, it is apparent that his communication must have been inerrant; verbal-plenary inspiration and the dictation theory are the only two views consistent with inerrancy, and the dictation theory cannot be correct (see below). One might ask why all the fuss about inerrant originals since all we have are imperfect copies. The answer is that we know to within about one part per thousand the original wording of the New Testament, and it is certainly better to have 99.9 percent of something that is 100 percent true, than to have 100 percent of something that is 50 percent true (with no means of sorting out the error). Verbal-plenary inspiration is the only reasonable means by which God could have spoken to man.

Biblical support for the verbal inspiration of the Old Testament

1. The Old Testament writers claimed to be speaking God's Word (Ex. 20:1; 32:16; Isa. 1:1-2; Jer. 1:1-2; Ezek. 1:3).

2. Jesus believed in the verbal-plenary inspiration of the Old Testament.

    a. He recognized the entire Old Testament (Jn. 5:39; Lk. 24:44-46), as well as all three of the major divisions of the Old Testament (Mk. 7:8-13; Mt. 13:13-14; Jn. 10:34-35) as the authoritative word of God.

b. He quoted authoritatively from many Old Testament books (Genesis cf. Mk. 10:6-8; Exodus cf. Lk. 18:20; Numbers cf. Jn. 3:14; Deuteronomy and Leviticus cf. Lk. 10:26-28; Samuel cf. Mk. 2:25; Kings cf. Mt. 12:42; Psalms cf. Mk. 12:10; Isaiah cf. Lk. 4:17-21; Daniel cf. Mt. 24:15; Malachi cf. Mt. 11:10).

c. He clearly believed the Old Testament to be historically reliable. For examples, note his treatment of the following Old Testament persons: Adam and Eve (Mt. 19:4-7), Abel (Lk. 11:51), Noah (Mt. 24:37-39), Moses (Jn. 3:14), David (Lk. 20:41), Jonah (Mt. 12:38-41), Daniel (Mt. 24:15).

d. He submitted himself to the authority of the Old Testament (Mt. 5:17-18; Lk. 18:31 [implied]).

e. He attributed Old Testament material directly to the Holy Spirit (Mt. 22:41-46).

f. He used the Old Testament in such a way as to indicate his complete confidence in what it said (Mt. 22:23-33 cf. Ex. 3:6).

3. The New Testament writers believed in the verbal-plenary inspiration of the Old Testament.

a. They quoted from, or alluded to most of the Old Testament books. According to *The Dictionary of Biblical Literacy* (compiled by Cecil B. Murphy, Oliver-Nelson Books, 1989), the book of Isaiah is referenced a total of 419 times in 23 different NT books, the Psalms are referenced 414 times in 23 NT books, Genesis is referenced 260 times in 21 NT books, Exodus is referenced 250 times in 19 NT books, Deuteronomy is referenced 208 times in 21 NT books, Ezekiel is referenced 141 times in 15 NT books; Daniel is referenced 133 times in 17 NT books, Jeremiah is referenced 125 times in 17 NT books, Leviticus is referenced 107 times in 15 NT books, and Numbers is referenced 73 times in 4 NT books, and this is only a partial listing. The book of Revelation draws information from 32 OT books, the book of Luke draws information from 31 OT books, the Gospel of John draws information from 26 OT books, Acts draws information from 25 OT books, the Gospel of Mark draws information from 24 OT books, Romans draws information from 23 OT books, Hebrews draws information from 21 OT books, 1 Corinthians draws information from 18 OT books, the Epistle of James draws information from 17 OT books, and the Epistle of 1 Peter draws information from 15 OT books, and again, this is only a partial listing.

b. The New Testament writers referred to many Old Testament characters as historical (Acts 1:16; 2:25-34; Rom. 4:6; 5:14; 9:10; 1 Cor. 15:22-45; Heb. 11:9-32; James 2:21; Jude 14;).

c. The New Testament writers referred to the Old Testament as "scripture," by which they indicated their belief that the Old Testament was divinely authoritative (Acts 17:11; Rom. 1:1-2; 2 Tim. 3:16).

d. They attributed the Old Testament to the Holy Spirit. Note the following instances:

Psalm 110 cf. Mark 12:36
Psalm 41:9 cf. Acts 1:16
Psalm 2 cf. Acts 4:24-26
Isaiah 6:9-10 cf. Acts 28:25-27

Support for the verbal inspiration of the New Testament

1. Jesus pre-authenticated the New Testament. Since the New Testament was not written until after Jesus ascended to Heaven, it was necessary for him to pre-authenticate it be-

fore it was written. Note that he validated all three of the major sections of the New Testament.

History (Matthew-Acts): pre-authenticated in John. 14:26

Doctrinal/didactic (Romans-Jude): pre-authenticated in John. 16:13-15

Apocalyptic [the future] (Revelation): pre-authenticated in John 16:13

2. The New Testament writers believed the New Testament to be inspired.

   a. John (Rev. 1:1-2; 22:6)
   b. Paul (1 Cor. 2:13; 14:37; 1 Thess 2:13)
   c. Peter — in reference to Paul's letters (2 Pet. 3:15-16)
   d. Jude (Jude 17,18)

Incorrect views of inspiration

We should not be surprised that a number of incorrect views of inspiration have arisen in the history of the church. Note the following.

1. *Natural inspiration:* Men of great creative genius wrote the Bible, but it is still just a human work, and no more likely to be true than any other human work.

2. *Mystical inspiration:* The biblical authors were inspired in the sense that people today are inspired to do great things like painting or poetry, but such inspiration does not guarantee that the Bible is God's word.

3. *Conceptual inspiration:* God gave the biblical authors the ideas and they developed those ideas, but they were not protected from introducing errors into their works.

4. *Partial inspiration:* Some parts of the Bible are more in- spired than other parts, and some parts are not inspired at all. This view allows for some portions of the Bible to be inspired and infallible, and for other portions to be uninspired, but it doesn't give any way to determine which is which. If this view were true, it would cast doubt on the validity of the entire Bible. Such a view appeals to those who want to develop their own brand of religion by selectively eliminating anything they don't like.

5. *Dictation inspiration:* God dictated every word and the human writers were merely transcriptionists. While this view sounds good on the surface, since it doesn't allow for errors in the original autographs, it is an overly simplistic view because it is evident that each human author used his own vocabulary and life ex- periences in the writing of the scripture, and that would not be what we would expect to see if the mate- rial were dictated.

Are copies of the original manuscripts inspired?

This is a particularly important question in light of the fact that we don't have any of the originals. Strictly speaking, inspira- tion refers to the original composition and recording of the text (*i.e.,* the actual autographs). A copy reproduces the inspired word of God to the extent that it accurately reproduces the original autograph. We will talk more about textual criticism later, how- ever, textual criticism is the attempt to recover the precise word- ing of the autographs from the copies we have.

Canonicity

Canonicity deals with how the early church knew which books should be accepted as scripture (like Genesis, Isaiah, Ro- mans, *etc.*) and which ones should be excluded (like Tobit, Judith, Baruch, and the Gospel of Thomas). The word "canon" means, "standard," or "measure." Canonical books are those that measure up to the standard of inspired literature.

There is a body of non-canonical literature that comes from the intertestamental period (between the writing of the Old and New Testaments), which is referred to as "apocryphal" (*i.e.*, "other writings"). Though this literature was not viewed by the Jews as scripture, some of it was included in Jerome's Latin translation of the Bible and adopted into the Roman Catholic Bible in the sixteenth century.

The real problem for the early church came from literature produced in the post-apostolic era. Since even false teaching has to appeal to some basis of authority, many books first saw the light of day in the second and third centuries of the church to support various heretical beliefs (usually concerning the nature of God, Christ, the Holy Spirit, sin, the material creation, the nature of evil, the fall of man, or redemption). This body of literature is often referred to as the New Testament apocrypha; however, most of these books are pseudepigraphal (forgeries) produced by gnostics. Because of the profusion of these spurious documents, it became necessary for the early church to make sure that such books were not included in the canon, or given weight in theological disputes [The early Church in the second and third centuries was, quite literally, in danger of being overrun by gnostic heresies. In the mid-second century, Valentinus, one of the leading gnostics of his day, was almost elected to be the Bishop of Rome.]

Many people mistakenly think that some group of church leaders sat down and voted on which books they thought should be in the canon, and that's how we got our Bible. But that isn't the way it happened. The target group to which each portion of scripture was addressed immediately recognized what they received as authoritative scripture. (This is true of both the Old and New Testaments.) The real issue facing the early church was keeping out spurious material that appeared in the post-apostolic era that was being used to support doctrines not found in the established teachings of Christ and the apostles. While this sounds complicated, it was not as difficult a task as one might imagine, and while these dubious documents created a lot of doctrinal disputation, the task of distinguishing them from the authoritative writings of the New Testament was fairly straightforward, and occurred with very little fanfare; so little, in fact, that we have had some difficulty in reconstructing the process.

We should not confuse a list of canonical books with the canon itself. Some people mistakenly think the church didn't have a canon until it had such a list; nothing could be further from the truth. The list was merely a tool for excluding spurious works that appeared late from being used as scripture. But list or no list, the early church knew what was authoritative, which is why many of the forgeries drew upon biblical imagery and often quoted or alluded to biblical source material to make them seem more "biblical." Note the following examples of how scripture was immediately recognized as the word of God.

1. Moses' writings were placed beside the ark of the covenant (Deut. 31:24-29), the most holy place on earth.

2. Daniel, a contemporary of the prophet Jeremiah, regarded Jeremiah's prophecies as authoritative scripture (Dan. 9:1-2, cf. Jer. 25:11).

3. Peter, a contemporary of Paul, regarded Paul's writings as scripture on a par with the Old Testament (2 Pet. 3:14-16).

In order to understand how we came to have the specific sixty-six books that are in our Bible, we need to look at the formation of the Old and New Testament canons individually.

The Old Testament canon

The question of which books should be included in the Old Testament was fairly simple and was settled before Christ was born. Note the following.

1. Except for the Sadducees, who accepted only the books of Moses (Genesis-Deuteronomy), the Jewish people regarded as scripture the same thirty-nine books as the protestant church today, though they arranged them in a different order. Also, some books have been split in the English Bible (*e.g.,* 1 & 2 Samuel, *etc.*).

2. The scriptures that Jesus read and used are the same as our present-day Old Testament (in Hebrew, of course).

3. The Old Testament apocryphal books officially accepted by the Roman Catholic Church were never regarded as scripture by Jesus or the Jewish people. They came into the Roman Catholic Church *via* the Jerome (Latin) translation. However, Jerome's own testimony was that those books were not considered by the Jews to be scripture and that he was reluctant to include them in the same volume as the canonical books.

4. Early quotations of the apocryphal books by some early church leaders (Irenaeus, Tertullian, Clement of Alexandria and Cyprian), none of whom were Old Testament or Hebrew scholars, occurred at a time when the extent of the Old Testament canon was not well understood, especially by non-Jewish religious leaders, and some may have mistakenly thought that these books had been an accepted part of the Hebrew canon, when in fact that was never the case.

The New Testament canon

Since the letters that were written to the early churches were scattered over the Roman Empire, it took some time for the churches to assess what they had. There was very little reason to draw up a list of canonical books until suspicious documents began to show up in doctrinal disputations; then it became necessary to establish an agreed upon list of books that were considered authoritative. This does not mean that the church had no canon until such a list was agreed upon. They had the canon; they simply needed to make certain that uninspired documents were not accorded canonical status.

It is extremely important to understand that the early church did not determine which books would become scripture; they merely endeavored to recognize which books were already received by the Church, at large, as scripture. They did this by developing tests that could be applied to a disputed book. The thirty-nine books of our Old Testament and the twenty-seven books in our New Testament were not seriously in dispute (of course those who had defected to amillennialism would like to have excluded the book of Revelation for obvious reasons). While it was not necessary for a book to meet all of the criteria, they were expected to meet most of it. The criteria were derived from what the church already knew about the character of scripture from the books of undisputed authenticity. (We can think of the criteria for canonicity as a kind of weed killer. Weed killer doesn't produce grass; it just gets rid of weeds.)

Some of the tests the early church applied to determine whether a book met the standard of canonicity were: the test of inspiration (Does the book claim to be inspired?), authorship (Is the book the work of an accredited representative of God?), genuineness (Does the book appear to be what it purports to be?), truth (Do the facts appear to be correct?), testimony (Is there credible historical evidence that the book has been regarded as authoritative?), authority (Does the book claim to be authoritative?), agreement (Does the book agree with received books doctrinally?), universality (Is the message of the book universally applicable to all generations?), spiritual and moral character (Is the message consistent with the character of God?).

Transmission

Given that God has communicated to man (revelation) and that man under the inspiration of the Holy Spirit has been able to accurately and faithfully record that message without error (including no additions or deletions), how do we know that the Bible we have today is anything close to the original that was written? Couldn't people have changed it over the years? Of course, the answer is "Yes." In fact, of the thousands of early manuscripts of the Bible (both Old Testament and New Testament) no two are identical. Providentially, however, in most cases the differences are minor and it is possible to determine the correct reading. We are aided by the fact that we have so many manuscripts to compare. There are about five thousand early Greek manuscripts, or portions of manuscripts of the New Testament alone. That's a lot of material with which to work. Besides, many of the differences are simply alternate spellings or accidents like skipping a word or line of text.

Textual criticism

How do Bible scholars determine which are the best manuscripts, and how do they resolve conflicts between manuscripts? These questions take us into the area of biblical studies known as "textual criticism." Textual criticism is the branch of biblical studies that deals with determining the most accurate reading of the biblical text. Scholars who engage in textual criticism usually specialize in the study of either the Old Testament or the New Testament. Textual criticism is necessary since we don't have any of the original documents.

Some of the basic principles used in textual criticism

1. Because manuscripts, when copied, tend to get longer with each copy, the shorter reading is more likely to be closest to the original. However, there may be good reasons for accepting the longer version. How do manuscripts get longer when they are copied? Sometimes explanatory notes in the margins of the manuscripts were copied into the text by later copyists thinking these were corrections or omissions.

2. Since copyists tend to smooth out difficult readings, the awkward wording may be closer to the original. Obviously this has to be taken with a dose of common sense. It doesn't mean that if a manuscript really butchers the text, it's the best version. It simply means that one should be aware of the signs of later editing.

3. The variation in reading that most naturally accounts for how another variation in reading occurred is probably the best. This means that if reading "B" could have come from making a simple mistake in copying "A," then "A" is probably closer to the original.

4. The variation that best exemplifies the style and vocabulary of the author and best fits with the context is probably the best.

Any of these principles taken to an extreme could result in an absurd conclusion. Obviously, they are only guidelines and must be applied with a large dose of common sense and sensitivity to both the content and context of the text.

The reliability of the present-day Hebrew and Greek texts

Since our translations are made from the Hebrew and Greek texts, those translations cannot be any more accurate than the texts from which they are translated. Therefore, the question of the reliability of our Hebrew and Greek texts is enormously important.

Observations on the present-day Hebrew text (Old Testament)

The present-day Hebrew text is based on the Masoretic Texts dating to about A.D. 900. Until fairly recent times we didn't have any way to check the accuracy of the Masoretic Texts, since they were the oldest manuscripts we had. However, the discovery of the Dead Sea Scrolls in the 1940's changed that. [The Dead Sea Scrolls are a collection of ancient manuscripts dating from about 150 B.C. to about A.D. 70. They were hidden in caves southeast of

Jerusalem near the Dead Sea, where they remained until their recent discovery.] Contained within the Dead Sea Scrolls collection are a number of ancient Hebrew manuscripts of the Old Testament; these manuscripts are about a thousand years older than the Masoretic Texts. The discovery of the Dead Sea Scrolls gave scholars the opportunity to check the accuracy of the Masoretic Texts to see if they had changed over the thousand-year period of hand copying from 150 B.C. to A.D. 900. What was discovered was that over that period the copying of the Old Testament resulted in very insignificant changes to the text. This was good news. If the Hebrew manuscripts could be copied from 150 B.C. to A.D. 900 with only minor variation, it isn't unreasonable to assume that they were copied from the time of their original composition with similarly great accuracy (after all, the original compositions were only written 250 to 1250 years prior to the date of some of the oldest Dead Sea Scrolls).

[Regarding the comparison of the DSS (Dead Sea Scrolls) texts to the Masoretic, of the 166 Hebrew words in Isaiah 53, only 17 letters (not words) were different. Ten of these deviations were the result of variations in spelling and four more were minor stylistic variations having no real effect on the reliability of the text. The remaining three letters comprise the word "light," which somehow became appended to verse eleven.] The reading of the Old Testament text is probably as settled as it's going to be, unless more old manuscripts are discovered.

Observations on the present-day Greek text (New Testament)

The reading of the Greek New Testament is well attested. Today we have over 24,000 early Greek manuscripts and translations of the New Testament. Although much of this material is fragmentary (not a complete manuscript), it is nonetheless an astounding quantity of material from which to determine the original reading of the text. Of these 24,000+ documents (or fragments), approximately 5,300 are Greek manuscripts; 10,000 are early Latin translations of the New Testament, and about 9,300 are other early translations (including Syriac {Aramaic}).

No other ancient manuscript is as well attested as the New Testament. New Testament scholars who study the transmission of the New Testament text believe that 99.9% of the text of the original is now well established. This means that only about one word in a thousand is in serious question (and none of those in question has any significant doctrinal impact). Also, no other ancient document has so many manuscripts so close to the time of actual composition (some within twenty-five to forty years). The abundance of early manuscript evidence means that we can be confident we know the original wording of the New Testament (at least within 99.9%).

There is a controversy within some circles over whether we should be using the "received" Greek text (The Textus Receptus, RT), or the more recent "eclectic" texts (produced by comparison of a larger body of manuscript evidence). Below is a quick rundown of the history of the Greek New Testament.

The earliest copies of the Greek text were probably made for personal use by non-professional copyists. Naturally, since these manuscripts were made by hand, over the years variations arose between manuscripts. Geographic isolation resulted in the development of manuscript families. Manuscripts reflecting certain family characteristics were copied time and again. With the advent of the printing press identical copies could be mass-produced; of course, everyone who could read wanted a Bible. The first Bible printed was the Latin Vulgate edition published in 1456.

Work on the Complutensian Polyglot, a multi-language parallel edition, was begun in 1502, but the book was not published until 1522. Meanwhile, Dutch humanist and Catholic theologian, Disiderius Erasmus, wishing to be the first to publish a Greek New Testament hurriedly put together a text for publication. Because this project was done in a great rush, Erasmus was limited to very few manuscripts, none of which contained the complete text of the New Testament. In fact, his only manuscript of Revelation lacked the last six verses, so Erasmus translated those verses from Latin back into Greek. The entire project took from July 1515 to March 1516, only eight months, including the hand typesetting and printing, and included Erasmus' own Latin translation of the text! It was truly a whirlwind production compared to the twenty years in preparing the Complutensian Polyglot. Erasmus' work was published by Johann Froben. The short of things is that Erasmus' Greek text became the first to be published. Martin Luther based the New Testament portion of his German translation of the Bible on the second edition (1519) of Erasmus' Greek New Testament, and William Tyndale may have used the third edition (1522) in his English translation. Four editions of the Greek text based on Erasmus' work were published by Robert Estienne between 1546 and 1551. His third edition was the first to contain a list of textual variations. Theodore Beza published nine editions of the Greek text, again based on Erasmus' edition and subsequent editions that were printed by Robert Estienne between 1565 and 1604. The Elzevir brothers published seven editions of the Greek text between 1624 and 1678. The introduction to the second edition contained the following statement: "You have therefore the text now received by all, in which we give nothing altered or corrupt." Although this notice was merely a statement affixed by the printer, the words "received text" stuck, and hence this text and subsequent editions became known as the "Textus Receptus."

Although the Textus Receptus came to be held by most as the text of the Greek New Testament, work on the text of the New Testament didn't stop. Scholars continued to believe it was possible to derive an even more accurate text by comparing more manuscripts and by applying a little logic. In 1707 John Mill published a Greek text based on more than a hundred manuscripts. However, by this time any challenge to the Received Text was viewed as almost heretical. Johann Albrecht Bengel published a Greek text in 1734. Bengel made a few changes to the Received Text (most of which had already been suggested in the footnotes of prior editions of the RT). Bengel also included a critical apparatus in his edition that compared and classified variant readings and rated those readings as superior or inferior. Bengel seems to have been the first to state that the more difficult readings are likely to be closer to the original. As such, Bengel is viewed by some as being the father of modern textual criticism.

Johann Jakob Wetstien published a Greek text in 1752 using the Textus Receptus, but offering variant readings. In 1831 Karl Lachmann completed the first edition of the Greek text that completely departed from the Textus Receptus, being based on a comparison of older sources. It was not well received. (Matter isn't the only thing in the universe subject to the law of inertia!) By this time the Textus Receptus had become firmly established. Other such texts were published by Samuel Prideaux Tregelles (1879) and Constantine Tischendorf (1841-1872). In 1882 two Cambridge scholars, Brooke Foss Westcott and Fenton John Anthony Hort published an edition, and along with it, a volume on the principles of textual criticism used in their work. There was a reaction to Westcott and Hort's text by those who were suspicious of their underlying principles. This was exacerbated by the fact that neither Westcott nor Hort were biblical conservatives (neither of the two believed in verbal inspiration). Since that time, numerous critical texts have been published, and they all share a basic conviction that comparison of the manuscripts using a set of reasonable principles will lead closer to the original reading of the text.

Basically, the present-day controversy continues to revolve around which Greek text ought to be used for translation and study. One school of thought is that the Textus Receptus should be used because it was translated from superior manuscripts (*i.e.*, manuscripts in the "western family" of texts; the western text was the dominant manuscript family in the western church, *i.e.*, the Roman Catholic Church, through the middle ages). By far the majority of present-day Bible scholars reject the notion that the western manuscripts are superior, and therefore conclude that we can, and ought to attempt to refine our understanding of the ancient Greek text of the New Testament by comparing the readings to older manuscripts and applying the principles of textual criticism.

Translation

The last step in making scripture available in other languages is translation. In many ways translation is the most challenging step in the process. The autographs were, of course, free of errors. As the manuscripts were copied over the centuries, various errors crept in. As we have seen, most of these errors can be identified and corrected through the use of textual criticism. However, the very nature of translation makes this step particularly vulnerable to the introduction of errors. The reason is that translators face a difficult task, and they must use a fair amount of discretion in the way they translate. One might ask why they can't just give a word-for-word rendering from the Hebrew and Greek, and let the reader decide the meaning. (Interlinear translations do this.) But that is not as good a solution as it might appear. Both Hebrew and Greek employ entirely different grammars than English. Simply rendering each successive word into English would result in tremendous confusion, because it would strip away the grammar, which is the key to understanding how the words are used. It would be like receiving a coded message without knowing the code.

The big problem in translation — finding balance

Translators generally try to produce a translation that strikes a balance between two objectives: accuracy and readability. Unfortunately these two objectives sometimes exist on opposite ends of the translation spectrum. Here's the way it sometimes works in translating either Hebrew or Greek into another language: The more accurate the translation, the harder it is to read, especially if the translation is English. The reason is that this type of translation tends to render the text as close as possible to the original language structure, and that structure is often unfamiliar to the English reader. On the other hand, translations that are highly readable tend to track poorly with the original language structure. Do you see the problem? Sometimes, the more precise the translation, the more difficult it is to read, and the more readable it is, the less precise it is likely to be. This fact, and commercialism (there's money in selling a new translation), has led to a profusion of English translations.

Illumination

The Bible is a book about spiritual things, and to understand those things we need the help of the Holy Spirit. Paul taught this principle in 1 Corinthians 2:9-16. Needless to say, anything that interferes with the work of the Holy Spirit has the potential to keep us from understanding and appreciating the message of the Bible. The presence of unconfessed sin and the lack of prayer are two of the greatest barriers to the Spirit's work of illumination.

Review Questions

1. What are the six steps in the word of God being communicated to man?

2. What is the difference between "natural revelation" and "special revelation"?

3. What are some of the ways God has revealed himself to man?

4. How common was special revelation in Bible times?

5. Define verbal-plenary inspiration.

6. Briefly summarize both the logical and the biblical support for verbal-plenary inspiration.

7. How does inspiration relate to copies of the biblical text?

8. Briefly summarize the formation of both the Old and New Testament canons (*i.e.,* how they came to be received as the word of God).

9. How do we explain the fact that some of the early church leaders (*e.g.,* Irenaeus, Tertullian, Clement of Alexandria, *etc.*) quoted from the Old Testament apocrypha as if it were a part of the Old Testament?

10. What branch of biblical studies seeks to recover the original wording of the biblical texts?

11. Briefly address the reliability of the present-day Hebrew text of the Old Testament.

12. Briefly address the reliability of the present-day Greek text of the New Testament.

13. Briefly describe the problem of translating the Hebrew and Greek texts into English.

The Person and Work
of Christ

The Person and Work of Christ

Christ is the focal point of the Bible. From its opening pages to its closing verses, the person and the work of God's anointed Messiah ("Christ") is the central theme. What is anticipated in the Old Testament is realized in the New. If all references to the work of Messiah, both direct and indirect, were removed from the Bible, there would be little left except some moral principles to which man could never attain, along with some interesting, but pointless ancient history.

When we ask about the "person" of Christ, we are asking, "Who is he?" This is the natural beginning point; for until we know who Christ is, it is impossible to understand or appreciate his past, present, or future work.

The pre-existence of Christ

The Bible tells us that Christ existed as a person prior to his birth in Bethlehem. This can be seen from the following four lines of evidence.

1. The testimony of the Old Testament

    a. He is an eternal being (Mic. 5:2)

    b. He appears in the Old Testament as, "the Angel of the LORD"

2. The testimony of John the Baptizer (Jn. 1:15 cf. Lk. 1:26)

3. The testimony of Christ himself (Jn. 8:58; 6:61-62; 17:5,24)

4. The testimony of the Apostles (Jn. 1:1-2; 1 Cor. 10:4; Phil. 2:5-7; Col. 1:17)

The deity of Christ

The deity of Christ refers to the fact that Christ is God, co-equal with the Father and the Holy Spirit. Before launching into an examination of Christ's deity, it is important to define two terms. The first is "deity" itself. As used here "deity" means absolute deity—not that Christ is "a god," but that he is "the eternal God"—Jehovah. Second, from time to time I will refer to a view the early church condemned; that view is called "Arianism." While we will discuss Arianism later, it is essentially a view that recognizes only the Father as God. According to Arianism, while Christ might be viewed as a lesser deity, on a par with angels, he is not viewed as absolute (eternal) deity. The early church rejected Arianism, and orthodox Christianity has always viewed Arianism as the most egregious heresy, since it denies the core tenant upon which the Christian faith is built. Arianism is forever cropping up in heretical groups like Jehovah's Witness. It certainly seems to be true that old heresies never die; they just get recycled. Why is that? Perhaps it is because so few people who profess to be Christians really understand the basis of the Christian faith. The deity of Christ is the one doctrine that every Christian must understand and believe, and it is the one doctrine that every Christian ought to be prepared to defend.

Christ's deity is taught in numerous ways. The following are some of the key observations from scripture.

1. The Bible explicitly says that Jesus Christ is God.

    Isaiah 9:6
    Jesus is identified as the "Messiah" ("Christ" is the Greek translation of the Hebrew word for "Messiah"). Isaiah said that the Messiah is "the Mighty God," "the Eternal Father," "the Prince of Peace."

    Isaiah 40:3,9 cf. Matthew 3:1-14, John 1:6-18
    According to Matthew 3:1-14 and John 1:6-18, John the Baptizer fulfilled the prophetic ministry described in Isaiah 40:3-11 of the one who would proclaim the coming of the

Messiah. For whom was John sent to prepare the way? It was the LORD God, *i.e.,* Jehovah (Isa. 40:3,9). Since John's prophetic ministry was based on Isaiah 40:3-9, and since John would have known that the one for whom he prepared the way was Jehovah, John's testimony concerning Jesus is nothing less than a prophetic proclamation that Jesus is Jehovah. John's prophetic proclamation is the fountainhead of the doctrine of the deity of Christ.

Isaiah 44:6 cf. Rev. 22:13-16 and Rev. 1:8

In this passage Jehovah said, "I am the first and I am the last, and there is no God besides Me." In Revelation 22:13-16, Jesus said, "I am the Alpha and the Omega, the first and the last, the beginning and the end." Consequently, Revelation 22:13-16 is a patent claim that Jesus is Jehovah (a claim already made by John). Interestingly, Revelation 1:8 begins by identifying the one who is "the Alpha and the Omega"; he is "the Lord God, who is and who was and who is to come, the Almighty"; thus, Jesus is identified in Revelation as the eternal God.

Psalm 45:6 cf. Heb. 1:8

In Hebrews 1:8, a quotation from Psalm 45:6, the Son (Christ) is expressly called "God" ("the God"), and thus identified as the God of the Old Testament.

John 1:1-3

This is a clear and emphatic statement of the absolute deity of Christ. It is little wonder that modern-day Arians, such as Jehovah's Witness, have sought to obscure these verses, since they reject the absolute deity of Christ. Actually, this passage provides three independent witnesses to the deity of Christ: In verse 1, Christ is expressly called "God." In verse 2, he is said to have been in the beginning with God (the Father), which could only be true if he were eternal, existing prior to the creation. In verse 3 we are told that he created all things (everything, without exception), which could only be true if he is eternal, since he could not have created himself. We will discuss verses 2 and 3 below; for now, we will focus on verse 1. Interestingly, every major English translation spells "God" with a capital "G," in recognition that it refers to absolute deity (*i.e.,* the God of the Bible). The Jehovah's Witness' New World Translation (NWT) reads, "a god." It is the position of Jehovah's Witness that Jesus is not absolute deity, but a lesser god, a created being on the same level as the angels. Such a view is untenable on at least two grounds. 1) Although Satan is referred to as, "the god of this world" (*i.e.,* a false god), to suggest that the New Testament presents Christ as such is to display deplorable ignorance of the scriptures. The Bible is clear that there is only one true God (Isaiah 44:6,8; 45:5,6,14,18,21,22; 46:9). Unless Christ is a false god, like Satan, then he must be the true God. 2) This entire discussion is built on a misrepresentation of the Greek text of this passage by Jehovah's Witness. In Greek, when a substantive isn't definite, an indefinite article ("a" or "an") can sometimes be inserted (but not if the word is otherwise indicated to be definite, which is often the case). Because "God" in verse 1 does not have a definite article ("the"), the translators of the NWT inserted an indefinite article and made the last part of the verse read: "and the Word was a god." However, this is completely erroneous since "God" is definite in the original. Although "God" (the predicate nominative) has no article, it is definite because the subject has an article, and it is impossible to have an indefinite predicate nominative with a definite subject. The reason the article is absent from the predicate nominative (God) is that John here uses an emphatic form to emphasize the deity of "the Word" (Christ); he switched the positions of the subject and the predicate nominative in the sentence, making the predicate nominative come before the verb. In such cases the article must be dropped from the predicate nominative so as not to confuse it with the subject. This grammatical feature is appropriately called, "the rule of the definite predicate"; it is a common and well-understood feature of Greek grammar with which any competent translator should be familiar. If the verse is translated giving the emphatic structure its full force, it says: "GOD, that's what the Word was."

John 1:18

The apostle John wrote that, "No one has seen God at any time; the only begotten God, who is in the bosom of the Father, He has explained Him." Did you notice what Christ is called by John—"the only begotten God." Remember, according to Isaiah 44:6,8; 45:5,6,14,18,21,22; 46:9, there is no God but Jehovah. Thus, John's proclamation is a claim that Christ is the eternal God referred to in Isaiah—the LORD God, Jehovah.

John 5:17-18

In this passage Jesus referred to the heavenly Father not as "our Father," but as "my Father" (*i.e.*, "my own father"), a transparent claim to be of the same substance as the Father. The Jews, understanding this claim, sought to kill him because he not only was breaking the Sabbath, but also was "calling God His own Father, making Himself equal with God" (v. 18). It might be charged that the Jews simply misunderstood what Jesus said; even in that unlikely case, it would have been incumbent upon John, the author of this Gospel, to point that out. Far from correcting any misimpression, John continued to reinforce the claim of Christ's deity throughout this gospel. If Jesus did not claim to be God, then John is to be greatly faulted for failing to present an accurate picture of what actually happened. There are really just two choices: 1) Jesus claimed to be God, or 2) John's gospel account is not inspired.

John 8:24, 56-58

Jesus said to his audience, "...unless you believe that I am, you shall die in your sins." Some versions read, "...unless you believe that I am *he*..."; however, there is no pronoun in the original. In the Old Testament, God called himself "I am" (Ex. 3:14) in view of his eternality. Here, Jesus was saying that unless men believe that he is the eternal God, they will perish in their sins. That this is the correct understanding of this verse is confirmed in verses 56-58, where Jesus again claimed to be "I am." Note that he didn't say, "...before Abraham was, I was," which would be correct if he were claiming merely to have pre-existed Abraham; he said, "...before Abraham came into being [Gr. *genesthai*, aorist infinitive], I am" [Gr. *egō eimi*, present tense]. In other words, Jesus was saying: I am the eternal God, the God who appeared to Moses by the name, "I am" (Ex. 3:14). While this might not be as clear to the modern reader, we can be certain that the Jews to whom Jesus was speaking understood exactly what he meant.

John 10:30-33
Here Jesus claimed to be one with the Father. Those who deny the absolute deity of Christ argue that this was a benign claim to be "in harmony" with the Father, not a claim of deity. However, the reaction of the Jews present at the time evidences that this was not simply a benign affirmation of unity with God, for they took up stones to stone him, giving the reason: "You, being a man, make yourself out to be God" (v. 33).

John 12:45
In this verse Jesus said the one seeing him is seeing the One who sent him (*i.e.,* the Father, cf. vv. 49-50). Of course one might argue that he was simply affirming that he (a man) was made in the image of God. However, if that is all he meant, why is it stated here in reference to believing in him, and why is it that no other God-fearing individual in biblical history made such a claim? Clearly Jesus was claiming to be God.

John 14:7-9
Here, as in John 12:45, Jesus claimed that to see him is to see the Father (v. 7). Philip, not comprehending what Jesus was saying, asked that Jesus would show them the Father.

To this Jesus replied, "Have I been so long with you, and yet you have not come to know Me, Philip? He who has seen Me has seen the Father; how do you say, 'Show us the Father?'" This statement could not be more clear; Jesus was claiming that he and the Father were of the same divine essence (v. 10), to see one is to see the other, a claim that this Jewish audience clearly understood to be a claim to be God (cf. 10:33).

John 20:28
Thomas had not been present on the previous occasion when the risen Jesus had appeared to the disciples (20:19-25), and he had said that unless he saw Jesus and put his finger into the place of the nails and his hand in his side, he would not believe. Thomas was not a man to be tricked; he demanded hard evidence, and we can appreciate that about him. Thomas got that evidence eight days later when Jesus reappeared to the disciples while Thomas was present. Thomas' response was to say to Christ: "My Lord and my God." Arians, such as Jehovah's Witness, typically respond that Thomas, in his excitement, was simply glorifying God instead of referring to Jesus as Lord and God. However, the text is clear that Thomas was referring to Jesus as Lord and God. (The words "Lord" and "God" are not in the vocative case, as this explanation would require.) Also, the text is clear that Thomas was speaking directly to Jesus when he said to him, "My Lord and my God." Thus it is clear that this could only be an appellative statement. It should be understood as: "[*You are*] my Lord and my God!" The omission of the verb with subject ("you are") was actually a rather common form of emphasis.

Acts 20:28
Here Paul instructed the church to be on guard for the flock over which the Holy Spirit had made them overseers, "to shepherd the church of God which He purchased with his own blood." The blood can only be the blood of Christ.

[Romans 9:5]

Did Paul say, "Christ...who is over all, God, blessed forever"? Or, did he say, Christ...who is over all. God [be] blessed forever"? The question of whether Paul here refers to Christ as God, or merely offers a doxology, boils down to a question of punctuation. And since the punctuation of the Greek New Testament is not inspired (it was added later), it is difficult to use this passage as a proof-text for the deity of Christ. [There is an excellent summary of the interpretive options for this passage given in, *A Textual Commentary on the Greek New Testament* by Bruce M. Metzger, which is the companion volume to the UBS *Greek New Testament* (3rd edition). However, we must take issue with the statement that Paul never referred to Christ as God in his "genuine" writings. First, Titus 2:13 is a very clear statement of Christ's deity, which forces Metzger (the textual committee) to reject Titus 2:13 as genuine (an *a priori* argument). Second, Paul clearly referred to Christ as God in his instructions given to the elders at Ephesus (Acts 20:28), an important fact not taken into account by Metzger and the textual committee. (Also see Paul's discussion in Philippians 2:6, that Christ existed "in the form of God.") However, due to the uncertainty of the punctuation, this passage probably should not be used as a proof-text.]

Philippians 2:6

Paul said that Christ, prior to his incarnation, "existed in the form of God." This is equivalent to saying that Christ is God; for who but God could exist "in the form of God"? The reason that Paul addressed the issue of "form" is that he was contrasting the visible appearance of Christ before and after the incarnation, for the purpose of illustrating humility. The thought of the passage is this: If Christ, being manifest as God, could humble himself, becoming manifest as a man, we who believe in him should also be humble. Incidentally, this passage illustrates a very important point regarding Paul's understanding and use of the doctrine of the deity of Christ. Many have questioned why Paul, if he believed Christ to be God, did not devote more attention to this doctrine. This has led some to conclude that the doctrine of the deity of Christ is of post-Pauline origin. However, quite the opposite is true. As we have already seen, Christ claimed to be God. From the very beginning the deity of Christ was the cornerstone of the gospel. The fact that Paul alludes to the deity of Christ as a primary truth from which other, secondary teachings could be derived, indicates that in Pauline theology the deity of Christ was already considered to be established beyond dispute. To Paul, Christians were people who believe in Christ, in his deity, in his substitutionary death, and his burial, resurrection, and ascension. In his letters to the churches, Paul assumed the deity of Christ to be common doctrinal ground, since it was part of the gospel the churches had been founded upon, and one does not need to state the obvious.

Titus 2:13
This passage so clearly teaches the deity of Christ that those who believe the doctrine to be of post-Pauline origin are forced to deny that Paul wrote this portion of Titus, even though there isn't a shred of textual or historical evidence for rejecting Pauline authorship of this verse. Paul emphatically declared Christ to be both God ("the" God) and Savior. Note that Paul here employs a single article ("the") for both "God" and "Savior" (*tou megalou theou kai sōtēros hēmōn, Christou Iēsou*), indicating that both titles, "God" and "Savior," apply to the same person—Jesus Christ. [It isn't uncommon for Arians to place a comma after "God" in order to separate Christ, as Savior, from "God." However, that isn't translation, it's alteration of the text, for the verse absolutely cannot be translated that way. Why? First, there is no indication from any ancient sources that the text was ever punctuated that way. Secondly, and more importantly, the rule of the "copulative *kai*" requires that two substantives modified by a single article and joined by *kai* (the conjunction, "and") must refer to the

same object. This passage is without any doubt the prime example of Pauline theology regarding the deity of Christ. It is clear and unassailable historically, textually, and grammatically.]

Hebrews 1:6-12
This is indeed an interesting passage, in that it expresses the deity of Christ in numerous ways, both direct and indirect. We will note here only the direct expressions of deity and comment on the indirect expressions below. In three verses (vv. 8,9, and 10) the author explicitly refers to the Son as God. In verses 8 and 9 he is expressly called "God" ("the" God), and in verse 10 he is called "LORD" (Jehovah). [The Hebrew word "Jehovah" (or "Yahweh"), the personal name of God given in the Old Testament, is not written in the Greek New Testament; however, verse 10, which is explicitly applied to Christ, is a condensed quotation taken from Psalm 102:22-25, where the word "LORD" (v. 22) is "Jehovah."] Thus, the writer of Hebrews explicitly identifies Christ as "Jehovah." Jehovah's Witness respond that two of these statements should be translated differently. They translate verse 8: "God is your throne forever;" and verse 9 as: "God, your God, anointed you." (Thus attempting to remove the direct attribution of deity to Christ.) Apparently they did not notice that in verse 10 the term "LORD," which is clearly applied to Christ, is a reference to Jehovah God in the Old Testament, and they let the common translation stand. Of course, if even one of these three statements stands, Christ is God; and even in their own distorted translation, the Jehovah's Witness acknowledge that Christ is Jehovah (in verse 10). However, let us go back and ask whether the translation they offer in verses 8 is legitimate. From a purely grammatical standpoint one could translate verses 8 and 9 as they appear in the NWT; however, grammar isn't the whole story in translation. In translation, when confronted with multiple possibilities of meaning, one must ask if the context or common sense provides some clue as to which translation

is preferable. In this case there is strong contextual evidence that Christ is here referred to as Jehovah God (v. 10). Also, there seems to be a hierarchical problem with the NWT. If God doesn't refer to Christ (because he isn't God), then Jehovah God would be inferior to Christ, who is not God, since Christ would be seated upon God, which makes no sense at all. To say that God secures one's throne is one thing, but to say that God is the throne upon which one sits is quite another thing. How could God be the eternal throne of an inferior being? Below we will look at the numerous ways in which this passage also implies the deity of Christ.

Revelation 1:8 (cf. Isaiah 41:4)
(See Isaiah 44:6, above.) Here "the Alpha and the Omega" is identified as "the Lord God, who is and who was and who is to come, the Almighty." In the same book (Rev. 22:13) John records Christ as saying, "I am the Alpha and the Omega." Thus, if the Lord God, the Almighty, is the Alpha and the Omega, and Christ is the Alpha and the Omega, Christ must be the Lord God, the Almighty. Revelation 1:8 is condensed from Zechariah 12:6-10, and there, the one who is LORD is Jehovah (cf. v. 7).

2. Biblical statements that imply Christ is God

    The following passages record statements made by, or about Christ that only make sense if he is God.

    Matthew 7:21 cf. 13:41
    Christ taught that he is the Lord of the kingdom of Heaven, and he referred to that kingdom as his kingdom.

    Matthew 11:27-30
    While all of the prophets called men unto God, Jesus called men unto himself.

Matthew 12:1-8
Christ said that he is greater than God's Temple and Lord of the Sabbath, a patent claim to be Jehovah.

Matthew 13:41
He claimed to be in command of God's angels.

Matthew 22:41-46 cf. Mark 12:35-37
At one point late in Jesus' ministry, each of the three leading parties of the Jews, the Herodians, the Sadducees, and the Pharisees, attempted to discredit him by asking disingenuous questions by which they intended to entrap him in a theological argument. Jesus outwitted them on each occasion. In this pivotal encounter, Jesus turned the tables. It was a strategic move, a move that permanently ended the intellectual dueling; for Jesus here displayed himself to be a vastly superior intellect than his opponents. Let's listen in as Jesus deals this final, crushing defeat to the theologians of his day. In contrast to the previous three engagements, Jesus initiated this encounter with a strategic question: "What do you think about the Christ, whose son is He?" This seems like an innocuous question, at least the Pharisees thought so, and so they answered, "The Son of David." That answer landed them right into Jesus' trap, for it is precisely the answer he knew they would give. The Pharisaic conception of Messiah was of a great leader, yet still only a man. Their charge against Christ was not that he claimed to be the Messiah (though they did not accept him as such); their charge was that he claimed to be God, and to them that was blasphemy of the worst sort—that a man should presume to be God. Jesus then closed the trap. He asked this simple question: "Then how does David in [by] the Spirit call him 'Lord.' Here he quotes Psalm 110:1; saying: "The LORD said to my Lord, 'sit at my right hand, until I put thine enemies beneath thy feet.'" We can imagine that the Pharisees started to sweat, for they knew that Jesus had slammed the trap shut. They had said it themselves: The Messiah is David's Son, yet Jesus had quoted a

Davidic psalm in which David, speaking by the Spirit of God stated that Messiah is, in fact, his Lord, proving that the Messiah is greater than David, his ancestor. Jesus closed the dialogue with a simple, "How is that?" and was greeted with stunned silence, not a word. In fact, we are told that from that day forward these shell-shocked experts of the Hebrew Scriptures never dared to ask Jesus another question.

Matthew 25:31-46
Jesus said that he will determine who will enter the kingdom of God, and who will go into everlasting punishment. In other words, he is the Judge before whom all men will one day stand.

Matthew 28:18
Jesus claimed to possess all authority in Heaven and on earth. He didn't simply claim to have some authority; he claimed to have all authority, not only on earth, but in Heaven as well. What a stupendous claim! Who but God could properly exercise such authority? Could the Father wisely commit such absolute authority into the hands of a mere creature?

Mark 2:3-12
Christ forgave sins committed against God. While one might forgive sins committed against one's self, it would hardly be appropriate for one to forgive sins committed against another. How much more inappropriate would it be for Christ, if he were not God, to forgive sins against God? This must be seen as an implicit claim to deity, and was clearly recognized as such by those present, since they regarded this act as blasphemous (vv. 6-7).

Luke 24:25-27
Jesus claimed that he is the focus of all the scriptures.

John 1:3,10; Colossian 1:15-17 (cf. Gen. 1:1-2)
He is referred to as the Creator of the world.

John 1:12
He has authority to make men God's children.

John 4:42 cf. Isaiah 43:10-11
He is referred to as the "Savior" of the world, even though the Old Testament stated that Jehovah is the only Savior!

John 3:15-16, 36; 6:47-51; 10:27-28; 11:21-27
Jesus said that he is able to impart eternal life, which would hardly be possible were he not eternal.

John 6:40,44
Jesus said that he would resurrect believers in the last day.

John 5:23
He taught that all men should honor him in the same way that they honor the Father. Even on the lips of an archangel, such words would be blasphemous. There are only two options: Either Christ is God Almighty (Jehovah), or he is a blasphemer.

John 9:35-38
Jesus claimed to be the Son of God and he accepted the worship of men. Yet he taught that men should worship God alone (Lk. 4:8). Even angels sent directly from God refuse to be worshiped (Rev. 22:8-9); thus, when Christ permitted others to worship him it was an implicit claim of deity.

John 10:27-33 cf. 5:17-18
He claimed to be of the same essence as the Father.

John 10:24-38
His Jewish audience clearly understood that in referring to himself as "the Son of God," he was claiming to be God.

John 11:38-44
Jesus raised the dead. Elijah and Paul also raised the dead, but they did not claim to be God while doing so. Remember, the purpose of miracles is to validate the message of the one who works the miracle. If Jesus claimed to be God and raised the dead to validate his claim, his claim is true.

John 19:7
The charge against Jesus at his trial was that he claimed to be the Son of God, a charge he did not dispute.

John 14:23
Jesus said that his work was co-extensive (on an equal level) with the Father's work.

John 16:14
He taught that the Holy Spirit (himself God, cf. Acts 5:3-4) would not speak of himself, but would glorify him.

John 17:5
Jesus claimed to have shared the Father's own glory before the world was created.

John 17:22
He claimed to share the very essence of the Father.

Acts 1:3 cf. Romans 1:4
Jesus arose from the dead, which was the validation of all of his claims.

Colossians 1:15; Hebrews 1:3
Christ is referred to as the very "image of God." "Being the image" and "being made in the image" are not the same. Christ is the image.

Hebrews 1:6 cf. Matthew 4:10
The Father commanded the angels to worship the Son. Yet only God is worthy of worship, and angels refuse to accept worship (Rev. 22:8-9).

3. Christ possesses the attributes of God. Some of those attributes are:

Eternality (Mic. 5:2; Rev. 1:11-18; Jn. 1:1-3; 17:5; Col. 1:16-17)
Omnipotence (Mt. 28:18; Philp. 3:20-21; Heb. 1:3; 2 Pt. 1:3)
Omniscience (Lk. 7:36-50; Jn. 1:43-51; Mt. 9:4; Jn. 21:17)
Omnipresence (Mt. 18:20; Eph. 1:22-23)
Immutability (Heb. 1:11-12; 13:8)
Sovereignty (Isa. 6:1-5 cf. Jn. 12:41; Col. 1:16-17)

The impeccability of Christ

Impeccability refers to the inability to sin. On the surface, the question of whether Christ was peccable (able to sin) or impeccable (unable to sin) seems irrelevant, since he did not sin. However, the position one takes on this issue has serious ramifications for other important doctrines. The issue of whether Christ could have sinned usually surfaces in regard to his temptation. Some take the position that Christ must have been able to sin, otherwise he could not have been tempted, and scripture is clear that he was tempted (Heb. 4:15). Generally, proponents of peccability maintain that while Christ's divine nature could not sin, the human nature could have sinned. This is the "weakest link in the chain" argument. However, this would call into question the hypostatic union of the divine and human natures of Christ (*i.e.*, that they formed a singular person). If one nature could have acted in disregard of the moral imperatives of the other, does that not argue that the two natures did not form one personal being? And if so, does that not call into question Christ's qualification as the God-man to be our Savior?

Fortunately, we do not have to maintain that Christ was able to sin in order to understand how he could be tempted. Since God cannot be tempted to sin (Jam. 1:13), it follows that God cannot sin. If Jesus was God, it must be the case that he could not sin. To suggest that he could sin is to suggest that he was not God. How do we deal with the remaining problem that Christ was genuinely tempted to sin? The answer is to be found in the fact that while he was, and is, the impeccable God, he was also a peccable man. Christ's humanity, had it been able to act independent of his deity, would have been fully capable of sin. So, if he had a peccable human nature, could he have sinned? The answer is "No." Why? — Because as a divine/human being whose natures exist in a personal (hypostatic) union, any personal act is an act of both natures (that's the nature of the personal union); thus, in order for Christ to sin, both natures would have to consent. To say that Christ could have sinned had he chosen to do so assumes that his human nature could have acted independently; but if that were the case, it would cast doubt on the reality of the hypostatic union, and hence on his qualification to die as the God-man for man's sin. Thus while Christ's humanity could be tempted to sin, the person, Jesus Christ, could not sin. This is the deep mystery of the virgin conception. This doctrine provides an opportunity to see how the answer to a seemly irrelevant question in one area of doctrine can have huge consequences elsewhere.

Historical views on the person of Christ

In the early history of the Church, there were numerous ideas as to whether Christ had both human and divine natures, and how those natures relate. The following is a survey of the major views.

1. The orthodox view (the majority view of the church)

    Statement: Christ is both God and man joined hypostatically such that he is one person. In Christ the divine person of the Son of God was joined with a complete human nature (body, soul, and spirit) to form a divine-human person (composed of divine spirit and a human body, soul, and spirit). According to the orthodox view, attributes of each nature pertain only to that nature. [The Lutheran view of the "ubiquity" (omnipresence) of Christ's body is slightly different in that it conceives of the divine attribute of omnipresence being transferred to Christ's humanity, such that his human body became omnipresent. In this regard Lutheran Christology deviates from the historic Christian position.]

2. Ebionism

    Statement: Jesus was the natural offspring of Joseph and Mary (he was not God). He so pleased God that he was chosen to be the Messiah. Jesus became conscious of this fact at his baptism. Actually, this view is similar to the Pharisaic view of the Messiah that Jesus refuted in Matthew 22:41-46.

3. Gnosticism

    Statement: The gnostics were dualists, believing that the physical is inferior to the spiritual. Most viewed the physical as not only inferior, but evil in some sense. Since the physical is inferior (evil), God could not become flesh; hence there could be no real incarnation. The two basic forms of gnosticism were: 1) that the divine Christ came upon the man Jesus at his baptism, and departed prior to his crucifixion (Cerinthian gnosticism); or, 2) that Jesus' body was not real, but a materialization from the spirit realm (Docetic gnosticism). Both of these views deny atonement on the cross.

4. Arianism

    Statement: Although called a god, Christ is not the eternal God (Jehovah), but a created being, "the firstborn of all creation." Through him God created the world. At the incarnation the Son of God entered a human body, taking the place of the human spirit; thus Christ was neither fully God, nor fully human since he had no human spirit. (Jehovah's Witness is a modern example of modern-day Arianism.)

5. Apollinarianism

   Statement: Jesus had a human body and soul, but not a human spirit. The divine Son of God took the place of the human spirit, thus Jesus was not fully human. This is similar to Arianism in its view of the humanity of Christ, but it differs in its view of the deity of Christ. The Apollinarians accepted the deity of Christ, Arians did not. As such, the Apollinarian view is closer to the orthodox view.

6. Nestorianism

   Statement: The divine Son of God indwelt the man Jesus. This view denies the hypostatic (personal) union of the divine and human natures. [Regrettably, this view is prevalent among Christians today. One indication of this is the widespread belief that Christ was peccable. See "impeccability" previously discussed in this chapter.]

7. Eutychianism

   Statement: The divine and human natures mixed such that each took on the attributes of the other. In this process both the human and divine natures were altered. Such a view conflicts with the doctrine of God's immutability, and also has serious implications for Christ's humanity and his qualification to be man's sacrificial substitute.

The work of Christ in the Old Testament

We encounter the Son of God in the Old Testament in various ways. We see him first as the Creator of the world. Secondly, we see him as the Angel of the LORD, a visible manifestation of Jehovah. Thirdly, we encounter him prophetically as the prophesied Messiah/Redeemer to come.

As the Creator

While all three members of the Trinity were involved in creation, the New Testament emphasizes the Son's involvement. The Apostle John writes that "the Word" (the Son) was already in the beginning before the creation of anything took place (Jn. 1:1-2). The verb "was" is imperfect, meaning that when the beginning took place, the Word had (already) been. Thus, the Word was not created. Furthermore, John tells us that the Word created everything that was created (Jn. 1:3). As we have remarked in our discussion of the deity of Christ, in order for Christ to be the Creator of everything created, he had to be eternal (uncreated), and thus God, which is the very truth explicitly stated by John in John 1:1-2. In 1 Corinthians 8:6 Paul said that all things owe their existence to the Son. In Colossians 1:15-17 Paul gave his most definitive statement on this subject; he said that Christ is the "firstborn of all creation" (*i.e.,* not the first to be created, but the Preeminent One). He is the Preeminent One because everything that was created was created by and for him (v. 16). In verse 17 Paul extended this thought by saying that Christ sustains all things (that he created). Modern-day Arians have made much over the fact that Christ is referred to as "the firstborn of all creation." However, in so doing they fail to recognize how the expression is used. Clearly Paul was not saying that the Son was the first being created, for he goes to great lengths to establish that the Son created everything, not everything except himself, but absolutely everything that was created, both in the heavens and on earth. Actually, Paul defines his use of "firstborn" in verse 17 when he says that he (the Son) is "before all things." That is to say that the Son is "preeminent." In ancient cultures, next to the father, the firstborn had greater status than anyone in the family. In view of what Paul said, as well as other biblical statements, it would be completely erroneous to conclude that "firstborn" as used here, means the first to be created.

As "the Angel of the LORD [Jehovah]"

In the Old Testament the Son of God is sometimes manifested as "the Angel of the LORD." A study of the Angel of the

LORD reveals that this is Jehovah. All theophanies (visible appearances of God) are "christophanies" (appearances of the preincarnate Christ). The Son is the only member of the Trinity that has ever appeared to man (Jn. 1:18). Some instances of the appearance of the Angel of the LORD are described in the following passages; note that for each, the context reveals that the one appearing is Jehovah: Genesis 16:7-13 (cf. Jn. 1:18); Genesis 22:11-18; Genesis 31:11-13; Exodus 3:1ff; Exodus 13:21-22; 14:19 (cf. I Cor. 10:1-3); Judges 6:11-23, 13:9-20.

As the coming Savior

The Son is revealed in the Old Testament as the Savior and Redeemer, 1) prophetically (Gen 3:15; Isa 52:13-53:12); 2) in types, *i.e.,* prefigurements: Adam (Rom. 5:14), Isaac (Gen. 22), Melchizedek (Gen. 14 cf. Heb. 5-7), the sacrifices, the priesthood, and the feasts of Israel.

The incarnation of Christ

The incarnation refers to the operation through which the Son of God was joined to the human family through the virgin conception. While it is common to link the incarnation with the virgin birth, the miraculous element was the conception, not the birth, though he was virgin-born as scripture plainly states (Mt. 1:18-25, esp. v.25). The Roman Catholic doctrine of "the immaculate conception" should not be confused with the virgin conception of Christ. The doctrine of the immaculate conception refers to the Roman Catholic belief that Mary, the mother of Jesus, was virgin born, and thus sinless also. The Bible does not teach, nor does it imply such a view of Mary.

The method of the incarnation

The method of the incarnation was the virgin conception. The biblical support for this truth is as follows.

1. According to Matthew 1:18, Mary conceived Jesus before she had sexual relations. Also, we are told in Matthew 1:25

that Joseph had no relations with Mary until after the birth of Jesus.

2. According to Matthew 1:20, Jesus' conception was through supernatural means (cf. Lk. 1:35).

3. The Bible repeatedly states Mary's virginity (Lk. 1:27, 34; cf. Mt. 1:18).

4. The genealogy of Jesus at Matthew 1:16 strongly implies the virgin conception. After giving Joseph's genealogy, it states that Jesus was the descendant of Mary, not Joseph! [The pronoun "whom" is feminine, and refers to Mary, not Joseph. Such a statement would have been a great insult had Jesus not been virgin conceived.] See also Jeremiah 22:24-30 for why Jesus could not be the physical descendant of Joseph.

5. Isaiah 7:14, as quoted in Matthew 1:23, prophesied the virgin birth. [Note: Matthew 1:23 translates the Hebrew *'almah,* meaning "maiden" using the Greek word *parthenos,* meaning "virgin." To the Hebrew mind, "maiden" and "virgin" were without distinction.]

The significance of the virgin conception and birth of Christ

The virgin birth was first and foremost a sign (Isa. 7:14). It may also have been the means through which Jesus was born sinless, though the Bible nowhere makes such a connection. The virgin conception also preserved Jesus from the curse placed on the kingly line of David during the time of King Jeconiah (Jer. 22:28-30), while at the same time allowing him to inherit the right to the throne as the legal heir of Joseph, who was of the kingly line (Mt. 1:1-17).

Objections to the virgin conception and birth

Numerous objections have been made against the virgin conception of Jesus. Among them are the following.

Objection: It would take a miracle.

Answer: Quite right!

Objection: Joseph is called Jesus' father (Mt. 13:55; Jn. 6:42; Lk. 2:33,48).

Answer: Joseph was Jesus' legal father (Greek has no specific term for an adoptive father); therefore Joseph is appropriately designed simply as Jesus' "father."

Objection: The virgin birth reflects the influence of pagan mythology.

Answer: In mythology there are examples of procreation between the gods and women; however, those examples involve the deity appearing in human form and having sexual relations. The biblical account of the virgin conception is of a totally different nature. The conception of Jesus did not involve sexual relations as is evidenced by the claim that Mary was a virgin after Jesus' conception, cf. Mt. 1:25. Rather, Jesus was conceived miraculously without the need for sexual relations. The virgin conception is unique to the Bible, and is found nowhere in mythology predating the New Testament; thus, the virgin conception of Jesus could not reflect the influence of mythology.

Objection: If the incarnation is true, then God is not immutable.

Answer: God is immutable, so the Son of God, who is God, is immutable with respect to his deity. However, this did not prevent him from taking on additional attributes (*i.e.,* the attributes of humanity) as long as the attributes of deity were not altered in the process. Remember, immutability only applies to deity.

The purpose of the incarnation

Why did the Son of God condescend to take upon himself the nature of man? Note the following four reasons.

1. So that the Son could die for sinners (Heb. 10:1-25, esp. v.5). God cannot die.

2. So that the Son might reveal to us the character of God (Jn. 1:18; Jn. 14:8).

3. So that he might become our high priest (Heb. 7).

4. So that he might fulfill the promises and prophecies of the Old Testament (Isa. 52:13-53:12; Mt. 1:22-23; 2:15; 4:14-16; 21:4-5; 26:56).

Christ's death

Before discussing the death and resurrection of Christ it would be helpful to have some basic terminology in mind. Note the following key terms.

1. *Atonement:* Atonement is the re-establishment of divine favor. It involves the transfer of guilt and penalty for sin to a suitable substitute.

2. *Expiation:* (see atonement)

3. *Forgiveness:* Forgiveness is the removal (remission) of divine judgment for sin. Forgiveness is made possible only because a suitable substitute bears the judgment on behalf of the sinner.

4. *Guilt:* Guilt refers to culpability (accountability) for sin.

5. *Justification:* Justification refers to the judicial act of God in which the believing sinner is declared to be free from sin and righteous before God. (Justification does not remove sin; it removes the guilt that a person incurs for sin.)

6. *Cleansing:* Cleansing is the actual removal of sin and its effects upon the sinner. Cleansing does not remove the sin

nature. The sin nature can only be removed as a result of final (ultimate) sanctification.

7. *Penalty:* Retribution, or just compensation for sin.

8. *Propitiation:* Propitiation refers to the satisfaction of God's justice. For those who place their faith in Christ, God's righteous demands for judgment are propitiated (satisfied) by Christ's sacrifice. When God is propitiated, he ceases to view the object of propitiation as deserving wrath; thus for the believer, Christ is said to be the propitiation for our sin (Rom. 3:25; 1 Jn. 2:2; 4:10).

9. *Reconciliation:* Reconciliation refers to man being brought back to God from whom he was alienated.

10. *Redemption:* Redemption refers to the payment that must be made to secure a sinner's release from divine judgment.

11. *Remission:* (see forgiveness)

12. *Righteousness:* Righteousness involves not only the absence of sin, but positive obedience. It is important to recognize that the mere absence of sin is not righteousness. Adam, prior to his fall was sinless, but he was not righteous.

13. *Satisfaction:* (see propitiation)

14. *Substitution:* Substitution refers to another bearing one's penalty for sin.

Theories of the atonement

Numerous theories have been proposed to explain the meaning and significance of Christ's death; they generally fall into one of the categories below.

1. Substitutionary atonement (the orthodox view)

   Christ died in the place of the sinner, bearing the penalty of sin and completely satisfying the justice of God. Scriptural support for this view is found in: Isa. 53:5ff.; Rom. 5:8; 1 Cor. 15:3; 2 Cor. 5:21; 1 Pet. 2:24; 1 Pet. 3:18; Mk. 10:45; Jn. 10:11; 1 Cor. 5:7; Heb. 10:1-14.

2. The accident theory

   Jesus' death had no ultimate purpose; he was killed by people who either did not understand, or did not appreciate his message.

3. Payment to Satan theory

   Satan has a claim on sinners and Christ died to satisfy that claim and purchase sinners back to God. (C.S. Lewis presents this view by way of analogy in *The Lion, the Witch and the Wardrobe*.)

4. Moral influence theory

   The purpose of the death of Christ was not to atone for sin, but rather an expression of divine love intended to motivate sinners to repentance and faith.

5. The martyr theory

   Christ's death as a martyr is an example of faith and should teach us to live true to what we believe, even unto death.

6. The governmental theory

   In order to maintain respect for his laws, God made an example of Christ to show man how much sin offends him and how much he will judge sin if man does not repent.

However, according to this theory Christ was not a substitute for the sinner.

The extent of Christ's atonement

The Bible is clear that Christ died for the sins of the whole world. This does not mean that Christ's death is applied to the sins of every person, but rather that it is available and sufficient for all who will call upon him in faith. This concept is often expressed in this way: Christ's sacrifice is sufficient for all sin, but efficient (*i.e.,* effective) only for those who place their faith in him. This view is in sharp contrast to the view of classic Calvinism, which holds that Christ not only did not die for the non-elect, but that God actually decreed their damnation, a view sometimes referred to as "double predestination" (see, *Institutes of the Christian Religion* by John Calvin, Book III, chap. 24). Note the following passages bearing on this subject: Jn. 1:29; 1 Tim. 2:6; Heb. 2:9; 2 Pet. 3:9; 1 Jn. 2:2. (The extent of the atonement will be discussed more thoroughly under the topic of "salvation.")

Christ's resurrection

The nature of the resurrection

There are two facts concerning the resurrection that are fundamental to understanding the nature of the event. First, it was a real historical event that occurred in time and space, not simply a spiritual truth. Second, it was a bodily resurrection; note the following evidences.

1. Jesus displayed himself as having flesh and bones (Jn. 20:19-31).

2. The tomb in which he was sealed was found to be empty (Mk. 16:6), and no dead body was ever found.

3. He ate food after his resurrection (Lk. 24:41-43).

4. After the resurrection, Jesus had the imprint of the nails in his hands and feet and the wound in his side (Lk. 24:34-39).

5. Angels declared that Jesus was not in the tomb, but had risen (Lk. 24:6-8).

The credibility of the resurrection account

The resurrection was a miraculous event, and as is the case with all miracles, they are neither subject to scientific analysis, nor are they repeatable. However, a number of factors indicate that the biblical accounts are accurate and credible.

1. There were competent firsthand witnesses to the events surrounding the resurrection, including at least one skeptic (Thomas), who demanded firsthand physical proof (Jn. 20:19-31).

2. There were numerous witnesses to the events. While it might be possible for a few people to be mistaken about what they saw, the large number of witnesses lends a high degree of credibility to the biblical account.

3. The witnesses to the events were people of good reputation and moral character who would not have been likely to lie about what they saw.

4. The recorded demeanor of the disciples fits what we would expect if the resurrection were true. (The disciples were unprepared, shocked, and in disbelief at first, but boldly proclaimed the resurrection once they were convinced.)

Also, numerous factors in the early history of the church would be unexplainable apart from the truth of the resurrection. Consider the following:

1. The account of the empty tomb.

2. The origin of worship on the first day of the week instead of the Sabbath.

3. The very existence of the Church was built on the proclamation of the resurrection.

4. The message of the New Testament. (If the resurrection did not happen, how do we explain that a group of morally upright people who taught against dishonesty of any kind claimed, even in the face of persecution and death, and for no personal benefit, to be eyewitnesses to the resurrection of Christ?)

The significance of the resurrection of Christ

The resurrection is one of the most significant events in history. Consider the following.

1. It provides additional verification as to Christ's identity — *i.e.,* that he is the Son of God (cf. Rom. 1:4).

2. It is assurance that Christ's sacrifice was acceptable to God (Rom. 4:25).

3. It serves as the prototype for the future of those who believe (1 Cor.15:20-23).

Christ's present and future work

At present Christ is the believer's high priest. As such, he represents believers before the throne of God (Heb. 7:1-28). He also continually intercedes for believers before the Father (Heb. 7:25). Christ's future work is summarized below.

1. He will rapture his Church into Heaven (Mt. 24:36-42; 1 Thess. 4:13-18; 1 Cor. 15:51-53).

2. He will pour out judgment upon the earth in the final days of this present dispensation, beginning sometime during the tribulation period (Rev. 6-19).

3. He will return to the earth to end the tribulation and to establish his kingdom (Rev. 19:11-20:4).

4. He will remove Satan and the demons from the earth, and rule in righteousness during the millennial phase of the kingdom (Rev. 20:1-3).

5. After the millennium is complete, he will dissolve the present heavens and earth (Rev. 20:9).

6. He will judge unsaved men and unholy angels, condemning them to the Lake of Fire for eternity (Rev. 20:10-15).

7. He will create new heavens and a new earth, over which he will rule in righteousness forever (Rev. 21-22).

Review Questions

1. How do we know that the Son of God existed before the birth of Jesus at Bethlehem?

2. What is the evidence for the absolute deity of Christ?

3. Of the passages that explicitly state that Christ is God, choose the two that you think are the best and summarize them.

4. Of the passages that imply that Jesus is God, choose the two that you think are the best and summarize them.

5. What attributes of God are ascribed to Christ in the Bible?

6. Is Christ the Father? Is Christ the Holy Spirit? Explain.

7. In regard to Christ, what is meant by the term "impeccability." Why is this truth important?

8. How might Nestorianism be related to the question of Christ's impeccability?

9. What are the two natures of Christ, and what is their relationship?

10. Which incorrect views state that Christ is not fully human?

11. Which incorrect views state that Christ is not absolute deity?

12. Summarize the work of Christ in the Old Testament.

13. In what ways is Christ presented as the coming Savior in the Old Testament?

14. What was the method of the incarnation? Explain how we know this method is true?

15. Why is the virgin conception important?

16. Does the account of the virgin conception and birth of Christ reflect the influence of pagan mythology? Explain.

17. Briefly discuss the purposes of the incarnation.

18. Briefly define each of the following: atonement, justification, cleansing, penalty, propitiation, reconciliation, redemption, remission, and substitutionary atonement.

19. Which view of the atonement is correct? Explain?

20. Discuss the extent of Christ's atonement. Include biblical support.

21. What important facts should be pointed out in regard to the nature of Christ's resurrection?

22. How do we know that Christ's resurrection was a bodily (physical) resurrection?

23. Why should we believe that the resurrection account in the Bible is reliable?

24. What is the significance of Christ's resurrection?

25. What two ministries is Christ currently engaged in? Describe each.

26. Briefly discuss the future work of Christ.

The Holy Spirit

The Person and Work
of the Holy Spirit

The Holy Spirit isn't simply a power, or a force; he is a person, and he indwells redeemed people. Having power within is one thing; having a person within is something else. Since many deny the personhood and (or) the deity of the Holy Spirit, it is important that these truths be firmly established.

The Holy Spirit is a person

Note the following characteristics of the Holy Spirit that demonstrate he is a person.

1. The Holy Spirit has intellect (1 Cor. 2:11).

2. He has a will (1 Cor. 12:11, 18).

3. He exhibits emotions (Rom. 8:26 — the word "groan" is *stenazo*; on the use of this word see 2 Corinthians 5:2,4 and Hebrews 13:17).

4. He is capable of interpersonal relationships (Mt. 12:30-32; Acts 5:3; Eph. 4:30; Heb. 10:29).

5. He engages in personal acts (John 14:26; Acts 13:2; Rom. 8:26f). (If the Holy Spirit is not distinct from the Father, to whom does he pray?)

The Holy Spirit is God

The following observations demonstrate that the Holy Spirit is God, equal with the Father and the Son.

1. The Holy Spirit is called "God" (Acts 5:1-5). He is called "the Lord" in both the Old and New Testaments (Isa. 6:8-9; Acts 28:25-26; 2 Cor. 3:17-18). In Jeremiah 31:31-34, he is referred to five times as "LORD" (Heb. *yhwh*, the Hebrew name of God sometimes translated, "Jehovah"), and once as "God" (Heb. *elohim*). [We must read Jeremiah 31:31-34 in the light of Hebrews 10:15-17, which identifies the speaker in Jeremiah 31:31-34 as "the Spirit," in order to see that the Holy Spirit is there referred to as "Jehovah."]

2. The Spirit possesses the attributes of God (Omnipresence: Psa. 139:7-10; Omniscience: 1 Cor. 2:10-11; his habitation is a temple: 1 Cor. 6:19).

3. He does the works of God (Creation: Gen. 1:1-2; Regeneration: Tit. 3:4-6; he raised Christ from the dead: Rom. 8:11; he inspired scripture: 1 Cor. 2:1-16; 2 Pet. 1:21; he sovereignly distributes spiritual gifts according to his own will: 1 Cor. 12:4-11; 2 Pet. 1:21).

4. The nature of the Spirit's association with other members of the Godhead demonstrates his deity (Mt. 3:13-17; Mt. 28:18-20; 2 Cor. 13:14).

According to scripture, the Holy Spirit is God, co-equal with the Father and the Son; however, he is not the Father or the Son. The three members of the Trinity are distinct persons sharing a singular divine essence.

The works of the Holy Spirit

General overview

The works of the Holy Spirit in regard to salvation are:

1. Convicting: Jn. 16:8

2. Calling: Rom. 8:30; 1 Thess. 2:12; 2 Thess. 2:7-14

3. Regenerating: Tit. 3:5

4. Baptizing into the Body of Christ (the Church): 1 Cor. 12:13

5. Sealing: Eph. 1:13; 4:30

6. Indwelling: 1 Cor. 6:19; Rom. 8:9

Other works of the Spirit are:

1. He was involved in creation (Gen. 1:1-2; Psa. 33:6).

2. He is the author of scripture (2 Pt. 1:21; 1 Cor. 2:13; 2 Tim. 3:16).

3. He gives illumination into the meaning of scripture (1 Cor. 2:11-14).

4. He was the agent of Christ's miraculous conception (Lk 1:34-35).

5. He was the source of Christ's power (Mt. 12:28; Acts 10:38).

6. He raised Christ from the dead (Rom. 8:11).

7. He convicts the world of sin, righteousness, and judgment (Jn. 16:8-11).

8. He grants gifts to the Church according to his will (1 Cor. 12:1-11).

9. He fills (controls) yielded believers (Eph. 5:18).

10. He empowers believers (Acts 4:23-31).

Key works of the Holy Spirit in regard to salvation

Regeneration and indwelling

We can group regeneration and indwelling together since they refer to different aspects of the same operation. Indwelling is simply the continuedness of the relationship that is established at regeneration. Regeneration is the work of the Holy Spirit in which a sinner, who is spiritually dead, is made alive. This operation happens when the sinner's spirit is cleansed of sin and brought into union with the Holy Spirit. Indwelling is simply the continuation of that union.

Baptism

Spirit baptism (not to be confused with water baptism) is the operation of the Holy Spirit by which one believing in Christ is placed into Christ's body, the Church. There are three sources of confusion regarding Spirit baptism.

1. The significance of Spirit baptism can only be understood in light of what it accomplishes—making one a member of the Body of Christ, the Church (1 Cor. 12:13). Apart from an understanding of the unique nature of the Church, the significance of Spirit baptism cannot be fully appreciated.

2. Sometimes Spirit baptism is obscured by an emphasis on water baptism. (That is not to suggest that water baptism is unimportant, only that it should be carefully distinguished from Spirit baptism.)

3. Spirit baptism is often incorrectly associated with the receiving of certain phenomenal gifts, like tongues, prophecy, healing, or other miraculous gifts. While Spirit baptism and the giving of these gifts did sometimes coincide in the very early days of the Church, not all believers who were baptized by the Spirit received such gifts (1 Cor. 12:13 cf. vv. 29-30).

Observations on Spirit baptism

1. Spirit baptism is unique to the Church age. According to Colossians 1:24, the Church is the Body of Christ. Paul said in 1 Corinthians 12:13 that Spirit baptism places one into the Body of Christ; thus, Spirit baptism places one into the Church (we are referring not to the visible local church, but the invisible, universal Church). There was no Spirit baptism in the Old Testament, and thus no Body of Christ (Church). Note that Acts 1:5 views Spirit baptism as a future work. The Spirit began the ministry of baptism on the day of Pentecost, A.D. 33, just a few weeks after the resurrection of Christ. (Christ was crucified on April 3, A.D. 33,

not A.D. 32 as is often incorrectly stated.) Peter recognized that Pentecost was the beginning of the Church (Acts 11:15-17). Understanding that Pentecost, A.D. 33, is the beginning of the Church, and that the Church is distinct from Israel is essential for the proper interpretation of biblical future prophecy.

2. All Church-age believers partake of Spirit baptism.

    a. This truth is explicitly stated in 1 Corinthians 12:12-13.

    b. Ephesians 4:5 implies this truth in that "one baptism" applies to the group that has "one faith" and "one Lord."

    c. This truth is implied from the fact that believers are nowhere urged to seek Spirit baptism.

3. Spirit baptism only occurs once in the life of a believer. It should not be confused with "filling" (controlling and enabling), which is repetitive.

4. The results of Spirit baptism:

    a. The believer becomes a member of the Body of Christ (1 Cor. 12:12-13; Eph. 4:4-5; Gal. 3:26-29).

    b. The believer is united with Christ in his death and victory over sin, and sin's power (Col. 2:8-12; Rom. 6:1-10).

    c. It is important to note that empowerment does not result from baptism, but from being filled by the Holy Spirit.

Sealing

Sealing is the operation of the Holy Spirit in which he seals the believer into Christ, thus ensuring the believer's salvation until the completion of redemption (Eph. 1:13; Eph. 4:30; 2 Cor. 1:21-22). (This truth will be discussed further under "salvation.")

Filling

Filling by the Spirit refers to being under the Holy Spirit's influence, control, and enablement (Eph 5:18). Instances of filling can be found in Acts 2:1-4; 4:8-13; and 4:23-31.

Gifts of the Holy Spirit

A spiritual gift is a God-given endowment of ability intended for the edification (building up) of the Body of Christ. In the very early days of the Church, Spirit baptism and the impartation of gifts on a very few occasions occurred subsequent to the exercise of faith; however, it quickly became normative for these works to occur at the moment faith was exercised. It is also important to recognize that spiritual gifts, once imparted to an individual, are never withdrawn. Hence in the early churches, some gifts (*e.g.,* the evidential and revelatory gifts) passed off the scene only as the believers possessing those gifts died.

Observations concerning spiritual gifts

1. Spiritual gifts are just that—gifts! *Charisma* (akin to *charis* = "grace") indicates that these gifts are not distributed on the basis of merit. A gift is by nature, unearned. It seems normative both in scripture and in Christian experience that an individual receives their spiritual gift(s) at the moment they receive the Holy Spirit, which is the moment they exercise saving faith. [Acts does record an exception, the Samaritans, who received the Spirit subsequent to salvation (Acts 8:4-17). However, that appears to have been a unique case during the transitional period of very early church history.]

2. Spiritual gifts are God-given abilities (*i.e.,* special supernatural endowments cf. 1 Cor. 12:6, 8-9, 11), not highly developed natural talents. The distribution of gifts is made

according to the sovereign will of God (the recipient has no control over the type of gift he or she receives, cf. 1 Cor. 12:11 and 18). [1 Corinthians 12:31 does not teach that believers can choose their spiritual gift(s). The verb "desire" used there (Gr. *zeloute*) is plural, referring to believers corporately (*i.e.*, the church), not individually. Paul was saying that the church (in this case, the local church) should desire that the greater gifts be manifested in their midst, not that individual believers should desire the impartation of gifts other than what they were sovereignly given by God. (See also 1 Cor. 12:27-30; 14:1 and 14:39, and notice the plurals—*i.e.*, "you" {plural} as a corporate body desire....) One possible exception to this may have been the gift of interpretation of tongues (for which the one who had the gift of tongues could pray); see 1 Cor. 14:13.]

3. Spiritual gifts are an endowment of special abilities. They should be distinguished from "offices" or "place of ministry." For example, one may have the gift of pastor and hold the office of pastor, or one may not have the gift of pastor, but hold the office. The same is true with some other gifts, such as evangelism and teaching. This raises an interesting point: Just because we do not possess a particular spiritual gift does not mean we have no responsibility for that area of ministry. For example, we might not have the gift of evangelism, but we are still to evangelize. We might not have the gift of giving, but we are still to give. Having a gift simply means that one has a special divine enabling in a particular area; it does not mean that we can focus on one area to the exclusion of all other areas of service. There may be times when it is needful to perform some function for which we are not specifically gifted. We must be careful not to let the lack of a specific gift become an excuse for avoiding responsibilities we don't like.

4. Spiritual gifts are given for the edification of the Body of Christ; they are not intended as private gifts for the personal benefit of the one possessing the gift. (That is not to

say that the gifted person could not benefit from the exercise of his or her gift, only that the purpose of the gift was for the edification of the Church.) Misunderstanding this can lead to abuse of spiritual gifts. (See, 1 Cor. 12:4-7; 14:1-12 and Eph. 4:11-16.)

Descriptions of various gifts

Duplicate gifts in the following lists have been eliminated, and the precise nature of some of these gifts is not known.

1 Corinthians 12:4-11

1. Word of wisdom: Possibly the ability to express the correct application of truth to particular situations.

2. Word of knowledge: The ability to know things that could only be known by supernatural means (cf. Acts 5:1-11).

3. Faith: The ability to trust and obey God to an unusual degree.

4. Healings: The ability to restore health almost instantly.

5. Miracles: The effecting of some work by direct supernatural means.

6. Prophecy: Speaking forth a divine revelation. Prophecy usually involved the giving of new revelation, but not always.

7. Distinguishing of spirits: The ability to distinguish between the sources of true and false revelations.

8. Tongues: The ability to speak the truth in an unlearned human language. This gift could substitute for prophecy in the church if accompanied by interpretation, though it was not specifically intended for such use.

9. Interpretation of tongues: The ability to interpret unknown tongues.

1 Corinthians. 12:28

10. Apostles: Individuals directly commissioned by the Lord and given authority over the churches (Eph. 2:19-20).

11. Teachers: Individuals given the ability to effectively communicate previously revealed truth.

12. Helps: The ability to aid those in need.

13. Administrations: The ability to manage the affairs of the local church.

Ephesians 4:11

14. Evangelists: The ability to effectively proclaim the gospel.

15. Pastor-teacher: A multifaceted gift that involved the ability to teach, guide, protect, and disciple the local body of believers. It appears that not all who are given the gift of teacher are given the gift of pastor (cf. 1 Cor. 12:28), but it appears that all who are given the gift of pastor are given the gift of teacher, and thus these gifts are linked in Ephesians 4:11.

Romans 12:6-8

16. Service: The ability to serve the local body. This probably differed from helps in that helps seems to have been focused on assisting individuals, whereas service appears to have been focused on assisting the body of believers corporately.

17. Exhortation: The ability to challenge believers to make application of truth and motivate people to action.

18. Giving: The ability to share one's resources to an unusual degree.

19. Mercy: The ability to show an unusual degree of compassion to those in some needy circumstance.

How does one identify their spiritual gift(s)?

You may have seen tests designed to help identify one's spiritual gifts. In most cases such tests only measure one's interest in certain areas, rather than the presence of a God-given gift. The best way to identify a spiritual gift is to be active in a local church where those gifts can become obvious.

Comments on the gift of tongues

Recently a great deal of controversy has surrounded the gift of tongues. For that reason we will explore this gift in greater detail.

The nature of the gift of tongues in the New Testament

The gift of tongues was the ability to speak a message directly from God in an unlearned foreign language; thus, this gift was both revelatory, in that the message came directly from God, and evidential, in that the method of delivery was clearly a miraculous sign. It is claimed by some that tongues, or a particular type of tongues, was a heavenly language intended for use in prayer and worship. However, there is no biblical support for that claim. Every instance of the gift of tongues in the New Testament was an unlearned, human language. The New Testament is clear that this gift was intended primarily for the purpose of evangelism (1 Cor. 14:22), in contrast to other revelatory gifts intended for use within the local church (1 Cor. 14:19). The speaker most likely had no idea of the specific content of the message he or she was delivering unless they also possessed the gift of interpretation. In addition, the validity of the message was always subject to validation by one who had the gift of "discerning spirits." Note the following observations regarding the nature of tongues in the New Testament.

1. There are three terms used to modify "tongues" as a spiritual gift. All of these terms indicate that tongues involved human foreign languages. For example:

    a. *Genos* (1 Cor. 12:10) –a general term meaning "kinds."

    b. *Heteros* (Acts 2:4) –meaning "different" or "foreign."

    c. *Dialektos* (Acts 2:6,8) –indicating the language of a particular region. We get our word "dialect" from this word.

    There is nothing in these modifiers indicating that the gift of tongues involved heavenly or angelic languages.

2. A historical analysis of this gift establishes that tongues were contemporary foreign languages.

    a. Acts 2:1-13

        This is the first instance of the exercise of the gift of tongues in the New Testament. It is especially important because the first instance of something new often gives insight into its nature. Here at the birth of the Church on the day of Pentecost we see that the believers were both filled with the Holy Spirit (2:4a) and began to speak in other tongues (2:4b). Because Pentecost, which followed on the heels of the Passover, was a major feast of the Jews, many Jews from other nations and languages were present in Jerusalem. When the believers began to speak in tongues, those from foreign lands heard them in the native tongue of their land. Some have suggested that maybe the way tongues worked was that when a person spoke in tongues, the listeners would hear the message in their own language, and if there were people of many languages present, each would hear the same speaker in their own language. However, such a view is problematic since it requires that the gift to be operative within the ungifted listener rather than the speaker. The reason that many people of different languages heard the message in their own native language on the day of Pentecost was that on that day a large number of disciples (about a hundred and twenty, cf. Acts 1:15), all in the same location in Jerusalem, received the gift of the Spirit at the same time and flooded into the street speaking in tongues. (Clearly this was a unique circumstance.) Since there were many tongues speakers present, the Jews visiting Jerusalem would have had little difficulty finding someone who was speaking in their language. In fact, we are specifically told some of the languages that were being spoken by the disciples (vv. 7-11), and they were foreign (earthly) languages; thus, there is no support in this passage for the notion that tongues was anything other than the ability to speak in an unlearned foreign language.

b. Acts 8:4-17

This is the second mention of receiving the Spirit in the New Testament. It does not specifically mention tongues, however, it is likely that tongues were manifested as individuals received the Holy Spirit. This is the first instance of receiving the Spirit through the laying on of hands (v. 17). The Samaritans had a system of worship that paralleled the worship of God in Jerusalem. They had their own imitation temple, their own imitation priesthood, and their own imitation sacrifices; and lest they develop their own imitation form of Christianity, God made sure that they understood that they were under the authority of Christ's apostles. He made this obvious by delaying the giving of the Spirit until Peter and John arrived from Jerusalem and prayed, laying their hands on the Samaritan believers.

Such a delay, however, was atypical, though we do see such a delay one more time in Acts 19:1-7, again for a special reason.

c.   Acts 10:44-47 cf. 11:15-18

This is the third mention of tongues in the New Testament, and we see no change in the gift from Acts 2:1-13. Peter had been directed in a vision to go and preach the gospel to a group of Gentiles. This is, in fact, the first occasion on which the gospel was specifically directed to Gentiles. Prior to this, the Jewish believers assumed that a Gentile must first become a Jewish proselyte and then believe in Christ in order to be saved. However, quite to the surprise of the Jewish Christians, God planned to extend salvation directly to the Gentiles. In this passage, as Peter explained the gospel to these Gentiles and they believed, they began to speak in tongues evidencing the same gift of the Spirit as the Jews had received at Pentecost. Notice that here there is no laying on of hands in order to receive the gift. When Peter was called to account for preaching to the Gentiles (Acts 11:1-18), he recounted the vision he had received, and how he had been directed to the Gentiles (9:32-10:22). When he explained that the Gentiles had received the same Spirit, as evidenced by the manifestation of the gift of tongues, the Jewish believers accepted the fact that God had opened the way of salvation to the Gentiles (11:18). Thus, in this instance the gift of tongues served as divine confirmation to the Jews that God had granted salvation directly to the Gentiles. It is important to note that the gift of tongues that God gave to the Gentiles was the same gift he had given to the believing Jews (11:15). Again, there was no change in the nature of the gift.

d. Acts 19:1-7

This is the fourth mention of tongues in the New Testament (if we count Acts 8:4-17), and again there is no
change in the gift from Acts 2:1-13. This passage and
Acts 8:4-17 are sometimes mistakenly used to teach
that the gift of the Spirit is "a second blessing" that a
person receives after they believe, since in both of these
instances the believers received the gift sometime after
they believed. [The disciples mentioned in Acts 19:1-7
were actually disciples of John the Baptist who had yet
to hear the gospel. When they heard it they believed
and were baptized, and received the gifts of tongues
and prophecy.] Why the men in Acts 19:1-7 did not
immediately receive the Spirit as did the Gentiles in
Acts 10:44-47 we are not told. Perhaps the conferral of
the gifts by the laying on of Paul's hands was intended
to help these men understand his apostolic authority.
In any case, there is no more mention of the receiving
of spiritual gifts through the laying on of hands in the
remainder of the New Testament, nor is the Church
anywhere instructed to lay hands on new believers for
the conferral of the Spirit or spiritual gifts. The two instances we have where gifts were conferred through
the laying on of hands were apostolic in nature, and
seem to have served a specific purpose unique to the
early development of the Church. That these two instances of the laying on of hands do not form a pattern
can be seen from the fact that the instance in Acts
10:44-47, which occurs between these two instances,
did not involve the laying on of hands. Again, there is
no indication from the text that the gift changed from
what it was in Acts 2:1-13.

e. 1 Corinthians 12:1-14:40 (esp. 14:2-4)

Why was it that only God understood what was said
by the tongues speaker? It was not because the gift of

tongues involved a heavenly language, but because believers were using tongues inappropriately (*i.e.,* uninterpreted) in the church, rather than for evangelism, and there was no one present who understood the language.

3. An examination of passages frequently appealed to in support of tongues as a heavenly language.

a. 1 Corinthians 14:2

In this passage Paul addressed the problem of the use of tongues in the local church (14:19). The gift of tongues was given as an evidential (miraculous) evangelistic gift, which means that it was designed for use with unbelievers, not with believers (14:22). However, in some churches, such as Corinth, it became commonplace for tongues to be used in the church. Since most of the people in a local church spoke the native language, in most cases the language of the tongues speaker would have been unintelligible to them, and therefore there was little or no benefit to the church. In fact, the use of tongues within the church undoubtedly took valuable time away from the exercise of gifts that would have been more helpful, like prophecy or teaching, from which the entire church could have benefited. Of course, there was nothing wrong with the gift of tongues, or with the use of tongues in the church; it was simply a matter of priorities and balance; when the church is assembled, why take time away from the gifts that can benefit the entire church in order to exercise gifts that benefit only a few, or no one (14:14-25)? Paul's statement in verse 2 that only God understands the tongue does not mean that tongues was a heavenly language; he was simply comparing tongues to prophecy. Only God would know what the tongues speaker was saying (not very profitable to the church), whereas everyone in the church could understand what the prophet said. In fact, the first twenty-five verses of this chapter are about the superiority of prophecy to tongues in the local church. Tongues was an important gift in the spread of the gospel in the early days of the Church, but each gift has its proper use, and as Paul emphasized in this chapter, tongues, while well suited for evangelistic work in the world, was not suited to use in the church. Using the gift of tongues in the local church was like using a wrench to drive a nail—it can be done, but if one has a hammer, why not use it instead?

b. 1 Corinthians 13:1

Note the use of *ean* ("if," third class conditional, subjunctive) indicating a hypothetical case. This is actually a hyperbolic expression that depends for its force on the impossibility of speaking in an angelic language. For instance: Suppose I said that if you have enough strength to lift a piece of paper, but don't have love, it profits nothing spiritually. Now suppose I said, "If you have enough strength to lift a battleship, but don't have love, it profits nothing spiritually." Which statement has the greater impact? Obviously the hyperbolic statement is more forceful. In fact, we could hardly imagine anyone making the first statement, since it sounds a little ridiculous. In this passage, Paul compared the gift of tongues (being able to speak in unlearned human languages) to a hypothetical example (*i.e.,* being able to speak in angelic language); even if one could do that, but didn't exercise such ability in love, it would amount to nothing spiritually.

c. Romans 8:26

In this passage Paul refers to the "groanings" of the Spirit that are "too deep for words." However, this is not a reference to the gift of tongues. Tongues are not mentioned anywhere in the book of Romans. Paul was simply saying that the Holy Spirit prays for us with groanings too deep for words. In fact, if one thinks about it, this could not be a reference to tongues, since the level of the Spirit's communication is specifically said to be beyond words (language).

The extent of tongues

In the New Testament only a portion of believers spoke in tongues (1 Cor. 12:30). This observation, coupled with the truth that the Holy Spirit sovereignly distributes gifts according to his will (1 Cor. 12:11), tells us that God never intended for every Christian to have this gift any more than he intended for every Christian to be an apostle or prophet. Note the following observations concerning the extent of tongues.

1. In 1 Corinthians 12:27-31 (esp. v. 30, cf. 12:13) we see that all believers are baptized into Christ's body (the Church) by the Spirit (1 Cor. 12:13). There is no such thing as being baptized "in" (or "into") the Spirit. This is a mistranslation of the Greek word *"en,"* which can be translated "by" (instrumental), or "in" (locative). The correct understanding is that we are baptized *by* the Spirit *into* Christ's body (the Church). 1 Corinthians 12:13 makes this very clear.

2. Spiritual gifts are distributed in accordance with God's sovereign will (1 Cor. 12:11,18) on the basis of grace. Therefore, we must conclude that it was never God's will for all believers to possess this gift, nor does there seem to be any other gift that is universally given.

The desirability of tongues in the church

The gift of tongues was a good gift; like all gifts, it came from God (1 Cor. 14:5a, 18). However, for use in the local church tongues was much less desirable than some of the other gifts. That only makes sense, since tongues was primarily an evangelistic gift. Paul said he wished that all of the Corinthian believers had the gift of tongues; however, in the same sentence he said it would be even better if they had the gift of prophecy (1 Cor. 14:5) so they could speak the truth plainly for people to understand. In fact, he said that in the church, he would rather speak five words plainly than speak ten thousand words in a tongue (1 Cor. 14:19)!

The purpose of the gift of tongues

The purpose of tongues was evidential; it was a supernatural sign that the message was from God. God's primary intention in the giving of this gift was evangelistic (1 Cor. 14:21-22), though we do find it used on one occasion as a sign to Jewish believers as confirmation that God was calling Gentiles into his kingdom (Acts 10:44-47 cf. 11:15-18). Note the following observations regarding tongues. Mark 16:17: Jesus referred to tongues as one of the signs that would accompany true believers after his ascension. 1 Corinthians 14:21-22: Paul states that the gift of tongues was intended as a sign to unbelievers. Hebrews 2:3-4: Although this passage doesn't mention tongues individually, it does refer to the "signs and wonders" and various miracles and gifts of the Spirit that were given to the early church (and which they recorded for us) in confirmation of the gospel. Acts 2:22: Peter's statement here was in regard to the miracles performed by Christ himself, nevertheless, he states that the purpose of those miracles (and we may surmise of miracles in general, including tongues) was attestation of the truth of God's message.

The use of tongues in the church (1 Corinthians 14:26-40)

Primarily because of the inappropriate use of tongues in the Corinthian church, Paul laid out a number of regulations for the use of the gift in the local church. The following is a summary of those regulations.

1. Any use of spiritual gifts that does not lead to edification is improper (v. 26).

2. Use of the gift of tongues should not dominate the service. Only two, or three at most, should exercise the gift in any service; and then, only one at a time (v. 27).

3. Uninterpreted tongues are strictly forbidden in public worship (v. 28).

4. Women are not to speak, either in tongues or prophetically, in the general assembly of the church when men are present (v. 34). This is often viewed today as a first century cultural phenomenon that does not apply to the modern-day church. However, in 1 Timothy 2:9-15 Paul includes teaching in this list and gives the reason as the order of creation, clearly not a culturally based reason. In other words, Paul said that it is inappropriate for women to give instruction to, or exercise authority over men in the local church due to the dignity of the man in the created order. (Of course it would be acceptable for women to teach other women, and they are encouraged to do so, cf. Titus 2:1-5.) While such a concept might not resonate well with the modern feminist theology, it is a universal principle taught in the New Testament that authority in the church is properly exercised through men.

Misconceptions about the gift of tongues

There are some widespread misconceptions regarding the gift of tongues. One is that God wants every Christian to have this gift; another is that Christians who do not possess the gift are to seek it. And finally, it is sometimes implied that speaking in tongues is a sign that a person has passed to a higher level of spiritually. Note the following points concerning these misconceptions.

1. Although the gift of tongues was important to the early church for the rapid spread of the gospel, tongues was never a necessary work of the Holy Spirit in the life of an individual believer (*i.e.,* something that every believer

must have). We know this because: 1) the Holy Spirit sovereignly gave each believer the gift, or gifts that he desired (1 Cor. 12:4-11); and, 2) the Spirit did not give everyone the gift of tongues (1 Cor. 12:28-31). Therefore, it should be clear that God never intended for every believer to have the gift of tongues. In fact, there doesn't seem to be any particular gift that was universally given. While Paul stated that he desired that all of the Corinthian believers have the gift of tongues (1 Cor. 14:5), he recognized that it simply doesn't work that way. Gifts are given according to the sovereign will of God.

2. The gift of tongues was not one of the more desirable gifts for the church. In 1 Corinthians 12:28 Paul lists the gifts of the Spirit in order of their priority. In scripture, enumerated lists are either chronological or prioritizations. Since all of the gifts of the Spirit were given at the same time (on the day of Pentecost, A.D. 33), the list given in 1 Corinthians 12:28 cannot be chronological so it must be a prioritization; in fact, we can easily see that from the structure of the list itself. In order of priority Paul lists: apostles first, prophets second, teachers third, then he lists miracles, and then he lists healings, helps, administrations, and finally, tongues. It is sometimes asserted that in 1 Corinthians 12:31 Paul instructed believers to desire to possess the greater gifts. However there are two problems with that interpretation: 1) The statement in 1 Corinthians 12:31 was addressed to the church as a whole (*i.e.*, you {plural} as a church are to desire to have the greater gifts in your midst). Paul was not suggesting that individuals should seek to possess greater gifts; he had already explained that gifts are distributed by the sovereign will of God. 2) Even if one were to seek to possess a particular spiritual gift, tongues would have been the least desirable gift. If some gifts are "greater," that implies that some are lesser. Paul clearly classifies tongues as the least of the lesser gifts in 1 Corinthians 12:27-31.

3. The exercise of the gift of tongues was not a sign of spiritual attainment or spiritual maturity. Spiritual gifts are simply that—"gifts." Even though there was an over abundance of tongues speaking in the Corinthian Church, which in part occasioned Paul's corrective letter, the believers at Corinth were characterized by gross spiritual immaturity (1 Cor. 3:1-3).

The cessation of tongues

All evidential ministries have a limited lifespan. They are always associated closely in time with the newly revealed truth to which they attest. The New Testament writers prepared the Church for the cessation of the revelatory gifts (prophecy, tongues, and word of knowledge). The question is: Have these gifts ceased, and if they have ceased, when did they cease?

In 1 Corinthians 13 Paul discusses the use of the revelatory gifts (prophecy, tongues, and knowledge, or "word of knowledge"). In the first eight verses he deals with the superiority of love to spiritual gifts (implying that any gift not exercised in love amounts to very little). Even tongues exercised without love is just noise (v. 1). In verse 8 he reveals that the gifts of prophecy, tongues, and hidden knowledge (such as Peter exhibited in Acts 5:1-11) will cease at some point in the future (from Paul's historical perspective). The remaining five verses in this chapter tell us when that will happen, and it is one of the most misinterpreted passages in the New Testament. Often these verses are interpreted to mean that when "the perfect one" (Christ) comes, there will be no more need for partial revelatory gifts. However, that is not what this passage says. "The perfect" is not Christ since the word is in the neuter gender; it is a reference to a perfect (or complete) thing. That "thing" is knowledge. Just as there is partial knowledge (revealed through prophecy, tongues, and word of knowledge), so there is complete knowledge (as revealed in the complete Word of God). The word "perfect" (Gr. *toteleion*) means "complete"; this is the word from which we get our word "total," meaning, "the whole thing." What Paul was saying was that as he wrote ("now," in A.D. 56), before the completion of the New Testament, knowledge of the truth was partial (piecemeal), revealed through prophecy, tongues, and word of knowledge; but there would come a time when that knowledge will no longer be partial, but complete (insofar as what God intended to reveal in this dispensation). At that time the revelatory gifts will no longer be needed and they will cease. It is a historical fact that at the completion of the New Testament, near the end of the first century, these gifts passed quietly off the scene. By the second century, the only groups that even claimed to manifest these gifts were those with serious doctrine problems. Thus in this case, history confirms this interpretation to be correct. When the last book of the New Testament was finally written, that was all God had to say to the Church; the New Testament finally constituted a completed revelation *in toto* and the stop-gap gifts of partial revelation were no longer needed. In light of this, the meaning of Paul's closing comment is quite plain. Just as there comes a time when a man grows up and puts away childish things, so (from Paul's historical perspective) there would come a time when the revelatory gifts given to the infant Church would no longer be needed. Misunderstanding the phrase "face to face" (v. 12) has caused considerable confusion. There was no word in the Greek of that time for "clearly"; they simply used an idiom (it does not denote that the thing seen was a person, only that something could be seen as clearly as if it were right in one's face). To those who would insist that the revelatory gifts are still active, perhaps we should ask: What is it that you claim is being revealed (that the Church really needs to know) that is not already revealed in the Word of God?

Review Questions

1.   Why is it important to understand that the Holy Spirit is a person, not simply a force?

2.   How do we know that the Holy Spirit is a person?

3.   How do we know that the Holy Spirit is God?

4.   What are the works of the Holy Spirit in regard to salvation? What are some of the other important works of the Holy Spirit?

5.   Compare and contrast "regeneration" and "indwelling."

6.   Define "Spirit baptism."

7.   Define "sealing" by the Holy Spirit.

8.   What is the result of being sealed by the Holy Spirit?

9.   What group of believers participates in Spirit baptism?

10. What is the result of Spirit baptism?

11. Define "filling" by the Spirit.

12. What do you think? Does a person have more of the Spirit when they are "filled" by the Spirit? Explain.

13. Why are spiritual gifts called "gifts"?

14. Explain how spiritual gifts differ from natural talents.

15. Can believers choose the gift they want? Explain.

16. Is it okay to engage in an area of ministry you know is not your spiritual gift? Explain.

17. What is the purpose of spiritual gifts?

18. What spiritual gift(s) do you think might be most important?

19. Have you thought about what your spiritual gifts might be? If so, what do you think they are? How did you come to that conclusion?

20. How is the best way to identify your spiritual gift(s)?

21. Describe the gift of tongues. What was the primary purpose for this gift?

22. How do we know that the gift of tongues was human languages?

23. Was everyone in the early church given the gift of tongues? Support your answer from the Bible.

24. Who decides which gift an individual receives when they are saved?

25. Was tongues one of the greater gifts to be desired in the church, or was it a good, but lesser gift? Explain.

26. What would be wrong with a group of ten men and women all speaking in tongues at the same time in a church? Support your answer from scripture.

27. What are some of the misconceptions regarding the gift of tongues?

Man

Man

Man's origin: The natural theory of evolution

Man exists, and his existence is either attributable to purely natural processes or it is not. Whether or not man's existence, indeed the existence of the universe can be explained in purely naturalistic terms has extreme implications. If a compelling natural theory could be proposed, it would seriously erode the purely rational case of theism. However, Christians do not need to be concerned. Natural philosophers have virtually exhausted the realm of possibilities, and are no closer to providing a compelling naturalistic theory of the origin of the universe, or man, than when they began. If anything, their inability to propose a workable theory has strengthened the case made by the classic cosmological and teleological arguments. Theism is as alive as ever, and thriving. Regrettably however, what natural philosophy has been unable to accomplish at the philosophical and scientific levels, it has sought to achieve at the popular level, through the co-opting of science (especially science education) and the media, in the service of cosmic and biological evolutionism. In a fallen world, the secular viewpoint can never be allowed to confirm or support a transcendent view of reality that acquiesces to the existence of a supernatural realm; to do so would be the death of secularism. The premise of naturalism is that everything has a purely natural explanation; there can be no exceptions. At the level of cosmology Stephen Hawking's book *The Universe in a Nutshell* (Bantum Books, 2001) amply illustrates the dilemma of modern naturalism. Hawking's quest is not to explain the origin of the universe; it is to offer a theory of how the universe could have a purely natural origin, for according to modern physics it did have an origin, and in this respect modern physics and the Bible are in agreement. Hawking's book summarizes the very interesting history of modern theoretical cosmology, giving the reader the impression that Hawking's conclusions are derived from science; however, Hawking's starting point is nothing more than a restatement of the presupposition of natural philosophy—that everything must have a natural explanation. Hawking's thesis, though very cleverly disguised, is that the universe emerged out of a more fundamental natural reality that included, at the very least, "imaginary time." Why does Hawking begin with imaginary time—because it is indicated by scientific observations? No, he begins with imaginary time because it is required by natural philosophy. Since quantum events require time, if the universe had its origin in a quantum event, which at present is the scientific presumption, then there must have been some other kind of time with no beginning before real time (the time of our universe). Of course the existence of imaginary time can never be confirmed, and so we see that naturalistic philosophy rests its case on faith in naturalism, just as theism rests its case on faith in supernaturalism. The difference between the two is that the case for theism is much more practical than that of naturalism, for theism has a ready explanation for all of the extreme improbabilities of a life sustaining universe and for the apparent design of life itself, all of which are left to unguided, impersonal physical processes in naturalism; indeed, naturalism has no explanation even for the physical processes. Natural philosophers have been so vexed by this problem that some have resorted to philosophical principles like the weak anthropic principle to explain these improbabilities. [The weak anthropic principle says that the natural processes of the universe tend toward the development of complex life; yet there is no explanation given as to why such a principle should exist in nature, or how such a tendency came about. Indeed the very suggestion of such a principle is an indication of the inherent weakness of natural philosophy to explain the existence of life in the face of staggering odds against life arising from unguided processes.] Thus, at the philosophical level, the case for supernaturalism is far superior to naturalism in terms of explanatory value, which of course is the principal criteria by which any theory should be judged. Since we will examine cosmology as a separate subject, our discussion here will be limited to brief remarks regarding biological evolution.

Historically, biological evolution is of fairly recent origin. Charles Darwin published his book, *On the Origin of Species* in 1859. However, it wasn't until the 1930's that Darwin's theory of natural selection (survival of the fittest) emerged as the default position of modern scientism. It is of supreme importance to realize that the question of human origin is the "acid test" of the validity of the Bible. The entire message of the Bible is predicated upon the creation story. To put it bluntly: If the Bible is wrong about the creation of man, it is wrong about everything of any consequence. The Christian who does not realize this, and who has not undertaken to understand the challenge of naturalism, is either blissfully ignorant, or incredibly naïve. There are, of course, some well educated but theologically naïve people who believe that the Bible and macroevolution can be seen as compatible. Such individuals almost invariably come from segments of Christianity that have a history of engaging in the allegorical interpretation of scripture, and they fail to look far enough down the road to see that non-literal interpretation of scripture leads invariably to theological apostasy. Biological evolution, by which I mean transmutation from one species to another, is completely incompatible with belief in a normal/objective understanding of the Bible.

The following are classic arguments one often sees in support of the evolutionary hypothesis. While some of these arguments are fading in popularity, most can still be found in any modern biology text. Since I will only mention these in passing, I have included only a brief counter-statement for each argument.

1. *The argument from comparative anatomy:* Similarities between the anatomy and physiology of animals suggest an evolutionary connection from a common source (*i.e.,* convergence).

   Counter argument: Anatomical and physiological similarities suggest a common design and a common Creator.

2. *The argument from vestigial organs:* Some organs seem to be left over from earlier evolutionary development.

   Counter argument: There are no vestigial organs, only organs for which the function has yet to be discovered. Science is now beginning to discover that organs once thought to be vestigial have useful functions that were previously unapparent.

3. *Argument from embryology:* The human embryo develops through stages that parallel human evolution. (Although this argument is no longer considered to be valid, it was included in biology textbooks as late as the early nineteen-seventies.)

   Counter argument: This argument is generally recognized as having been wishful thinking on the part of evolutionists.

4. *Argument from biochemistry and physiology:* Animals are similar in their chemical and physiological makeup, which argues for an evolutionary connection.

   Counter argument: Similarities argue for a common design and Creator. Also, many biochemical systems are irreducibly complex, and cannot be accounted for by gradual evolutionary processes.

5. *Argument from paleontology:* The sequence found in the fossil record argues for an evolutionary development from simple to complex.

   Counter arguments: 1) The sequence referred to is not a naturally occurring phenomenon. There is no single location where the evolutionary sequence can be seen intact. The sequence to which evolutionists refer is an elaborate extrapolation of sampling data from many locations, based on evolutionary and geologic assumptions. 2) There are no intermediate species, either in the fossil record, or living. Although some evolutionists point to a small number of intermediates, even evolutionists cannot agree on their intermediate status. There should be countless intermediates between each stage of macroevolutionary development for each individual species, which would mean that for each species there would be almost an innumerable number of intermediates. It cannot be argued that the intermediates are not in the fossil record because they were unsuccessful, since they would need to have been the successful precursors of the organisms that survived. The most telling fact is the complete absence of living intermediates in nature. While some have argued that evolution proceeds so slow that it cannot be observed in nature, it is not true that the accumulated effects of evolution could not be observed. Indeed, the complete absence of living intermediates is proof-positive that macroevolution is not now occurring nor has it occurred in the recent past; and the absence of intermediates in the fossil record is proof that evolution has not occurred in the more distant past. For the sake of argument, even if we were to allow that a thousand undisputed intermediates had been identified in the fossil record (even though evolutionists claim only a handful of cases), that fact alone could not account for the existence of the diversity of life we see in nature. The fact is that the hard evidence (nature and the fossil record) do not suggest that macroevolution has occurred in the past, or that it is occurring at the present, and nothing short of a few billion fossils, and/or an abundance of living intermediates will suffice for evidence. We must, however, give credit where credit is due. Evolutionary biologists have succeeded where every other scientific discipline has failed. They have managed to retain a theory that is completely contradicted by all of the available hard evidence of both nature and the fossil record. That rivals even the missionary zeal of the Christian Church!

6. *Argument from genetics:* DNA provides a means of evolutionary development and suggests that given enough time evolution could occur.

Counter arguments: 1) Natural selection explains only why certain organisms do not survive; it does not explain how or why other organisms would become more complex. Interestingly, there are no current, viable theories as to how organisms might have become more usefully complex other than a combination of pure chance and natural selection (and natural selection does not produce, it simply selects). If random variations gave rise to useful complexity, evolution should make sense statistically, but it doesn't. To date, evolutionists have failed to produce a single mathematical model that suggests that evolution is anything more than the most remote possibility conceivable. In fact, some evolutionists seem obsessed with refuting mathematical models that show the extreme improbability of evolution. Of course, it is easy to attack statistics, especially an evolution statistic, since they necessarily involve many assumptions and limitations. Some, in refuting such statistics have resorted to extreme assumptions, such as postulating that alternate forms of life could have arisen based on nucleotides and amino acids not actually found in nature. One tactic used to refute anti-evolution statistics regarding protein synthesis is to suggest that the statistics are flawed because alternative forms of life could have arisen (*e.g.*, with a six base set of nucleic acids); thus many forms of life were possible, and we simply happen to be the one that occurred. However, such arguments are flawed because they fail to demonstrate that such life forms could actually have arisen and persisted in nature; if a life form did not arise, how can we know that it could have arisen, and that it could have persisted? When we confine ourselves to the real world, that is, nature, as it actually exists, the odds of life evolving by natural processes, no matter who does the calculations and no matter what the assumptions, is not promising for evolution. While no statistic about the origin of life is apt to be what one might call accurate, they do give a strong sense of direction; and what they tell us is that the arrival of life by purely natural processes is just about the most unlikely thing imaginable. To the evolutionist who remains unconvinced, I would ask: If a stock had the same odds of success that are conservatively calculated for evolution (let's pick a number much smaller than the smallest number anyone has calculated for the random evolution of even the simplest form of life, say 1 in 10^{20}), would you invest your own money in that company? If the answer is "No," I submit to the evolutionist that his or her financial judgment is far better than their scientific judgment. Of course it might be argued that in finance one has something to lose; but we must not forget that if one is wrong about creation, they have far more to lose than money. 2) As already mentioned, mutation and natural selection cannot account for how irreducibly complex systems could have arisen. This is highly problematic. If critical complex systems are unlikely to have arisen from simpler precursors, then evolution is equally unlikely to be the answer to the origin of life. Of course, some scientists talk about "evolutionary necessity" or an innate tendency toward life in nature (the anthropic principle, which says that evolution happens as it does because it must), but here they cross over from science to naturalistic philosophy and religion (which is okay, as long as it isn't purveyed as science).

One of the major challenges to a literal understanding of the biblical account of creation is the dates given by modern science for the age of life, dates that far exceed the time frame allowable for biblical history. It is important to note that scientific dating beyond a few thousand years (certainly prior to 5000 BP, the approximate time of the biblical flood), including radiometric dating, is highly speculative. There are problems with both stratagraphic dating and radiometric dating. Stratagraphic dating is based on evolutionary assumptions and does not consider the implications of a global flood. Radiometric dating is based on three major assumptions, all of which are potentially problematic. First, the popular carbon-14 dating method assumes that the carbon-12 to carbon-14 ratio prior to the industrial revolution was fairly constant. This assumption has been shown to be inaccurate.

In 1950 Nobel Prize winner Willard Libby demonstrated that carbon-14 is forming more rapidly than it is decaying (Walt Brown, *In the Beginning: Compelling Evidence for Creation and the Flood*, 8th ed., 2008, p. 343). This observation was confirmed in 1977 by Melvin Cook (Brown, pp. 343, 344 endnote 3). As Brown has pointed out, due to the lush vegetation, the pre-flood atmosphere would have had far more carbon-12 than the present atmosphere (Brown, pp. 342-343), diluting the concentration of carbon–14 (which, as has been pointed out was probably less abundant than currently assumed in radiometric dating); this would make pre-flood samples appear to be much older. Second, radiometric dating methods assume a constant rate of nuclear decay (for example, the half-life of carbon-14 is assumed to be 5,730 years); recent research into nuclear decay rates calls this assumption into question (see: "Evidence For Solar Influences On Nuclear Decay Rates", arXiv: 1007.3318v1 [hep-ph], July, 2010, by E. Fischbach, J.H. Jenkins, J.B. Buncher, J.T. Gruenwald, P.A. Sturrock, and D. Javorsek II; for a summary see: "The strange case of solar flares and radioactive elements," in the *Stanford University News*, August 2010). Third, another major problem for radiometric dating is sample contamination and leaching of atoms from the sample prior to collection and testing. It is often impossible to know whether leaching has occurred and it is always possible that assumptions regarding leaching could result in incorrect dates being assigned to samples. Fourth, internal inconsistencies in radiometric dating are ubiquitous. Take for example the case of carbon-14 found in coal samples generally believed to be hundreds of millions of years old. The most sensitive means of measuring carbon-14 is the AMS (Accelerator Mass Spectrometer) method. However, given the half-life of carbon 14, there should be no measurable carbon 14 in samples older than about 100,000 years (approximately seventeen half-lives), since any remaining carbon-14 would then be below the AMS detection level. [See: Hebert, J. 2013. "Rethinking Carbon-14 Dating: What Does It Really Tell Us about the Age of the Earth?" Acts & Facts. 42 (4): 12-14. Also see: Baumgardner, J. 2003. "Carbon Dating Undercuts Evolution's Long Ages." Acts & Facts. 32 (10).] For detailed information on problems in radioisotope dating from a creationist perspective see: *Radio Isotopes and the Age of the Earth*, by Andrew A. Snelling, Eugene F. Chaffin, and Larry Vardiman, {848 pages}, ICR, 2005).

Christians must decide whether they are going to accept the biblical testimony, or the conclusions of modern science. Some Christians have decided to make a compromise by accepting scientific dating and adjusting biblical interpretation accordingly (*via*, the use of non-literal, allegorical interpretation). However, that solution abdicates the core principle upon which biblical Christianity is based — that the Bible communicates important objective truths upon which man must act. If the objective truth of the Bible is redefined (or jettisoned) whenever it contradicts current scientific ideas, then one can never be certain that anything taught in the Bible is objectively true. In such an environment faith becomes merely subjective experience. Note Paul's assessment of the value of faith in the absence of objective truth (I Cor. 15:1-19). According to Paul, faith that is not rooted in reality is "worthless."

Man's origin and original nature

Special creation

The Bible describes the origin of man as a direct creation of God, that is to say that man was not created through an intermediate process such as evolution. This does not mean that micro-evolutionary changes do not occur in nature; the capacity for variation and adaptation was built into living things by God, and there can be no doubt that natural selection plays a part in the survival of species. However, according to the Bible, evolutionary change did not give rise to new species. Although many have attempted to square the biblical account of creation with evolutionism, when the Bible is understood in a normal/objective manner the details simply do not agree. The Bible declares that the animals were created as distinct "kinds," that man was a direct creation of God, and that the creation of man preceded the creation of the first woman.

Man's nature

Man was created in the image of God

Students of the Bible have debated the meaning of Genesis 1:26-27. What does the scripture mean when it says that man is made in the image of God? The obvious place to look for an answer is to ask the question, "In what ways does man's nature reflect God's nature?" First of all, man is intelligent and self-aware. Of course animals exhibit a level of intelligence too, but they don't build spaceships or nuclear reactors, and they don't write encyclopedias or novels; and so far as we know, they don't contemplate the nature of their own existence, or God's existence. Incidentally, no animals (if man is excluded) are known to be atheists! Man is also emotive (capable of experiencing emotions). Some have suggested that the ascribing of emotions to God in the Bible are simply examples of "anthropopathisms" (a figure of speech in which a human emotion is ascribed to something incapable of emotion), but there is no biblical basis for such a position. Why would we think that God has no capacity for emotion? If God has no capacity for emotion, then how do we explain that he created man with such a capacity? Psychologists tell us that people with little or no emotional capacity are seriously handicapped, unable to develop healthy relationships, and far more likely to engage in sociopathic behavior. Emotions are an important part of our created nature. Of course, like everything else, man's emotions have been impacted by the fall, and further impacted by personal experiences, which are often negative. Man is also volitional, having the capacity to make choices including the capacity to do good or evil. Adam and Eve originally had the capacity to originate righteousness by choosing to love God more than self. While the fall has rendered man in his present state unable to exercise that capacity, it was part of the original constitution of man. In his present state between regeneration and the complete redemption of his nature, even the believer can only perform truly righteous acts by the enabling work of the Holy Spirit, and then only inconsistently. While it may appear to fallen men that they possess a free will, their choices are limited to the range of choices consistent with a fallen nature. Thus, while fallen men do exercise choice, they cannot choose to be righteous. (This will be discussed further under "salvation.")

Man's complex constitution

There has been disagreement over the nature of man's constitution. The debate has centered on how many components there are to man's constitution, and to a lesser degree on the function of those components. Some think that man is dichotomous, having two basic elements (soul or spirit, and body), others that man is trichotomous, having three basic elements (spirit, soul, and body). The difference centers on whether man's immaterial nature can be subdivided. The arguments used in support of dichotomy are as follows.

1) God breathed into man a living soul (Gen. 2:7), which seems to imply a simple (unitary) immaterial nature.

2) In some passages "soul" or "spirit" seems to be used to refer to the immaterial nature generally (Gen. 41:8 cf. Ps. 42:6; Mt. 10:28 cf. 27:50); thus these appear to be two names for the same thing.

3) Body and soul are spoken of as constituting the entire man (Mt. 10:28; 1 Cor. 5:1-5, esp. v. 5).

4) Some say that man is conscious of only two parts of his nature, the immaterial and the material. (Personally, I find this to be untrue, as I am frequently in conflict with myself, cf. Rom. 7:15-25.)

The following are arguments used in support of trichotomy.

1) Some biblical statements make a clear distinction between spirit and soul (cf. 1 Thess. 5:23; Heb. 4:12).

2) The arguments used in favor of dichotomy can be explained as figures of speech in which either soul or spirit is

used figuratively to represent the entire immaterial nature, which is actually composed of two elements.

Interestingly, dichotomy and trichotomy can be two ways of looking at the same information. Since soul and spirit together comprise man's immaterial nature, the question of whether man is tripartite or bipartite is a matter of how specific one wants to be. Some passages distinguish between soul and spirit, others do not. This is not a contradiction; it's simply a matter of specificity. Some passages require a higher degree of specificity in order to relate a particular truth. Seen in this light, the answer to the question, "Is man tripartite or bipartite?" is "Yes."

Man's original moral state

According to the biblical account man was made sinless. That does not mean that he was righteous. Righteousness is a positive quality obtained by obedience to the will of God. Had Adam and Eve passed the moral test presented to them in the Garden, they would have become righteous, but that did not happen. Nevertheless, they were sinless. A sinless creature can go in either direction; he or she can choose to yield in obedience to God's will and become righteous, in which case they become inclined toward righteousness (*i.e.*, righteousness becomes their nature), or they can choose to sin, in which case their nature becomes inclined toward sin.

The proof of man's original sinlessness can be seen from the following: 1) Man, being a direct creation of God, could not have been sinful originally unless God made him that way. For God to make man sinful would be inconsistent with his holy nature. 2) The biblical record of creation indicates that everything God made, including man, was "very good" (Gen. 1:31). 3) It is apparent from the account of man's fall in Genesis 3:1-24 that man's sin originated in his moral choice made in the Garden. It is important to recognize that the fall of the human race into sin was the result of Adam's sin, not Eve's (Rom. 5:12-21).

The fall of man

The necessity of a literal view of the Genesis account

An understanding of the fall of man and it consequences is essential in understanding many other important truths. We cannot understand or accept the concept of original sin (referring to the sin of Adam) apart from a literal understanding of the Genesis account of man's direct creation by God. Those who hold to an evolutionary view of man's origin almost invariably deny the fall. Apart from an understanding and acceptance of original sin, it is impossible to understand both man's historic and current dilemma (spiritual, intellectual, and physical). Also, apart from an understanding and acceptance of the fall we have no basis for understanding and appreciating the work of Christ on the cross (cf. Rom. 5:12-21). Our entire concept of the message of the Bible, and hence, Christianity, stands or falls on our view of the fall of man, and that view rests on the validity of the account of man's creation.

The particulars of the fall

Although Satan tempted Eve, his real target was Adam and Adam's race. Satan struck at Eve because he knew he could leverage Adam's relationship with Eve against his relationship with God. Satan deceived Eve by casting doubt upon God's goodness, suggesting that God was withholding something desirable from her (Gen. 3:4-5). Satan's deception also involved a direct contradiction of God's word to Adam and Eve (v. 4). Satan attributed evil motives to God, suggesting that God told Adam and Eve to leave the tree alone because he did not want them to discover they could be like him (v. 5). He made deceptive promises to Eve, telling her that if she ate of the fruit she would be like God (V. 5). Satan's tactic as seen in this temptation has been repeated countless times down through history. He attacks where we are weakest. His method is simple but effective: He pits one affection against another, entices us to disbelieve God's goodness, incites us to actions that contradict God's clear commands, and holds out deceptive promises about the outcome of our actions.

The consequences of the fall

In surveying the consequences of the fall, we need to distinguish between the kinds of consequences. There are various types of consequences: Immediate consequences happen almost instantly, remote consequences happen in time. Some consequences are natural (cause and effect), others are the result of divine judgment. Adam and Eve's sin involved all of these.

Immediate consequences of the fall

Adam and Eve immediately sensed that something had changed. Whereas previously they had no self-consciousness, they now felt vulnerable, exposed, naked, corrupt, and ashamed (Gen. 3:7). Of course there was nothing wrong with their nakedness; they were naked before. The problem now was that in their fallen state they experienced alienation, both from God and from one another (vv. 8-10). For the first time they experienced a fear and dread of God and repulsion to his holiness. They didn't want to be in his presence. This was evidence of their spiritual death, for at the very moment of their sin, the indwelling presence of God was withdrawn. Their fellowship (the life giving union that existed) was instantly terminated. There arose within Adam and Eve a self-serving and self-preserving instinct. They began to pass blame for their actions (vv. 12-13). Before their sin Adam and Eve had experienced a deep unity at every level (spirit, soul, body), now they were left with only a psychophysical unity. The flame of their relationship withered to merely a smoldering ember of what it had been. The relationship between the man and woman would now be strained and burdensome as a result of the fall (v.16). Any worldview that minimizes the distinct and complementary nature of men and women denies the truths taught in the account of man's creation and fall. (Note the connection between modern feminism and homosexuality: If woman is not a distinct, uniquely designed complementary mate to man, then male/male, or female/female relationships differ little from male/female relationships.) In addition, the environment was cursed and became hostile to man's survival; the serpent was cursed, perhaps as a symbolic remembrance of the fall; and finally, Adam and Eve were expelled from the Garden forever (vv. 23-24).

In regard to man's spiritual condition, the fall rendered Adam and Eve completely unable to redeem themselves, or even to assist God in their redemption; this condition is called "total depravity." Total depravity does not mean that a fallen man is as bad as he or she could possibly be, it simply means that sin has affected every part of his being (spirit, soul, and body). A depraved person will naturally recoil from God just as Adam and Eve did after their sin. Therefore fallen men in their natural state do not seek God; God must seek them (Rom. 3:9-18).

Remote consequences of the fall

Adam and Eve began the long process of physical degeneration and death. While it took many centuries for Adam to die, we may assume that the effects of physical degeneration were soon noticeable. There were additional physical complications for Eve and women after her; reproduction would be burdensome (v. 16). Since in Adam the entire human race fell, every descendant by natural conception would be born in sin, already spiritually separated from God (*i.e.*, spiritually dead). This is usually referred to as the problem of "original sin." While the fall of the human race was immediate, its full effect would only be seen in the course of time.

Questions concerning the fall of man

The fall of man raises several important questions that need to be addressed.

Question: How could the impulse to sin arise within a sinless being?

Answer: In the post-fall world, we sin because we have a sin nature that is inclined toward sin. To put it another way, we have a tendency, or propensity to sin, just like a ball under the influence of gravity has a tendency to roll downhill. Of course

Adam had no sin nature, and thus no propensity to sin; so, how can we explain his action. If he had no inclination to sin, what moved him in that direction? The answer is in the nature of choice, or what we call "free will." All sin is first committed in the heart before it is acted out. Since Adam was created with a free will (the ability to freely make moral choices), he had within him the God-given ability to move in either moral direction. Today, man no longer exercises a completely free will. He has a will, and he does exercise a degree of free choice, but because of his fallen nature his choices have become limited to those choices that are consistent with his sin nature. For example, prior to the fall Adam could have chosen to do a truly righteous act, but the natural (unregenerated) person is incapable of producing righteousness (Rom. 8:5-8). A righteous deed is motivated from a heart that sincerely desires to please God above all else. Even redeemed people can perform righteous deeds only with the enabling of the indwelling Holy Spirit (Rom. 8:9-10). [Some Arminians differ on this point. They believe that not only can man exercise free will, but that believers can reach a state of sinless perfection wherein they are no longer tempted to sin. Such a view is completely without biblical support, cf. Rom. 7:24-25.]

Question: How could a good God permit man to be tempted?

Answer: It is because God is good that he designed man with the ability to choose, and allowed him to experience a real-life choice. Remember, God did not tempt Adam and Eve to sin (Jam. 1:13); he created them with the ability to make moral choices. So why did God deliberately place a tree in the Garden and command them not to eat from it? Wasn't God placing a stumbling block in their path? The answer is that in order for Adam and Eve to be truly free to choose to obey God and become righteous, they had to be free to reject him and become sinful. If God had created Adam and Eve with the ability to choose, but had provided no practical way for them to express their choice, they still would not have been able to choose. In that case their actions would have been determined by the lack of an alternative. God provided a choice for Adam and Eve, and warned them of the consequences of disobedience. God knew before he created Adam and Eve that they would fall, but their choice was nonetheless free, since foreknowledge of an event is not determinative. [If foreknowledge were determinative, then all things would be predetermined, since God knows all things. In that case God could not justly punish sinners, since he would have predetermined their actions.]

Question: How could so great a penalty be attached to so small a sin?

Answer: The problem here is in the assumption made in the question, that is, that sin is finite. If we consider that every sin is committed against an infinitely holy God, then every sin is an infinite offense and merits eternal damnation. In understanding the nature of sin, we must always seek to understand it against the backdrop of God's holiness. We cannot minimize sin without also minimizing God's holiness.

The human condition after the fall

How did Adam's sin affect the human family? Historically, three key positions have been advanced to answer this question; they are: total depravity, Pelagianism, and semi-Pelagianism. The view one takes with regard to how Adam's sin affects his posterity has radical consequences with respect to the doctrines of salvation. This is really where the dividing line is drawn between liberal and conservative theology; and with respect to conservative theology, it is the dividing line between Calvinism (in its varying forms) and Arminianism.

Total depravity (Rom. 5:12-21; 8:5-8; Col. 1:21)

Adam's sin resulted in the fall of his entire person (body, soul, and spirit). When Adam sinned, his nature became such that he no longer possessed the capacity for righteousness, and thus he lost the capacity to exercise faith unto salvation. This posed quite a dilemma; for if faith is required for salvation, and if man has lost his capacity to exercise such faith, how is he to be saved? The answer is that God imparts faith as a gift (Eph. 2:8-9).

Total depravity does not mean that unregenerated people are as bad as they could possibly be, and it does not mean that unregenerated men cannot do good works; it simply means that the natural man is incapable of saving faith and righteousness. An unsaved soldier might sacrifice his life for the cause, or for a friend. Nevertheless, such deeds while noble from the human point of view, are not righteous because righteousness is motivated by intentional obedience to the will of God. As Paul said, the natural man is in a state of hostility against God and cannot yield himself to God (Rom 8:7; Col. 1:21). Actually, total depravity explains a great deal of human history. Man may become more prosperous and more educated, but the basic propensity toward sin is unchanged. Even regenerated men and women find that holiness involves a constant struggle against the propensity of that part of our nature that is not yet sanctified (*i.e.*, the mind and body). As we will see further along, the doctrine of the total depravity of fallen man is pivotal in understanding how men and women come to be saved.

Two other views on the effect of Adam's sin on the human race need to be considered.

Pelagianism (5th Century A.D.)

Pelagianism is the belief that man is not fallen, and that Adam's sin merely set a bad example for his descendants whereas Jesus' life set a good example. Modern liberal Christianity is largely based on this view. Pelagianists deny the fall of the race and the transmission of sin and a sin nature from Adam to his descendants; and as such, stands in clear contradiction of the teaching of the Bible (cf. Rom. 5:10-21, esp. vv. 18-19).

According to Pelagianism all men have a free will and are free to choose righteousness or sin. However, Christians are assisted in performing righteousness by divine grace. A man's free choices thus determine his standing before God. Pelagianists see no need for sacrifice, and they reject substitutionary atonement. In practice, Pelagianism is often expressed as a system of works in which good works should outweigh sin. Salvation, if it can be called such, comes by works of righteousness. Early forms of Pelagianism tended to be strictly moralistic (legalistic) and often ascetic. Modern forms of Pelagianism tend to dismiss most sins as dysfunction rather than moral acts incurring divine judgment. Pelagianism was condemned by the early church at the Councils of Carthage (A.D. 412, 416, and 418), and that condemnation was ratified at the Council of Ephesus (A.D. 431).

As a theology, Pelagianism has serious defects; it denies total depravity (Rom. 5:10-21; 8:5-8 cf. Psa. 51:5; Eph. 1-3), as well as the Old and New Testament doctrine of atonement. Also, it does not explain the universal propensity toward evil among members of the human family. Pelagianism is an example of an early deviation in which human reason was substituted for divine revelation in the development of theology. Throughout church history this basic procedural defect has resulted in a great deal of theological error.

Semi-Pelagianism (5th century A.D.)

Semi-Pelagianists believed that Adam's descendants were affected by the fall, but through a special endowment of the Holy Spirit given to all men (called "common grace") it is possible for men to exercise free will and thus saving faith. Just as semi-Pelagianism was a fifth century reaction to Augustinianism, "Arminianism," a revival of semi-Pelagianism in the early post-reformation period, was a reaction to sixteenth century Calvinism. Semi-Pelagianists believe that saving faith originates within man's free will. The difficulty with semi-Pelagianism is the same as with Pelagianism—it is inconsistent with the biblical teaching of total depravity, and it does not explain man's universal propensity to sin.

Both Pelagianism and semi-Pelagianism hold that all men can exercise free will; whereas total depravity holds that when Adam sinned he fell into bondage to sin and lost the capacity to freely choose to love and obey God, hence to exercise saving faith. Since these positions contradict one another, they cannot all be correct. For those who accept the full verbal inspiration of scripture, it is a fairly straightforward process to eliminate Pelagianism as inconsistent with the general teaching of the Bible (Rom. 5:20-21, esp. vv. 18-19). Also, semi-Pelagianism lacks biblical support, and is contradicted by the New Testament teaching concerning total depravity and election. While some people are clearly Calvinistic (believing in total depravity) and others are clearly Arminian (believing that through common grace men can exercise faith unto salvation), much of contemporary Christianity is eclectic, or a fusion of these doctrines. Often this is seen in the acceptance of eternal security (which is consistent only with total depravity and sovereign grace) along with a conditional view of election (which is completely inconsistent with total depravity and sovereign grace, being based on free will). Regrettably, it appears that many Christians are unaware that eternal security and free will are mutually exclusive. While Calvinism and Arminianism are each coherent systems, the combination of these is not coherent; thus in this case it appears that a great many people hold to a hybrid system of belief that is theologically conflicted.

The transmission of sin

In our discussion above we examined the three major views of how Adam's sin has affected the human family. We now need to address a related question: How can Adam's descendants be held liable for Adam's sin as total depravity insists? Before we deal with the various views as to how Adam's sin is transmitted to his descendants, we must first discuss a related topic: the origin of the soul. There are two major views on how man obtains his soul. One view is called "creationism" (unrelated to cosmological creationism), and the other is called "traducianism."

The origin of the soul

Soul creationists believe that for each newly conceived child God creates a sinless soul that will eventually be joined to the physical nature propagated by the parents. Proponents of this view are not agreed as to when the soul is joined to the physical nature. Some believe the union of soul and body occurs at conception and others that it occurs later, as late as birth. There are a number of problems associated with this view. First, it requires that the sin nature be transmitted through the physical nature, since that is all that man passes down. Such a view seems contrary to the New Testament, which teaches that the source of man's sin resides in his inner (immaterial) nature (cf. Mark 7:21-23). As early as the late first century Christianity began a shift toward an anti-cosmic worldview. This was due to the influence of Platonism, which was prevalent in the Roman world. Platonism exerted a profound influence on the development of Christian theology from the early second century forward, with the material world being viewed as inferior at best, and evil at worst. This anticosmic influence on Christian theology was expressed in such doctrines as amillennialism (the belief that the kingdom of God is a present spiritual reality rather than a physical reality to come) and the doctrine of soul creation. An additional problem with creationism is that it seems contrary to God's moral nature to create a sinless, eternal soul and then condemn it to inevitable corruption by joining it to a sinful material nature. This would seem to be the moral equivalent of chaining an innocent victim to a sinking ship.

Traducianism (the word "traduce" means "to carry over") is the position that the human soul is passed from parent to child, though the means for accomplishing this is unknown. Traducianism is a helpful theory for several reasons: 1) It avoids the problems inherent in soul creationism. 2) It helps us to understand how the entire human race fell when Adam sinned. If the soul is passed from parent to child, then working backwards we can see that at one time all the soul of the human family was in Adam (in unindividuated form). Consequently, in Adam the entire human family fell. While this line of reasoning might seem strange from a modern perspective, we have to remember that it must be viewed from the biblical perspective. According to traducianism we have in us a portion of the same soul that was in Adam. As such, we have inherited a fallen soul with a sin nature. So, we are what Adam became: sinful. While this may be difficult to accept, there is a strong biblical basis for this view. In Hebrews 7:4-10 the writer makes the point that when Abraham paid tithes to Melchizedek, Levi, who would not be born for several generations, was still within Abraham; thus, when Abraham paid a tithe to Melchizedek, Levi paid a tithe to Melchizedek. This is a highly significant case because the writer of Hebrews argues that this action on the part of an ancestor was really, substantively attributable to one yet to be born. Again, the challenge is to be open to see things from God's perspective.

Traducianism explains not only how we can be responsible for Adam's sin, but also why we sin—because we have a fallen, sinful soul from the very beginning of our individual existence (cf. Ps. 51:5). The traducian view also may help to explain the reason for the virgin conception of Christ. If the sin nature is passed through the male, the avoidance of natural conception could have been the means through which God supernaturally brought his Son into the world without sin. While it is generally believed that there is a connection between the virgin conception and Christ's sinlessness, we should note that no such connection is explicitly stated in the Bible.

Theories on the imputation of sin

This is a complex area of theology; one of the reasons is confusion over whether the imputation of sin to the race occurred immediately when Adam sinned, or mediately as the race was propagated, or through some combination of these. If one takes the view that sin was imputed to the entire race immediately, then they would hold to either the federal view, in which Adam by divine covenant represented the entire race in his choice, or that Adam was the natural head of the race and thus all of humanity (being substantively in Adam when he sinned) actually participated in his sin. Alternatively, some have taken the position that sin is passed down generationally (mediately) from parent to child. The following table illustrates the relationships that exist between the views on the origin of the soul and whether the imputation of Adam's sin was immediate or mediate.

	Creationism or Traducianism	Traducianism
Immediate Imputation	Headship view: Adam chose for the entire human race, whether as the natural head or the divinely appointed head.	Substantive view: The entire race, being within Adam, became sinful when Adam sinned
Mediate Imputation		Seminal view: The race became sinful as sin was passed down from parent to child

In the headship view, Adam is seen as making a representative choice on behalf of the entire human race. This could be due to either natural headship (as the father of the race), or to his appointment by God (federal headship). The federal view presumes the existence of a covenant between God and man establishing Adam's federal (representative) headship; since no such covenant is found in scripture, this view requires such a covenant to be inferred. (This is the position of covenant theology.) The other alternative is based on some type of substantive or seminal connection. The substantive view is that all humanity was within Adam when he sinned and therefore the entire race participated in Adam's sin and fell immediately. The "seminal" view is an alternate view that sin is passed down as the race is propagated generationally. The headship view can be compatible with either creationism or traducianism. However, soul creationists must hold to some form of headship, since the non-headship views are only compatible with traducianism. Note how Paul expresses the imputation of sin in Romans 5:12-21.

> 12Therefore, just as through one man sin entered into the world, and death through sin, and so death spread to all men, because all sinned — 13for until the Law sin was in the world, but sin is not imputed when there is no law. 14Nevertheless death reigned from Adam until Moses, even over those who had not sinned in the likeness of the offense of Adam, who is a type of Him who was to come. 15But the free gift is not like the transgression. For if by the transgression of the one the many died, much more did the grace of God and the gift by the grace of the one Man, Jesus Christ, abound to the many. 16The gift is not like that which came through the one who sinned; for on the one hand the judgment arose from one transgression resulting in condemnation, but on the other hand the free gift arose from many transgressions resulting in justification. 17For if by the transgression of the one, death reigned through the one, much more those who receive the abundance of grace and of the gift of righteousness will reign in life through the One, Jesus Christ. 18So then as through one transgression there resulted condemnation to all men, even so through one act of righteousness there resulted justification of life to all men. 19For as through the one man's disobedience the many were made sinners, even so through the obedience of the One the many will be made righteous. 20The Law came in so that the transgression would increase; but where sin increased, grace abounded all the more, 21so that, as sin reigned in death, even so grace would reign through righteousness to eternal life through Jesus Christ our Lord. (NASB)

Paul said that through one man sin entered the world, and death entered through that sin (v. 12, *tēs hamartias,* "the sin"). Eve's sin resulted in her own death, but Adam's sin resulted both in his death and in the death of his descendants—including even those who lived prior to the giving of the Law, who in the absence of law could not have committed any personal sin (vv. 13-14). In fact, Paul declared that the spreading of death to all men derived from the fact that in Adam's act all men sinned (v. 12). [If we were to suppose that Paul meant that all men die (eventually) because all men sin (eventually), then we would be left with no explanation as to why those who lived prior to the Law died; for Paul states that they did not sin after the likeness of Adam (v. 13-14), who committed a personal transgression by disobeying a divine command. Thus it seems that Paul's teaching requires us to understand that Adam's sin and condemnation was attributed to the entire race.] Actually we can find elements of all of these views in Paul's statement in Romans 5:12-21.

The doctrine of original sin raises a serious christological question: If Adam's sin was imputed to the entire race, how is it that Christ could be sinless? A possible answer could be the fact that because Christ is "the second Adam" and thus the head of a new race, he was not reckoned a sinner along with Adam's race. A better possibility is that the virgin conception, or some other miracle, prevented sin from being passed to him. Of course, no explanation is going to be entirely satisfactory since we don't have all of the pieces to this puzzle. In summary, the following points should be considered.

1. When Adam sinned, the entire human race became sinful and died. Christ is the only exception, though we do not know precisely how that was accomplished. Romans 5:12-21 is clear that Adam's sin is reckoned to be the sin of every one of his natural descendants.

2. Every one of Adam's natural descendants begins life with a fallen nature, which has been passed down from one generation to the next (cf. Gen. 6:5; 8:21; Psa. 51:5; Eccl. 9:3; Jer. 17:9; Mk. 7:21-23; Jn. 3:19; Rom. 3:9-12, 23; 8:7,8; 1 Cor. 2:14; Eph. 4:17-19; 5:8; Tit. 1:15).

3. As a result, all of Adam's natural descendants are born under condemnation. Man enters the world lost (Jn. 3:16), condemned (Jn. 3:19; Rom. 6:16ff.; 8:1), spiritually dead (Eph. 2:1), and hostile to God (Rom. 5:10, 8:7; Col. 1:21).

4. There seem to be both immediate and mediate aspects to the imputation of sin. When Adam sinned the act was attributable to the entire race; however, the corrupt nature is passed from one generation to the next.

Review Questions

1. Briefly state the arguments commonly used in support of biological evolution.

2. How could you respond to each of the arguments used in support of biological evolution?

3. What are some of the problems with trying to fit evolutionism into the Bible? Explain.

4. In what ways does man reflect God? Can you think of some ways in which man does not reflect God?

5. Define "dichotomy" and "trichotomy," and explain how the two views can fit together.

6. How do we know that man was created sinless?

7. What is the difference between "sinless" and "righteous"?

8. Discuss the key elements in Satan's temptation of Eve. What specific strategies did he use?

9. Discuss the immediate consequences of man's fall.

10. Discuss the mediate (remote) consequences of Adam's fall.

11. Respond to the question: "How could the impulse to sin arise within a sinless being?"

12. Respond to the question: "How could a good God permit man to be tempted?"

13. Respond to the question: "How could so great a penalty be attached to so small a sin as Adam and Eve's sin?"

14. Explain total depravity. Discuss both what it means and what it does not mean.

15. Define "Pelagianism" and discuss any problems with this view.

16. Define "semi-Pelagianism" and discuss any problems with this view.

17. Define "creationism" as used in relation to the origin of man's soul.

18. Define "traducianism."

19. What advantages does traducianism have over creationism?

20. Which view (creationism or traducianism) do you think makes the most sense? Explain.

21. Describe the representative views of imputation (natural headship and federalism).

22. Describe the realistic views of imputation (the substantive and seminal views).

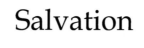

Salvation

Salvation

The area of doctrine concerned with salvation is called "soteriology." In our study of Christ and the Holy Spirit, we have already been introduced to some of the concepts that will be developed here in greater detail.

The necessity of Christ's death for man's sin

According to some theories of the atonement (the accident theory, the moral influence theory, and the martyr theory) the death of Christ was not necessary for man's redemption; however, the Bible is clear that Christ's death was necessary in order for man to be redeemed. Scripture states that Christ died in our place; this view is called substitutionary atonement (Heb. 9:28; 1 Pet. 2:24; 2 Cor. 5:21). The Greek word most commonly denoting substitution is *huper*, meaning, "on behalf of" (Gal. 3:13; Eph. 5:2; Heb. 2:9, 14-17; Rom. 3:21-26; Heb. 10:1-14). These passages tell us that Christ's death satisfied God's righteous demands for judgment upon sin, both Adam's original sin and our personal sin. We are told that Christ quite literally traded places with us, taking our sin and imparting to us his righteousness (2 Cor. 5:21). This is an amazing truth. However, it is important to remember that this transaction is not automatic (as held by universalists); it is applied only to those who receive (*i.e.*, yield themselves to) Christ for what he claims to be, which is nothing less than God, Savior, and Lord. Those who refuse Christ remain liable for their own penalty, which is eternal damnation (Rev. 20:11-15).

The extent of Christ's atonement

While Christ died for all men, his sacrifice secures forgiveness and reconciliation only for those who respond in faith to his offer of salvation. Another way of stating this is that Christ's death is sufficient for all, but efficient only for those who respond in faith. There is a popular misconception that Christ's death satisfied the penalty for all sin regardless of whether a person believes in Christ or not, and therefore the only sin for which any unbeliever will be held liable is the sin of unbelief. However, this view is seriously flawed. First, if Christ paid for all sin, how is it that unbelievers could be held liable for the sin of unbelief? Obviously, the penalty of some sin (unbelief) was not satisfied. (Actually, all sin can be traced to unbelief.) Second, this view contradicts scriptural statements. Revelation 20:12 says that the final judgment will be based on two considerations. First, the Book of Life will be consulted to determine that the one being judged is not redeemed, and thus responsible for his or her sins. Second, another book containing a record of each person's deeds will be consulted, and each one will be judged according to their deeds written in the book. This indicates that Christ's sacrifice is not applied in the case of those who do not accept him.

Key scriptural support that Christ's sacrifice is sufficient for all sin (the position referred to as "unlimited atonement," or "general redemptionism") is found in 1 Timothy 2:6, and 4:10; John 1:29; Hebrews 2:9; 2 Peter 2:1, and 3:9; 1 John 2:2.

The application of Christ's atonement

In order for Christ's atonement to become effective for an individual a number of things must occur. In some cases a sequence for these events can be determined; in other cases several events happen instantaneously (and thus simultaneously). The individual elements leading to salvation are as follows.

Election

The word "elect" means, "to choose" (Heb. *bahir*, and Gr. *eklektos*). Israel is referred to as an elect nation (Isa. 45:4), meaning that God chose them from among all the nations to be the recipients of special promises. Election is also used to denote the fact that God chooses men and women unto personal salvation (Eph.

1:1-12); this is sometimes referred to as personal, or individual election. Historically, two views of personal election have been offered; one is called "conditional election," the other is called "unconditional election." Both views place election prior to the creation of the world. Some of the major passages on election are: Romans 9:1-29, esp. vv. 6-24; Ephesians 1:3-10, also John 6:37 cf. vv. 44, 65. (In John 6:37-65, note that the single greatest defection Jesus experienced in his followers was on the occasion that he spoke concerning personal election, cf. v. 66.) Regrettably, election has proved to be a stumbling block for many. The question is not: Does the Bible teach election? There can be no doubt that the Bible teaches some view of election; the question is: What view does it teach? This issue is largely settled by one's prior conclusions regarding man's fallen nature. If one accepts total depravity as true, then only the unconditional view could be correct, for a totally depraved person would never freely choose to yield himself or herself to God apart from God's sovereign election.

Conditional election

Conditional election is the view that God chose people to salvation based on his foreknowledge that they would exercise faith in Christ. According to this view election is conditioned upon foreseen faith, making faith the cause and election the effect. Conditional election is strictly a semi-Pelagian view in that it bases faith in man's free will. Most of the passages used in support of conditional election deal not with election, but with the general call to salvation (*i.e.*, invitations to "whosoever"), which proponents view as incompatible with unconditional election. However, as will be seen, the general call of God to all men and Christ's death for all men is not incompatible with unconditional election. The two principal arguments used in support of conditional election are as follows.

1. *The argument from fairness:* Of the two views, the conditional view seems on the surface to be more fair than the unconditional view, since God simply validates the individual's free choice.

2. *The argument from foreknowledge:* There are two principal
    passages that appear to link election to divine foreknowl-
    edge: Romans 8:29-30 and 1 Peter 1:1-2. It is argued on the
    basis of these passages that God based election on the
    choice he foresaw that men would make. (Foreknowledge
    is sometimes referred to as "prescience.")

However, there are serious problems with the conditional view.
Note the following:

1. There is a lack of biblical support for conditional election,
    since neither Romans 8:29-30 nor 1 Peter 1:1-2 states that
    God based election on foreseen faith; they state only that
    God foreknew the individuals elected, which would be a
    prerequisite for either view, since God could not elect
    anyone, conditionally or unconditionally, that he did not
    foreknow.

2. Conditional election is completely incompatible with to-
    tally depravity, since a totally depraved person would
    never freely choose to yield himself or herself to God.

3. The greater fairness of the conditional view is merely an
    illusion, because it assumes that God could have deter-
    mined to elect conditionally or unconditionally. However,
    if total depravity is true, then conditional election is
    impossible, and it cannot be argued that an impossible
    position would have been fairer. (That would be like
    saying that imaginary candy is sweeter than real candy.)

4. The conditional view reverses the cause and effect relation-
    ship indicated by 1 Peter 1:1-2, where election (being "cho-
    sen") is indicated to be the cause of faith (referred to there
    as, "obedience to the truth").

5   The description given of election in some passages seems
    compatible only with the unconditional view (Rom. 9:6-24;
    Eph. 1:13-14, esp. vv.5, 11); on the other hand there seem to

be no passages in which the description is compatible only with the conditional view.

Unconditional election

Unconditional election is the view that God chose individuals to salvation according to his own will for reasons unknown to man. The view does not attempt to answer the question of why God chose some and not others. According to this view faith is given to elect individuals on the basis of grace (*i.e.*, it does not originate in man's free will). Consider the following arguments.

1. The argument from cause and effect supports unconditional election (1 Peter 1:1-2; Jn. 10:26; 17:2,6,9,24).

2. Total depravity is consistent only with unconditional election. Men, being totally depraved, are not spiritually neutral; they live in a state of hostility toward God, and are unable to voluntarily submit themselves to God (Rom. 8:5-8, esp. v. 8).

3. Unconditional election is the view that is described in the New Testament (Eph. 1:1-12, esp. vv. 5 and 12; Rom. 9:6-24). Romans 9:6-24 is an especially important passage. One of the key reasons for believing Paul was teaching the unconditional view is that he anticipated that his readers would protest with the objection: "That's not fair!" (vv. 14 and 19)—an objection that would never have been made against the conditional view. After all, don't most people who hold to the conditional view do so because they think it to be fair? Thus the fact that Paul anticipated a strong objection of unfairness clearly indicates which view he taught.

On the surface, unconditional election seems unfair when compared to conditional election. However we must consider several factors. First, given the fact of man's total depravity, the conditional view is not a viable option. Perhaps God has elected the greatest number of people possible that can be elected; maybe the redemption of the total human family was never a possibility. Second, perhaps the choice of who was elected, and who was not, was pragmatic rather than preferential. In other words, maybe God elected whom he did, not because he preferred some to others, but because by electing whom he did, he could extend redemption to the greatest extent of the human family possible. If this were true, then we could see how God could sovereignly elect some and not others, and still be impartial. Jesus himself seems to imply that this might be the case in the parable of the wheat and the tares (Mt. 13:24-32 and vv. 36-43). In this parable a man sowed seed in his field and both wheat and tares came up. Since he had sown only good seed, he knew that an enemy had sown tares to ruin his crop. When asked by his servants whether they should pull up the tares, the planter said, "No, lest while you are gathering up the tares, you may uproot the wheat with them" (NASB). In this parable Jesus clearly implied that the presence of the non-elect (the tares) is a necessary evil that must be endured until the elect (the wheat) are brought safely into the kingdom. This is a difficult truth, but clearly some choices on God's part limit future options even for him. We can illustrate this by asking a simple question: Could God redeem a person who persists in rejecting Jesus Christ as Savior? Obviously the answer is "No." Why? Because the way God established things precludes such a possibility, and even the scripture asserts this to be true (Acts 4:12). It is possible that once Adam fell, the redemption of the complete human family was never a possibility. To further illustrate this point, let us recall that many people would never have been born except for the presence of evil in the world (war, famine, broken families and marriages, slavery, rape, incest, *etc.*). Also, many people have been brought to the point of surrender and faith in Christ only in times of great national, family, or personal tragedy. It has taken a foxhole with bullets flying overhead to motivate some people to do serious business with God, even though they were elect. Let us remember that election doesn't save anyone; men and women are saved by grace through faith at the moment that faith is exercised. Election is simply the choice on God's part to do whatever it takes, even if it means tolerating evil dictators and wars, to bring a particular individual to faith in Christ. To those who may be disturbed by this, consider the following: God obviously knew prior to creation that if he created, billions of souls would spend eternity in Hell, yet he did it anyway. That incontrovertible fact tells us that God is willing to sacrifice many in order to save a comparatively small number. In light of that fact, where does that leave the fairness argument?

One issue that is raised against unconditional election is that it diminishes man's responsibility to exercise faith. However, men still must exercise faith to be saved. Even the elect cannot be saved apart from faith. Unconditional election simply recognizes that the ability to exercise faith is a gift from God (Eph. 2:8-9), not an act of free will. It is also alleged that unconditional election diminishes our motivation to evangelize since the elect will be saved anyway. That is not true. The proclamation of the gospel is essential in order for anyone to come to faith (Rom. 10:14-17). Note what this objection implies: that men will only be faithful to evangelize if the salvation of others hangs in the balance; yet how fair would it be for God to make the salvation of one person contingent upon the actions of another person?

Some believe that unconditional election implies double predestination (the election of some to life and others to damnation). Such is, in fact, the historic position of Calvinism. Nevertheless, there seems to be no general scriptural support for double predestination. Some point to Romans 9:17 and verses 22-23; however, this harkens back to the issue that was addressed previously, that God tolerates, even uses the non-elect in order to bring about the salvation of his elect. However, such does not require or even imply double predestination. God does not need to secure the perdition of the non-elect; they are already condemned. On this point it is important that we distinguish between God not electing, and in actively decreeing perdition. If God is the active cause of the perdition of those finally lost, by what criteria will he judge them? In such a case the lost could simply argue that they pursued the only course open to them, and thus cannot be justly faulted for doing so. Thus, double predestination is both biblically and theologically problematic.

Calling

Calling is a special ministry of the Holy Spirit; it is related to conviction (cf. Jn. 16:7-11). There are two kinds of calls referred to in scripture. One is a general call, in which God issues a genuine invitation to all men to come to him (Jn. 3:16); the other is an effectual call in which God brings men unto himself (Rom. 8:28-30). The effectual calling is sometimes referred to as "irresistible grace."

The general calling of God

The general call is the invitation that God extends to all men everywhere to come to Christ and be saved (Mt. 11:28; 28:19; Jn. 3:16; 4:14; 11:26; Rev. 22:17). The general call is a genuine offer of salvation to all men and is based upon the death of Christ for all.

The effectual calling of God

The effectual call is the invitation and impetus that God grants to the elect that cannot fail to result in the exercise of saving faith (Rom. 8:28-30; 1 Cor. 1:26-31; 2 Tim. 1:9).

Questions about calling

Question: If unconditional election is true, is the general call of God to the non-elect sincere? In other words, why would God issue a call to one that he has not elected?

Answer: Yes, the general call of God is sincere, because God has provided for the salvation of all men and women in Christ, and he genuinely desires their salvation (Jn. 3:16), even though man's condition, as a result of the fall, renders the redemption of the entire human family unattainable.

Question: Why would God issue a call to people he knows have been rendered unable to respond by virtue of total depravity?

Answer: We don't know, but we do know that man's inability to respond in faith stems from his fallen nature, for which each man is responsible, which is why he is in need of salvation in the first place. Thus, a man's self-imposed inability to respond does not absolve him of responsibility for making a choice; it simply makes the outcome a function of a prior choice — the choice to sin at the fall, for which all men are responsible. [This is analogous to the case of a drunk driver who causes the death of another person. The drunk cannot plead that he is not responsible since he was drunk when the accident occurred, because he is responsible for his drunken state. Similarly, while a sinner's nature renders him unable to come to God, he is nonetheless responsible for his sinful state *via* his participation in humanity's original sin.] One thing we know is that God loves every person, and desires the salvation of every person, and as evidence of his love he has provided a sufficient sacrifice for all men and calls all to himself.

Question: If the effectual call is irresistible, does this violate man's choice; in other words, is salvation forced upon the elect?

Answer: No, because God is capable of making an irresistible offer that employs rather than preempts man's will. (We do this frequently with children, offering them something we know will induce them to a particular choice.)

Repentance and faith

Repentance and faith are two sides of the same coin. It is impossible to consider one without the other.

Repentance

Repentance is rejection of sin previously embraced; it is a sincere reversal of thinking about sin. Note the following observations regarding repentance.

1. God's grace is the source of repentance (Acts 5:31; 11:18).

2. Godly sorrow is the motivation of repentance (2 Cor. 7:8-10).

3. Repentance makes faith possible (Acts 20:21).

4. Repentance and confession are the same concept expressed in different terminology (1 Jn. 1:9).

Faith

Saving faith is obedience (voluntary submission) to the gospel truth. There are three essential ingredients necessary for faith.

1. Truth

    Saving faith is based on truth; without truth, one cannot exercise such faith (Rom. 10:17). Paul said that faith that is not based on truth is worthless (2 Thess 2:13; 1 Cor. 15:12-17). However, knowledge of the truth doesn't always lead to faith; sometimes people know and reject the truth. The minimum truth required for salvation is the knowledge of who Christ is and what he accomplished for our salvation (*i.e.,* the gospel).

2. Voluntary obedience

    Note the connection between faith and works in James 2:14-26. What James said is that a person can distinguish true faith from non-saving faith because the nature of true faith is that it yields to truth, and therefore will naturally be manifested in the way one lives his or her life. James made a very interesting observation: He said that the demons believe too. In other words, demons know and believe the truth, but their belief is not saving faith, because while knowing the truth (*i.e.,* the facts), they choose to rebel against that truth. One can know what the Bible says and believe every word, and still be lost if they do not yield to that truth. Mere acceptance of truth as fact is not faith; faith is a response to truth, a submission of the will to the truth that God has revealed (1 Pet. 1:22; 2:8; 3:1; 4:17; Rom. 2:8).

3. Opportunity to choose

The reason that opportunity is essential for faith is that one cannot yield to truth unless there are choices to be made. For example, suppose God had placed Adam and Eve in the Garden but had not given them an opportunity to make a morally significant choice, how would they have been able to yield to God in faith? God allows us to experience trials in order to give us the opportunity to yield to him and to grow in faith. Trials are actually opportunities in disguise (Jam. 1:2-4, 1 Pet. 1:3-7).

Forgiveness

In regard to salvation, forgiveness means that God does not exact from the sinner the penalty due for his or her sins, since that penalty has been paid by Christ (Rom. 4:7; Eph. 1:7 cf. Col. 1:14). Forgiveness of the penalty for sin, which is accomplished once when a person exercises faith in Christ (Col. 2:1314; Heb. 10:11-14) and forgiveness of the discipline for sin, which occurs as often as a believer confesses sin (1 Jn. 1:9), should not be confused. When a person is redeemed, the penalty for all sins is forgiven. This operation will never need to be repeated. However, when a redeemed person sins, though the penalty is forgiven, God may find it needful to discipline his child in order to get him or her back on the right path. Keep in mind that the ultimate goal of redemption is holiness. We must be careful not to confuse punishment and discipline. Punishment is what the unredeemed will suffer in Hell, discipline is God's corrective training of his child, and though unpleasant at the time, it is actually a means of grace. If a saved person commits sin and is unrepentant, God uses discipline to bring about correction in his or her life. Through sincere repentance of one's sin, the believer may avoid discipline, though they still might suffer the natural consequences of sin. We should not think of confession as simply giving God a list of our sins; he already knows what we have done. The word "confess" in 1 John 1:9 (Gr. *homologia*) means to have the same attitude or judgment upon one's sin as does God. In other words, God wants his children to come to see their sins the way he sees them, insofar as that is possible. When the child of God does that, discipline serves no further purpose.

Justification

Justification is a judicial act of God in which a believing sinner is declared righteous and completely acceptable to God (Rom. 3:21-28; 4:1-25; 5:1, 15-21; 8:30; Gal. 2:16). Justification does not change the person; it changes their standing before God. Note the following observations in regard to justification.

1. Justification involves the transfer of penalty from the sinner to Christ (Rom. 5:12-21).

2. Justification involves the transfer of Christ's righteousness to the believing sinner (2 Cor. 5:21).

3. Justification involves a restoration to God's favor. Whereas previously sinners were under condemnation and enemies of God, having been justified they are restored to favor and blessing.

Regeneration and indwelling

Regeneration is the act of God in which the spiritually dead sinner is made alive. Regeneration and indwelling are two aspects of the same operation. Indwelling is the continuation of what begins with regeneration (Titus 3:5). [The Greek term *palingenesia,* translated "regeneration," means to be "born" (*genesia*) "again" (*palin*). A similar expression (Gr. *anagennao,* {*ana* = "again" + *gennao* = "to bring forth"}) is used in 1 Peter 1:23 and is translated "born again."]

Before man's fall, he lived in continual communion, or fellowship with God. Man's spirit and God's Spirit were in vital (life-giving) union, such that man was spiritually alive. When Adam sinned, God, because he is holy, withdrew from that relationship, leaving Adam spiritually dead. That condition Adam passed on to all of his naturally conceived descendants. The only remedy for spiritual death is regeneration, which is the re-establishment of vital union between God and a man or woman. This can only happen if a person's spirit is first cleansed of sin. By dying in our place, Christ made it possible for us to be forgiven when we accept him as our Savior/God. Once a person is cleansed of sin, God, through the Holy Spirit, instantly establishes a vital union with that person's spirit, infusing spiritual life. The continuedness of this relationship is referred to as "indwelling."

Union with Christ

Union with Christ refers to the union in which the believer experiences a dynamic and life-giving relationship with Christ. This work is virtually indistinguishable from indwelling, except that the focus is on the connection to Christ rather than the Holy Spirit. There are a number of New Testament analogies to illustrate this truth. For example: 1) a foundation and a building (1 Cor. 3:10-15); 2) a husband and a wife (Eph. 5:22-30; Rev. 19:6-9); 3) a vine and its branches (Jn. 15:1-6); 4) a head and a body (Eph. 4:15-16); 5) Adam and Adam's descendants (Rom. 5:12-21). There are several other biblical expressions that indicate the union between Christ and the believer: 1) being "in Christ" (Jn. 14:20); 2) Christ being "in us" (Jn. 14:20; Col. 1:27); 3) "partaking" or "sharing" in Christ (Heb. 3:14; 2 Pet. 1:4). The believer's union with Christ should not be misunderstood as a combining of essence, rather the two are brought into a special spiritual life-giving relationship. This idea can be extended to the entire Body of Christ. If Christ is in union with every believer, then every believer is joined, through Christ, to every other believer (cf. 1 Cor. 12:12-27; Eph. 4:7-16). It is important to realize that this is a real and spiritually substantive relationship, not merely a figurative truth. (There is a difference between a figure being used to illustrate a truth, and a truth being figurative.)

Sealing

Sealing is the work of God by which the believer's standing before God is made secure (Eph. 1:13; 4:30). The Holy Spirit's work of sealing the believer into Christ is directly related to perseverance, which is often referred to as "eternal security." The believer is sealed into Christ by the Holy Spirit to be safely delivered to God at the day of his or her final redemption, when they will be glorified eternally. In order for a redeemed person to lose their salvation, either Christ or the Holy Spirit would have to fail, which of course makes the loss of salvation impossible.

Adoption

Adoption is the work of God by which he makes the believer in Christ a member of his family with all of the privileges and blessings of family membership. The figure of adoption is used only by Paul (Rom. 8:15, 23; Gal. 4:5; Eph. 1:5).

Spirit baptism

Spirit baptism is the work of the Holy Spirit in which the believer is made part of the Body of Christ, the true (universal) Church (1 Cor. 12:13ff is the definitive passage). Note the following observations concerning Spirit baptism.

1. Spirit baptism is unique to the Church age (from Pentecost A.D. 33 to the conclusion of the Church age at the rapture). The rationale for this statement is as follows:

   a. The Church is the Body of Christ (Col. 1:24).

b. Spirit baptism places one into the Body of Christ (1 Cor. 12:13).

c. In Acts 1:5 Christ referred to the baptizing work of the Holy Spirit as future. In other words, prior to Pentecost (A.D. 33) there was no Spirit baptism, and thus, no Church.

d. In Acts 11:15-17, Peter identified Pentecost as the beginning of the Church and the beginning of the baptizing work of the Holy Spirit.

2. All Church-age believers partake of Spirit baptism. Note the following evidence:

a. This truth is expressly stated in 1 Corinthians 12:12-13.

b. Ephesians 4:5 implies that all who are part of the Body of Christ have been baptized into Christ.

c. Believers are nowhere exhorted to seek Spirit baptism; thus it is reasonable to presume that it is automatic.

3. Spirit baptism occurs only once in the life of a believer.

4. The results of Spirit baptism are:

a. The believer is made part of the Body of Christ (with all of the benefits and privileges (1 Cor. 12:12-13; Eph. 4:4-5; Gal. 3:26-29).

b. Believers are united with Christ (Col. 2:8-12, esp. v.12; Rom. 6:1-10), and with one another (1 Cor. 12:1-31).

A proper understanding of Spirit baptism is essential to many other doctrines, especially to the doctrine of the Church and to eschatology (the doctrine of the future). Certain prophetic promises were made to the Church; unless we understand that the Church is distinct from Israel, to whom other prophetic promises were made, we will have a tendency to confuse these prophetic programs. Confusion on this point leads to significant theological differences.

Sanctification

Sanctification refers to how a redeemed person is made holy; it is a necessary part of the salvation process since God's holiness limits the relationship he can have with sinful men. While some see sanctification as an operation distinct from salvation, it is actually an integral part of the salvation process, along with forgiveness, justification, regeneration, union with Christ, sealing, adoption, Spirit baptism, and ultimate glorification.

Theologians have attempted to explain sanctification from various perspectives. One common approach is to view the believer's ongoing struggle with sin as owing to the fact that he has two natures: a holy (sinless) nature, and a sin nature. According to the two-nature view, the nature that the believer chooses to nurture manifests itself to the greatest extent. While this model does illustrate the conflict between righteous and sinful impulses that occur within the believer as described by Paul in Romans 7:13-25, it fails to address the key issue in sanctification: how transformation of the believer's human nature (the totality of his being) takes place. The two-nature view simply lacks enough explanatory value to be of much use. Additionally, there is considerable ambiguity over what is meant by the term "nature." If the new (holy) nature is one of the two natures and the sin nature is the other, then which nature is being transformed? The new nature is already holy and the sin principle cannot be made holy (Rom. 7:13-25). On the other hand, if the unsanctified part of the believer's human nature is simply under the domination of a sin principle operative within, then while the sin principle itself cannot be made holy, the human nature can, but this leads us back to a single nature. The ambiguity of the two-nature model and the precise identification of the two natures and their relationship lead to some rather fruitless theological discussion.

Looking at other perspectives, one common approach is to focus on the positional aspect of sanctification, emphasizing that the work of sanctification is essentially a divine work, already accomplished both declaratively (judicially) and according to the reckoning of God who sees the end from the beginning, and can view the process as complete though it is not actually complete (with respect to the present). Support for this view is drawn from 1 Corinthian 1:2; 6:11, and Hebrews 10:8-18. In 1 Corinthians 1:2, Paul addresses his letter to "the church of God which is at Corinth, to those who have been sanctified [Gr. *hēgiasmenois*, perfect participle—denoting a present condition resulting from past action] in Christ Jesus, saints by calling...." In 1 Corinthians 6:11 he says, "...but you were washed, but you were sanctified [Gr. *hēgiasthēte*, aorist passive—denoting completed action], but you were justified in the name of the Lord Jesus, and in the Spirit of our God." The grammar in these passages seems to imply that washing (associated with regeneration, cf. Tit. 3:5), sanctification, and justification (all aorist verbs) occur simultaneously. In Hebrews 10:10 the writer says, "By this will we have been sanctified [Gr. *hēgiasmenoi*, perfect participle] through the offering of the body of Jesus Christ once for all." This is theologically identical to Paul's teaching in 1 Corinthians 1 and 6. Also, in Hebrews 10:14 the writer says, "For by one offering He has perfected [Gr. *teteleiōken*, perfect tense] for all time those who are sanctified [Gr. *haiazomenous*, present passive participle, *i.e.*, "those who are being sanctified"]. We see here clearly the two ideas of the "already" and the "not yet." The idea that God has perfected what is being sanctified seems to have a declarative element (with respect to the judgment of God), as well as a temporal element that is reflected in the believer's progressive experience.

Another view is what might be regarded as a temporal view, and it is organized around the timing of the various operations leading to total sanctification. According to this view the redeemed person is made holy in some limited sense at the moment of redemption, then continues to be sanctified in their present walk, and will be fully and finally sanctified at the appearing of Christ in the future. This too seems to be a valid model, but it leaves some questions unanswered. For instance, the temporal perspective neither specifies what part of man is sanctified when, nor does it give us a clue as to the specifics of the sanctification process. Nevertheless, understanding that sanctification occurs within a temporal frame of reference involving past, present, and future, is important.

A somewhat existential view emphasizes that when a person is regenerated, they are separated from the penalty of sin; then as they grow in their walk with the Lord they are progressively separated from the power of sin; and finally when they are with Christ they will be separated from the presence of sin. This is very similar to the temporal view, only the emphasis is placed on how the believer's state of being is impacted with respect to sin as the overall process is brought toward completion. While this view does not specify what part of the believer (spirit, soul, body) is affected at each stage, it does deal with the state in which the believer exists as the process unfolds.

Finally, a view that might be regarded as an objective view explains that the believer's spirit is made holy at the moment of salvation, while the soul (including the mind and emotions) are progressively sanctified, though not completely, throughout the Christian life; and last, the body will experience its sanctification at the appearing of Christ to transform the believer's body. This perspective is similar to the last two (the temporal and the existential views) in that it incorporates a temporal element, but in this case the focus is on the believer's own objective nature (spirit, soul, body).

All of these views in varying ways attempt to deal with the relationship between "what is" and "what is to come," and they all have some explanatory and illustrative value, though none is complete by itself. Since it is difficult to build a comprehensive view around abstractions like "time," "justice," and "divine reckoning," it is helpful if we use man's objective nature (spirit, soul, and body) as the basis of a more integrated view. If nothing else, this might make it easier to conceptualize how some of the elements of the various views fit together. In the following discussion we will explore how the objective view, which focuses on the sanctification of the human nature, is developed biblically, and then how the elements from the other views can be correlated to this view. Obviously, this is only one way of organizing and correlating this information.

The Bible describes sanctification as occurring in three stages: sanctification of spirit, soul (inclusive of heart and mind), and body; they are the objects upon which the work of sanctification is performed, and together they comprise the sum total of the believer's human nature.

Immediate sanctification of the believer's spirit

Immediate sanctification is the sanctification of one's spirit the moment he or she is regenerated. In order for the Holy Spirit to be united with the person who exercises faith in Christ, the believer's sinful spirit must be made holy. Sin was the cause of man's spiritual death in the first place, and in order for union with God to be re-established there must be, minimally, a reversal of what caused man's spiritual death (though certainly more than the minimum is accomplished in redemption). Because God is holy, union with God is predicated upon holiness. When a person is regenerated he or she must also be cleansed, not only judicially, but actually. Paul alluded to this aspect of sanctification when he said: "If Christ is in you, though the body is dead because of sin, yet the spirit is alive because of righteousness" (Rom. 8:10). In Romans 7:14-25 Paul described the conflict between the already sanctified inner man (7:22) and the unsanctified part of his nature, which he termed "the flesh" (vv.14,18,25) or "the bodily members" (vv. 23,24), but which we should understand to include the soul (the heart and mind) since the body does not have an independent capacity to make moral choices apart from the heart and mind. Paul said,

> [14]For we know that the Law is spiritual, but I am of flesh, sold into bondage to sin. [15]For what I am doing, I do not

understand; for I am not practicing what I would like to do, but I am doing the very thing I hate. [16]But if I do the very thing I do not want to do, I agree with the Law, confessing that the Law is good. [17]So now, no longer am I the one doing it, but sin which dwells in me. [18]For I know that nothing good dwells in me, that is, in my flesh; for the willing is present in me, but the doing of the good is not. [19]For the good that I want, I do not do, but I practice the very evil that I do not want. [20]But if I am doing the very thing I do not want, I am no longer the one doing it, but sin which dwells in me. [21]I find then the principle that evil is present in me, the one who wants to do good. [22]For I joyfully concur with the law of God in the inner man, [23]but I see a different law in the members of my body, waging war against the law of my mind and making me a prisoner of the law of sin which is in my members. [24]Wretched man that I am! Who will set me free from the body of this death? [25]Thanks be to God through Jesus Christ our Lord! So then, on the one hand I myself with my mind am serving the law of God, but on the other, with my flesh the law of sin. (NASB)

When a person is regenerated, their spirit is immediately sanctified (Rom. 8:10). This is a final (completed) operation. Thus, for the regenerated person, their spirit is as holy as it will ever be. Man can contribute no more to the sanctification of his spirit than he can contribute to his own redemption, which is absolutely nothing; it is entirely of God. Because this occurs instantly at the moment of regeneration, it can be referred to as, "immediate sanctification."

Progressive sanctification

Progressive sanctification refers to the sanctification of the soul (the heart and mind). This aspect of sanctification is not instant as is the case with immediate sanctification, rather it begins at the moment of regeneration and progresses over the remainder of the believer's earthly life. No one reaches a state of perfection in this life. Nevertheless, it is God's will that his children be progressing in the direction of holiness. Perhaps the level to which one attains is less significant than the fact that there is continued progress toward the goal, which will be fully formed in us only when we are finally changed by Christ at his appearing. How does God sanctify the soul of man? He does it through the process of transformation. The sin principle itself (*i.e.*, evil, cf. Rom. 7:21, 23,25) cannot be transformed, but its power over the believer can be ameliorated as the human nature is transformed into the image of Christ (2 Cor. 3:18). Paul said in Romans 12:1-2, "I urge you therefore brethren [note the responsibility of the believer], by the mercies of God [*i.e.*, "on account of," or "in view of God's mercy shown to you"], to present [*parastēsai*, aorist infinitive, denoting decisive action] your bodies a living and holy sacrifice, acceptable to God, which is your spiritual service of worship [*tēn logikēn latreian humōn*, "which is your reasonable service" to God in view of what he has done for you]. And do not be ["be being," present tense] conformed to [*suschēmatizesthe*, "molded into the shape of"] this world, but be transformed [*metamorphousthe, i.e.*, reflecting in one's life a profound transformation originating from within] by the renewing of your mind, that you may prove what the will of God is—[that] which is good and acceptable and perfect." Paul said that as we assimilate the word of God by faith, we are transformed such that our outer life reflects the renewal within. In progressive sanctification our progress will depend, to a large degree, on our own choices, though we must not forget that God can, and often does bring about circumstances to move us in the right direction. Given these facts, we should not be surprised to find that not all believers progress at the same rate or to the same degree. If we choose to live carnally, according to the sinful impulses of our fallen nature, our progress will be negatively impacted. That was happening to some of the believers at Corinth in Paul's day (1 Cor. 3:1-9), and it happens to the rest of us to one degree or another, at one time or another. That being the case, it is important to yield ourselves to the control of the Holy Spirit, what the Bible calls "walking in ("by," or "according to") the Spirit/spirit," cf. Gal 5:16, and being "filled (controlled) by the Spirit" (Eph 5:18). On this aspect of sanctification see: Romans

12:1-2; 1 Peter 1:13-16; 1 Corinthians 2:6-16; and Ephesians 4:11-16, 17-23.

Progressive sanctification differs from immediate sanctification in that it is a process rather than an instantaneous operation, and it depends upon the believer's active participation. We can only assume that whatever is lacking in the sanctification of the soul, which in all cases will be considerable, will be completed by God upon the believer's death or rapture, as the case may be.

Final (ultimate) sanctification

Final, or ultimate sanctification refers to the last stage in the overall sanctification process, the sanctification (glorification) of the believer's body. This will occur when Christ comes and either resurrects or changes believers, giving them a glorified, eternal body. Since the final sanctification of the redeemed person is an immediate (direct and instantaneous) operation, the believer cannot contribute anything to his or her final sanctification. Paul alluded to the final sanctification of the believer in Romans 8:18-25 when he said:

> [18]For I consider that the sufferings of this present time are not worthy to be compared with the glory that is to be revealed to us. [19]For the anxious longing of the creation waits eagerly for the revealing of the sons of God. [20]For the creation was subjected to futility, not willingly, but because of Him who subjected it, in hope [21]that the creation itself also will be set free from its slavery to corruption into the freedom of the glory of the children of God. [22]For we know that the whole creation groans and suffers the pains of childbirth together until now. [23]And not only this, but also we ourselves, having the first fruits of the Spirit, even we ourselves groan within ourselves, waiting eagerly for our adoption as sons, the redemption of our body. [24]For in hope we have been saved, but hope that is seen is not hope; for who hopes for what he already sees? [25]But if we

hope for what we do not see, with perseverance we wait eagerly for it. (NASB)

He goes on to describe the actual event that will result in the transformation of the bodies of believers in 1 Corinthians 15:51-58 and 1 Thessalonians 4:13-18; and John says, "...We know that, when He appears, we shall be like Him, because we shall see Him just as He is" (1 John 3:2b).

The body is the last part of man's nature to be sanctified. Once this operation occurs the process is complete. However, since no one but Christ has received a glorified body, no one has yet been completely sanctified. The final sanctification of Church-age saints will occur at the rapture of the Church.

Correlating information from other perspectives on sanctification

When a person is regenerated their spirit is immediately sanctified. For the one having placed his or her faith in Christ this is a past action, and it was at that time that they were released from all penalty for sin, past and future. In the believer's present experience, to the extent that he or she is being sanctified, they are being delivered from the power that sin has over them. At some point in the future every believer will be delivered from the presence of sin, at least the presence of sin within, when their nature is fully transformed. Of course God can see the end from the beginning, and in some respect chooses to regard his redeemed as though this process were already accomplished, which in fact it is from a declarative (judicial) standpoint. The status the believer enjoys before God is referred to as his "position" and his present state as his "experience."

The permanence of salvation

When a person exercises faith in Christ the process of salvation that is begun is irreversible. In other words, it is impossible for a person, once redeemed and regenerated, to ever be lost again. The two views on this subject, the view of divine sovereignty, represented imperfectly in classic Calvinism, and the free will view (represented in Arminianism), see the process of salvation in fundamentally different ways, and as one might expect, they hold divergent views regarding the permanence of salvation. The view of divine sovereignty is that God initiates faith and secures man's salvation. Arminianism holds that man initiates faith by an act of free will enabled by common grace, and thus, man procures his own salvation, but that salvation is only secure as long the person, through his or her own free will, continues to exercise faith. Hence, Arminians hold to a doctrine called, "the security of the believer," by which they mean that a person is secure as long as they remain a believer. Obviously such a teaching should not be confused with the doctrine of eternal security. The biblical teaching is that God is absolutely sovereign in both the initiation and continuance of salvation. Such a view is the only view compatible with total depravity and unconditional election.

There are a number of reasons why a saved person can never become lost. These reasons relate both to the nature of saving faith and to the preserving work of each of the members of the Trinity. It is important to understand that this truth is not intended to suggest that believers are free to live unrighteous lives. Rather, an appreciation of this truth causes us to acknowledge a great debt of grace as we realize that we have not saved ourselves, nor can we by our own efforts add anything to the grace freely given to us. We are saved, now and always, for one reason: because of what God has willed and worked (Rom. 9:16). This should be is a very humbling truth.

A conclusive argument for eternal security

One of the simplest lines of evidence for eternal security is the following argument. In order for a saved person to become lost again one of two things would need to happen: 1) he would either have to be separated from God by something other than himself; or, 2) he would have to separate himself from God. According to Romans 8:31-39 the first option is impossible. Paul clearly includes everything in his list of things that can never separate a believer from Christ. He even says that nothing in the present or future can separate us from Christ, and he includes physical things, circumstances, and supernatural powers, even life itself. The second option is also impossible because the believer would have to be included in the list of things that cannot separate him or her from Christ. In other words, when Paul said "nothing," it is clear that he was excluding everything (meaning, "absolutely nothing"), and that would include the believer also. The Apostle John addressed this point in 1 John 2:18-19, when he said that those who profess Christ, only to renounce their profession later, were never saved. Had they been saved, they could not have returned to a state of unbelief. The logical implication is clear: The nature of true faith is that it perseveres to completion.

Why is it that a saved person cannot lose his or her salvation? The answer is that it is God's work to bring the believer's salvation to completion. Note how each member of the Trinity is involved in preserving the child of God.

The preserving work of the Father

1. It is God's responsibility to bring salvation to the point of completion (Philp. 1:6).

2. God will not allow a saved person to reach the point of perdition (lostness), cf. 1 Cor. 11:28-33, also 5:5.

The preserving work of the Son

1. Christ's sacrifice is sufficient for all sin for all time (Heb. 10:14).

2. Christ's high priestly ministry ensures forever the salvation of those who come to him (Heb. 7:25).

The preserving work of the Holy Spirit

The Holy Spirit places the believer into Christ and seals him or her unto the day of redemption (Eph. 1:13-14; 4:30). The purpose of sealing is to preserve something unspoiled. Each believer is in Christ, and Christ is in the Father (Jn. 10:28-30); the Holy Spirit has sealed them there and all three members of the Trinity are intent on preserving the believer until their redemption is finally completed. We can think of it this way: If a sheep gets lost whose fault is it, the sheep, or the shepherd? It's the shepherd's fault, right?

Passages frequently misunderstood

There are some New Testament passages that when taken out of their proper biblical context, or when simply misunderstood, seem to suggest that a saved person could become lost again. While we cannot discuss all of the passages here, we will mention some representative problems.

Passages describing personal apostasy are often misunderstood as applying to believers

Most of the difficulty involves a misunderstanding of personal apostasy. (This subject is discussed in more detail further in this chapter.) Virtually every New Testament book mentions personal apostasy. The early church, like the present-day church, attracted many people who had not genuinely yielded their lives to Christ. These people became part of the local church, and some even became leaders. In the course of time, some of these reformed but untransformed individuals turned back from their profession of faith, going back to their old religion or on to the next. They knew the truth, but they had never trusted the Savior. They had come to the full knowledge of who Christ is, even experiencing a measure of sanctification through exposure to biblical truth and observing the power of the Holy Spirit working in the midst of the church, but they had never taken the plunge of personal faith. Because this was a widespread problem, those in the local churches who professed faith were exhorted to make sure their faith was genuine (2 Cor. 13:5). The descriptions of apostasy and exhortations to self-examination are easily misunderstood. The most common mistake is to misunderstand the spiritual status of an apostate. An apostate is a person who ultimately rejects their profession of faith in Christ because they never possessed saving faith. They may have been reformed but they were never transformed; they professed faith, but never possessed faith. When they turn away from their profession of faith, these individuals are doing what is in keeping with their true nature of unbelief. A doctrinal problem emerges when one reading these New Testament warnings mistakenly assumes that these individuals were saved. Some of the primary passages describing personal apostasy are: 1 Timothy 4:1-3; 2 Peter 2:1-22; Hebrews 3:1-14; 6:4-12; 10:26-31; 12:14-29; John 15:1-6, cf. Mt. 13:1-43 — the parables of the kingdom of Heaven. (For discussion of these passages see the section on personal apostasy further in this chapter.)

Grammatical difficulties

Some passages are misinterpreted to imply loss of salvation because of confusion over, or inattention to grammatical details. For example, see Colossians 1:21-23. The key to the interpretation of this passage is the conditional particle (Gr. *ei* = "if"), which is a first class conditional (indicative, not subjunctive) and should be translated, "since." When the meaning of this word is clear, it is apparent that Paul was not suggesting that some of the Colossians might run the risk of losing their salvation; rather, he was confident they did have genuine faith leading to salvation.

Corporate salvation

If by corporate salvation one means eternal salvation (*i.e.,* redemption from the penalty of sin) based upon some group membership, no such thing is taught in the Bible. In the Bible salvation is always individual, based on personal faith (Jn. 1:12; Rom. 4:1-25). While God did bless national Israel corporately under the Mosaic covenant, such blessing did not constitute eternal salvation. The Bible does refer to the salvation of Israel in the future (Isa. 44:1-5, 21-23; Jer. 3:15; 23:14-18; 31:1, 27-34; Ezek. 11:19-20; 20:1-44; 36:25-32; 37:11-14, 21-28; 43:6-9; Hos. 6:1-3; 14:4-8; Joel 2:12-17, 28-32; Mic. 7:18-20; Zech. 13:7-9; Rom. 11:25-27); however, that is not corporate salvation, since each individual Jew must place their faith in Christ to be part of that group. In fact, those who do not believe will be purged from Israel during the tribulation period (Zech. 13:8-9; Ezek. 20:33-38). (See the discussion of law and grace below.)

The function of law and the superiority of grace

Salvation is wholly by grace; the reason is simple: God's standard is perfection, and no human being, other than Christ, can reach that standard by his or her own effort. Every man, other than Christ, and every woman who has ever lived is a sinner (Rom 3:23), and in their natural, unredeemed condition they stand condemned before a holy God (Rom. 6:23). The question is, "What part, if any, does the Law play in salvation, and subsequently in the Christian life?"

God gave the Law at Mt. Sinai. He never intended for it to be a means of salvation, but rather that it should show man his sinfulness and his need for repentance and faith in the promised Savior. Religion, as it is commonly practiced, turns the purpose of the Law upside down. Men took what God intended as a means of driving them to seek his mercy and grace, and repackaged it as a goal to be obtained by works. Of course, in order to sustain such a notion that man can keep the Law it is necessary to either elevate man's capacities, or to diminish the absolute holiness represented in the Law; in essence, either raising man to God's level, or lowering God to man's level. If one buys into such a view of the Law, the result is legalism, the belief that man can produce righteousness of his own that is acceptable to God. Legalism is an extremely dangerous belief. In its most radical form it can keep one from exercising faith in Christ, which is essential for salvation, and in the case of Christians who fall into this error, it is only one step removed from the notion that our salvation depends not so much on God as on ourselves, and is thus subject to loss.

In Jeremiah 31:31-33, God declared that the covenant made at Sinai (the Law) would be replaced by a better covenant; in so saying, he acknowledged that the covenant of the Law was both inadequate and temporary. The writer of Hebrews developed this theme in Hebrews 8:13 by pointing out, "When He said, 'A new covenant,' He has made the first obsolete. But whatever is becoming obsolete and growing old is ready to disappear." The covenant of promise that God made with Abraham is the foundation of all the kingdom promises of the Bible; it is the covenant of promise made with Abraham that the New Testament writers refer to as the basis for understanding the work of God in history (both past and future); its promises relate both to personal redemption (Gal. 3:6-9) and to the visible kingdom of God to come in the future (Rom. 4:13; 11:25-32). The covenant of promise is the central covenant of the Bible; everything else in the Bible must be seen in light of this covenant in order to be fully appreciated. The Law, which came 430 years later, did not, indeed could not, supercede the promises made to Abraham (Rom. 4:1-25; Gal. 3:15-19), nor was the Mosaic covenant given as a means of fulfilling the promises made to Abraham. The Law, as a covenant, was temporary. It was a stop-gap measure until the new covenant, which implements and enables the promises made under the Abrahamic covenant, could be brought into force by Christ's atoning work on the cross. The Law was, in essence, a spiritual band-aid, not a cure. It was like a crutch to a cripple; Christ, on the other hand, is the cure. Once the cure has been applied the crutch is no longer needed, indeed it becomes an impediment. Some argue the point that since the Law embodies the moral precepts of God and since morality does not change, the Law must be eternal. Such thinking is flawed. The Law is not holiness. (Wasn't God holy before the giving of the Law?) The Law simply conveyed the standard of holiness to man, along with specific civil penalties and the certainty that the transgression of any of these expectations not sufficiently atoned for (ultimately in God's perfect sacrifice) would bring condemnation. When Christ died, he completely satisfied the demands of the Law (*i.e.*, the penalty for the abrogation of the requirement of perfect moral holiness), such that those who believe in him now fully meet God's demand for perfect holiness and are no longer even capable of breaking the Law, since Christ is the end of the Law for righteousness for everyone who has faith in him (Rom 10:4). The true believer in Christ is incapable of breaking the Law because the Law no longer has jurisdiction over him (Rom. 7:1-25; 8:1-11). To use an illustration, I live in the state of North Carolina (USA). If, while in North Carolina, I do something that is illegal in Turkey, I cannot be charged with breaking Turkish law, because I'm not under the jurisdiction of Turkish law. In the same way, if I break one of the moral precepts of the Law, I cannot be condemned because I'm not under the Law, but in Christ (wherein all of the Law has been fulfilled by Christ on my behalf). Does this excuse my sin of doing what is contrary to God's holy nature? Of course not, my sin is still sin; it can ruin my testimony and incur many other unpleasant consequences. So it's foolish and wrong to do those things, most especially because they displease God and may incur his discipline if not properly dealt with (1 Jn. 1:9); but the one thing my sin cannot do is result in my condemnation, because I am no longer under the Law's jurisdiction.

So the Law, as law, has no applicability to the believer in Christ. The question remains, "Do the moral precepts contained within the Law have applicability to the Christian life?" The answer is "Yes," but only as moral precepts, not as law having the power to condemn. Most of the moral components of the Mosaic Law are repeated in the New Testament. This is often taken as evidence that the Law is still applicable to the believer. However, it must be understood that the Mosaic Law is never repeated in the New Testament as law. The moral precepts are repeated as moral precepts so that believers can live free from the natural consequences of evil that can still ruin our lives and rob us of our time, talent, testimony and effectiveness for Christ, but there is no divinely imposed penalty for their violation, only natural consequences — which can be considerable.

The Law is neither the means, nor the measure of holiness. The Law is powerless to produce even a single drop of righteousness. Not only that, the Law isn't even a good indicator of personal sanctification; if it were, we would have to conclude that most of the Pharisees who rejected Christ were sanctified, for externally (and that's all the Law deals with) their lives conformed to the Law. Conversely, we might conclude that a person exhibiting outward conformity to the Law to be progressing in sanctification, but if that person harbored sin inwardly we would be wrong. It is amazing to see how selective people can be in determining which laws they will use in evaluating their spirituality. Most of us can do a pretty good job, at least outwardly, of keeping commandments like "Don't steal," "Don't make idols," "Don't commit murder," but there are few legalists claiming to keep the two most important commands (which both Jesus and Paul state are the keys to all the rest), that is, to love the Lord with all one's heart, soul, and mind, and to love one's neighbor as one's self (Mt. 22:37-38 cf., Deut. 6:5). In light of so high a standard, who among us is showing much progress as compared to the Law? Paul certainly didn't feel happy with how he stacked up against the Law (Rom. 7:1-25). Herein is the problem with externalism: Instead of promoting the work of the Holy Spirit within, it focuses one's attention on external behavior, which is a very poor indicator of spiritual development. In so doing it either depresses us if we are honest, or we develop a distorted, unrealistic, and self-righteous view of ourselves, thinking that we are succeeding when we are actually failing.

Let's take a look at some of the New Testament teaching regarding the superiority of faith to the Law. We will focus on Hebrews 7-9, Galatians 2:11-5:26, and Romans 3:21-10:15.

The superiority of grace to law argued from Hebrews 7-9

Hebrews chapters 7-9 were written to address the obsolescence of the Law and its replacement by the new covenant. Let's simply step through these three chapters and see what they have to say about the present applicability of the Law.

Hebrews 7:1-10

Melchizedek was a priest-king in the pre-Israelite city of Salem (later called Jerusalem). All that is known of him from the

Old Testament is recorded in Genesis 14:17-20 and Psa. 110:4. According to Hebrews 7:1-10 he seems to have been a prefigurement of Christ. That is not to say that he was somehow an appearance of the pre-incarnate Christ; he was not (since a thing cannot illustrate itself), but that in some ways he illustrated what Christ would be like when he came. The writer of Hebrews goes to great length to demonstrate that the priesthood of Melchizedek was superior to the Levitical priesthood under the Law. His argument is simply that Abraham, and thus by extension Levi (who was as yet unborn within Abraham) paid tithes to Melchizedek; and since the lesser pays tithes to the greater (v. 7), Melchizedek must have been the greater, and thus his priesthood greater. As we are about to see, the superiority of the Melchizedekian priesthood is a precursory argument leading to the conclusion that the new covenant is superior to and replaces the Law.

Hebrews 7:11-17

In verses 11 and 12 the writer makes the point that the priesthood and the covenant (*i.e.,* the Law) cannot be separated; a change in one requires a change in the other. Verses 13 through 15 demonstrate that a change of priesthood has already taken place: Christ is a priest after the order of Melchizedek—a superior priesthood. The stage is now set for the argument that since the priesthood has changed, the covenant (the Law) has been set aside. Some argue that this is antinomian, and they have sought to castigate others as lawless on that basis. Such an argument is baseless. The Law did not create righteousness; righteousness has its roots in God's eternal character, and the passing of the Law does not leave us without righteousness. The Law was a mere candle in a dark, sinful world to allow fallen men to walk without stumbling, until God sent a greater light. Christ on the other hand, is like the noonday sun! He not only illuminates the way, but also infuses life and transforms our lives.

Hebrews 7:18-28

If there has been a change of priesthood, it is indicative that there has been a change of covenant (law, covenant, and commandment are used somewhat interchangeably in this epistle). Why was the former covenant set aside? — Because it was weak and useless; it had no power to perfect, or transform. Note that this is God's assessment of the Law. Did God do a poor job in giving the Law? No, it was only a temporary light, a candle, and when seen for what it was, the Law was good and served its purpose. Jesus said in Matthew 5:17-18, "Do not think that I came to abolish the Law or the Prophets; I did not come to abolish, but to fulfill. (18) For truly I say to you, until heaven and earth pass away, not the smallest letter or stroke shall pass away from the Law, until all is accomplished" (NASB). It is sometimes claimed that this statement supports the eternality of the Law, but those who make that claim fail to hear what Jesus was saying. It is not uncommon to see the last few words of this passage ("...until all is accomplished") omitted when the passage is quoted, and no wonder, those words tell us that the Law is not eternal. Both the Law and the prophets will be fulfilled; the Law was fulfilled in Christ's righteousness and atoning death (Rom. 8:1-4; 10:4; Heb. 10:1-18), and the messages of the prophets will be fulfilled just as they were spoken, even to the smallest letter. (The term "law" as used in verse 18 encompasses the entire Old Testament, which is variously referred to as "the law," "the prophets," "the writings," or some combination of these terms.) Christ's priesthood is evidence of a better covenant (vv. 20-22), and his priesthood abides forever (vv. 23-25); thus, "He is able to save forever those who draw near to God through Him...."

Hebrews 8:1-13

Hebrews chapter 8 serves to summarize and reinforce the concepts communicated in chapter 7. The amount of space devoted to this subject underscores its importance. Notice how this section begins with a summary statement: "Now the main point...is this." And what is the main point? We have such a high priest as has been described in the previous section; it is an accomplished fact. He is now seated at the right hand of the Father, demonstrating the completeness of his work. He ministered the true sacrifice in the true sanctuary, of which the earthly was only a copy, and therefore inferior. He is the mediator of a better covenant (v. 6) enacted upon better promises (*i.e.,* the unconditional promises made to Abraham, cf. Gal. 3:15-18). Again, he states the temporary nature of the Law in verse 7 and backs up the statement by quoting the prophecy of the new covenant from Jeremiah 31:31-34. In verse 13 he restates the main point that the Law is now "obsolete" and ready to disappear. (At the time this letter was written, the ceremonial system of worship was still in place and Jewish Christians still participated as they had been taught for generations, but this would soon change with the destruction of Jerusalem and the temple in A.D. 70.) The writer next begins a supplemental line of argumentation based on the nature of worship in the temple.

Hebrews 9:1-10

The writer goes on to describe the earthly tabernacle (or temple) in which the sacrificial provisions of the Law were carried out. He describes the outer area (the holy place) wherein were kept the lampstand, the table, and the holy bread. Behind the holy place separated by a veil was the holy of holies, containing the ark of the covenant. Having given the physical description, he goes on to describe the system of worship that took place in the temple. While the priests regularly entered the outer room (the holy place), only the high priest entered the holy of holies, and only once a year, having offered the appropriate sacrifices for himself and for the people. The point is this: As long as the outer tabernacle stood, it signified that the way into God's presence was not open, man could only approach God through the sacrificial system given under the Law. (Men were, of course, still saved by faith alone.) No doubt the hearers would have been familiar with the fact that upon Christ's death the veil of the temple (a covering several inches thick) was ripped from the top to the bottom (Mt. 27:51). While the rending of the veil was an immediate sign of the obsolescence of the Law, it would be the final destruction of the temple in A.D. 70 that would bring and end to the practice of temple worship. What is the implication of this line of argumentation? Simply that the old covenant is passé. In the light of what Christ accomplished on the cross, the former covenant is no longer needed, and it is precisely the implication of that point that many miss; if the Law were still needed, that would imply some insufficiency in the atoning work of Christ.

Hebrew 9:11-17

Since Christ has entered the greater and more perfect tabernacle, what need is there for the copy? He entered not through the blood of sacrificial animals, but by his own blood. He entered once and for all — the Just for the unjust — and obtained our eternal redemption. We see here the great difference between the shadow and reality. The sacrifices made under the Law could only sanctify the flesh, merely covering sin from sight (10:4), but Christ's sacrifice cleanses the conscience (the inner man) from dead works to serve the living God. It is not the Law working externally that empowers one for divine service, but the transformation from within, made possible only by faith in the atoning work of Christ. There is no greater source of power and motivation for holy living than that of inner transformation, something the Law is powerless to accomplish. So, which covenant is superior, the Law, or the new covenant in Christ's blood? To which will we resort? If we re-establish the Law that God has removed out of the way, we simply make ourselves prisoners to the powerlessness of dead works; we return voluntarily to the same prison cell from which Christ has freed us.

Hebrews 9:18-28

Christ is the mediator of a new covenant (v. 15). That covenant was sealed with his blood and is the only basis of sanctification from sin. Even sins committed by God-fearing worshipers in the Old Testament could only be remitted, ultimately, as a result of what Christ did on the cross. Under the Law the sprinkling of the blood of animals sanctified the earthly tabernacle and its implements, but the blood of Christ sprinkled the heavenly tabernacle. The earthly tabernacle was only a shadow of the heavenly. Why return to the shadow when one has the reality? To illustrate the folly of this, we may well imagine a young woman who has fallen in love with the picture of a man, who when he appears in the flesh finds that she does not love him so much as his picture. In the same way, some are unwilling to give up the shadow for the reality; they are so stuck in externalistic thinking that they are blinded to the true nature of the redemptive work of Christ, a redemption of the world not through Law, but through the power of a resurrected Savior, who as scripture says, will come again in power to claim what he has purchased, and personally rule in righteousness forever.

As a binding covenant the Law is obsolete, because it was satisfied at the cross. Paul said in Colossians 2:13-15: "When you were dead in your transgressions and the uncircumcision of your flesh, He made you alive together with Him, having forgiven us all our transgressions, (14) having canceled out the certificate of debt consisting of decrees against us, which was hostile to us; and He has taken it out of the way, having nailed it to the cross. (15) When He had disarmed the rulers and authorities, He made a public display of them, having triumphed over them through Him" (NASB). For the one who places his or her faith in Christ, the Law is completely fulfilled at the cross, much as a note of debt is marked "paid" when the debt is satisfied. One might well ask what purpose the Law still serves (*i.e.*, if it still has a use beyond historical and informational purposes). This is the principal question addressed in Paul's letter to the Galatians.

The superiority of grace to law argued from Galatians 2:11-5:26

In this letter Paul addressed what he termed a "desertion" (NASB) from God to a different gospel (1:6). This was a serious theological matter and quickly brought with it a forceful response from the Apostle (1:8). Those who introduced their heretical teaching of Christian bondage to the Law had done so amid sharp personal attacks upon Paul, his character (1:10-14), and his apostleship (1:18-2:10). Paul begins his retort to this vexing problem brought on by the Judaizers with a historical discussion of the issue as it relates to the Church in general (2:11-21).

Galatians 2:11-21

Paul recalled how Peter, a Jew, while visiting in Syrian Antioch had dispensed with certain elements of the Law in his personal life, but upon the arrival of other more strict observers of the Law, Peter hypocritically separated himself from the Gentiles. Paul recalled how he rebuked Peter, asking if he, being a Jew, lived like a Gentile, how could he justify compelling the Gentiles to live like Jews? After all, the Law never justified anyone (2:16).

Paul went on to address the question of whether justification by faith and the believer's release from the curse of the Law makes Christ the cause of sin. The answer is a resounding "No!" Such thinking, as Paul now refutes, is characteristic of legalism. It goes like this: "The teaching of grace and release from the Law produces lawlessness." But such legalistic thinking results not in righteousness, but a rebuilding of what was once destroyed (the curse of the Law) and a re-imprisonment of the soul as a transgressor in bondage to the penalty of the Law. Legalism never produces true righteousness; it only makes its adherents slaves and prisoners. Paul said in verse 19, "For through the Law I died to the Law, that I might live to God." What does that mean? How does "dying to the Law" result in the ability to live to God? He explains in verse 20 the truth to which legalists are blind, that those who are in Christ have already died with Christ and that all of the requirements of the Law have been fully satisfied. This is not a setting aside of the Law, but rather the fulfillment of the requirements of the Law in Christ. As such, grace becomes not an excuse to sin, but the power to continue serving God in spite of the fact that we frequently fail, for we are yet imperfect in soul and body. The Apostle John said those who taut grace as license to sin do not know Christ, or the power of the Spirit of God (cf., 1 Jn. 1:1-6; 3:9-10). Are we so foolish as to think that the Law could accomplish more than the living and indwelling Christ and his Holy Spirit?

The idea that righteousness comes through external regulation is the philosophy of legalism, but as Paul concludes in verse 21, if the Law was a means of righteousness, then Christ died in vain. For Christians to rebuild the Law as a means of obtaining righteousness is to nullify the grace of God. Paul next turned his attention to the question of what, if any, use the Law has for the Christian.

Galatians 3:1-9

Paul began with a severe reprimand: "You foolish Galatians, who has bewitched you." The implication is clear: The church had fallen, as it were, under the influence of a spell. These are tough words both for the Galatians and for those who had misled them. Paul's first argumentative question is simply this: "Did you receive the Spirit by the works of the Law, or by hearing with faith?" He has a purpose in asking such a question. The Galatians had received the Spirit of God at the time they placed their faith in Christ; this had undoubtedly resulted in the manifestation of the Spirit through the exercise of spiritual gifts within the church. Paul knew this. He wants them now to consider the absurdity of their shift from grace to law. If the Holy Spirit, whose presence is the evidence of salvation in progress, could not be attained on the basis of law, but by faith alone, how could they now think that the process of salvation could be completed by observance of the Law? It's easy to see why Paul uses the analogy of witchcraft, for to Paul it seemed that only one under an evil spell could be so thoroughly deceived. Will a man enter salvation by faith and then seek to complete that salvation by the deeds of the Law? That would be like accelerating a five-hundred horsepower speedboat up to top speed, and then switching off the engines and trying to maintain the momentum with a broken paddle! If the Law had sanctifying power, Christ would not have had to die in the first place (cf., 2:21)!

In 3:6-9 Paul makes the case that faith, as the means of obtaining righteousness before God, was established long before the Law was given, since Abraham "believed God and it was reckoned to him as righteousness." Thus the principle was established in the Old Testament that justification is by faith, and the Law, which came later, could not change that; it could only lead men to the conclusion that they need God's forgiveness and righteousness, supplied by his perfect Son, of which the Old Testament sacrifices were merely a prefigurement.

Galatians 3:10-18

Paul now begins to deal with the true effect of the Law (3:10-18) and how this relates to God's intended purpose for the Law (3:19-4:7). We may well skip to Paul's question in 4:21, "Tell me, you who want to be under law, do you not listen to the law?" What does the Law accomplish? Paul says it places one under a curse (3:10), that it has no power to justify (v. 11), and that the Law is not of faith (v. 12). This ought to be obvious, but Paul was pointing out that faith and Law are two completely incompatible principles. What is the implication of this statement? Simply put, one who walks by the Law is not walking by faith. Could it be that legalists do not realize that in looking to the Law they are rejecting the principle of faith? The incompatibility of the two is certainly evident in this passage. One might ask how faith and Law could be incompatible if they both have their origin in God, but in so saying they miss the point of the Law entirely; the Law was not intended to be a means of obtaining righteousness, but as a light to show man his sinfulness. When I go into a lavatory, I turn on the light so I can see that my face or hands are dirty. I don't wash with the light; I wash with soap, for soap has the power to cleanse, whereas light has only the power to reveal. In the same way, the Law has only the ability to reveal our sins; it has no power to cleanse. Law and grace both come from God, and when used properly they are compatible; they only become incompatible when one attempts to use the Law to do what only grace can accomplish.

Legalists object that the Law is not too difficult to keep (often citing Deuteronomy 30:11-14). However, when God commanded the children of Israel to keep the Law (Deut. 29:9) and told them that it would not be too difficult for them (Deut. 30:11-14), he was referring not to the moral code alone, but to the Law comprehensively, which through the sacrificial system made provision (at least typically and symbolically) for failure to perfectly keep the moral code. In other words, the provision of sacrifice under the Law anticipated failure on the part of the worshipers to keep the moral code (even outwardly, to say nothing of keeping it inwardly), yet when the provisions of the sacrificial system were applied, the Law (when viewed comprehensively) was considered to have been kept. In other words, the system contained a remedy of sorts, albeit only symbolic, of God's ultimate sacrifice of his Son. The point is that while the Law, as a system, could be kept (if one includes the remedy of sacrifice), the moral component of the Law by itself could not be kept by men in their fallen state. When legalists imply that the Law can be kept, they mean that the moral code can be kept. This is a thoroughly unbiblical idea even from a strictly Old Testament perspective, and not only is it an unbiblical idea, it is contrary to the principle of faith. Faith does not say, "What can I do to establish my own righteousness," but rather, "I believe that God has done for me what I could not do for myself." These two principles are mutually exclusive; to live by one is to deny the other. Paul is clear on this point and he quotes Leviticus 18:5 as support. It was Christ who redeemed us from the curse of the Law (v. 13) in order that we might receive the blessing of the promise (Jer. 31:31-33) on the basis of faith alone. Faith is the divinely appointed means of obtaining righteousness, and the Law that came over four hundred years later did not, indeed could not change that (vv. 16-18), for the eternal covenant of promise had already been ratified (v. 15).

Galatians 3:19-4:7

Here Paul addressed the purpose of the Law. He began with the question: "Why the Law then?" In other words, given what has already been said—that the promise (of salvation) was by faith, and the Law is not of faith—he now addresses what must certainly be the question remaining in the minds of his hearers: If the promise was to be received by faith, why did God subsequently give the Law 430 years later? His answer is straightforward: The Law was added because of transgressions until Christ, the promised seed, should come. In other words, Paul said that the Law was a stopgap measure, never intended to be permanent. It was, as it were, a bandage until the wound could be cured. He quickly addressed an additional question sure to arise in the minds of his readers: If faith and law are incompatible principles, is the Law somehow contrary to the promises of God? Paul's answer is "No," the Law does not contradict the promise by faith simply because the Law was never an alternative to faith. That is to say, the Law was never intended as a means of obtaining righteousness; its only purpose was to shed enough light in the darkness of sin to point the way to the only true solution to the problem. That solution is Christ (vv. 23-24). The Law pointed the way to Christ through the power of condemnation (foreclosing all options save one—faith in Christ alone). Some insist that those who teach grace through faith alone as the means of obtaining the promise of salvation are opposed to the Law, but that is untrue. The Law, when properly understood, was never an alternative to faith; it is rather an inducement to faith. But once faith appears, the Law serves no further purpose; indeed its continued application would be injurious to faith. Those who teach grace through faith alone as the means of obtaining the promises simply understand the proper relationship between the Law and faith. One could make the case that the real antinomians are those who distort the purpose of the Law by attempting to make it into something that it is not, thus perverting the true intent of the Law.

Galatians 4:8-20

Paul reminded the Galatians that before they came to know God, or rather came to be known by him, indicating God's sovereignty in their salvation, they were slaves of a religion consisting of rules and regulations. These things, Paul said, are "weak" and "worthless," mere "elemental" (elementary) things. Paul expressed his concern that perhaps his ministry had been in vain, for (by implication) Paul's ministry, and by extension all of his apostolic letters were tuned to a completely different frequency, indeed a different form of religion. This is serious talk, and it underscores Paul's firm belief that faith and Law are completely incompatible when the Law is viewed as a means of obtaining righteousness.

Galatians 4:21-31

Paul now draws upon familiar source material from the Old Testament. He is not interpreting that material, merely using it as an analogy to illustrate his point. Legalists among the Galatians advocated a blending of faith and law, but Paul warns that faith cannot co-exist with law. The very presence of law is injurious to faith, for it tells us to draw close to God through self-regulation, and to measure our progress by the same. Paul's point is that just as Isaac and Ishmael could not co-exist together, without Ishmael's presence being detrimental to Isaac, neither can faith and law co-exist. Any attempt to combine the two will ultimately end in the destruction of faith, for faith is by definition trusting someone else to do what one acknowledges he cannot do for himself. Just as God commanded that the bondwoman and her son were to be cast out, so now Paul applies the same to the Law; there is simply no place for legalism in the life of faith because legalism is destructive to faith.

Galatians 5:1-12

The Law represents slavery, and Paul urged the Galatian believers, having been freed from that yoke, not to return to it. His warning in verses 2-4 is poignant. He tells them that if they return to the Law, Christ will be of no benefit to them. He says in verse 4, "You have been severed from Christ, you who are seeking to be justified by law; you have fallen from grace" (in terms of their doctrine). These were people who having made a profession of faith in Christ were seeking to be perfected in the flesh (according to the Law, cf. 3:3), and in so doing were manifesting the shallowness of their faith. Paul had in mind that if those in the Galatian churches who were involved did not heed his warning, they might ultimately prove not to be true believers. This is consistent with other New Testament teaching regarding personal apostasy (1 Tim. 4:1-3; 2 Pt 2:1-21; 1 Jn. 2:19; Heb. 3:1-14; 6:4-12; 10:26-31; 12:14-29).

It is faith, not the Law, and certainly not faith plus Law that leads to righteousness (v. 5). The Law (symbolized by circumcision) means nothing to those who are in Christ (v. 6). Before the legalists entered the picture the Galatians were running well, but the legalists proved to be a stumbling block to their faith (v. 7). Paul asserts that this legalism did not come from God (v. 8), and he was concerned that the entire church could become corrupted by this false teaching (v. 9). Nevertheless, he expressed his confidence in the Galatians, that they would adopt the correct understanding of this issue, that salvation (all of it from start to finish) is of faith (vv. 10-12). That isn't to say that faith doesn't result in works; true faith always results in works, but not works of the Law under threat of penalty, but rather obedience from a transformed and grateful heart flooded with joy at pleasing God.

Galatians 5:13-26

Does freedom from the Law mean freedom to sin? Certainly not! It means freedom to live apart from condemnation. It means freedom to please God out of a heart of love, joy, and gratitude. The Law is completely fulfilled by love, and that is Christ's command to his Church (Jn. 13:34) — what more do we need? We are saved by grace through faith, and commanded and empowered by the Holy Spirit to love one another. What advantage does the Law offer?

Given what Paul has said, the question that naturally arises is this: Does the Law have relevance in the present era (the age of grace)? The Law is of two parts; there is in the Law that part wherein the perfection and holiness of God is seen (the moral code) and which the Law merely illuminates, though dimly in comparison to Christ; and there is that part which prescribed the obligations of the Jewish nation with respect to the covenant made with them. The knowledge of God and the holiness he requires will always result in condemnation to those who fall short of God's perfect standard of holiness. However, the covenantal aspect of the Law, that is, its operative principle of external working through regulations, penalties, ceremonies, *etc.*, has been replaced by the inner working of the Holy Spirit in accordance with the new covenant. Sin is still sin. But the operative principle has changed; "the law" (the moral compass) is now written within, and transgressions are not the domain of civil or ceremonial/sacrificial law; they are matters of relationship, matters of the heart (Jer. 31:31-33). What the Law could not do working from without, the implanted law, the Law of the Spirit, accomplishes from within; thus is the demise of the principle of legalism, and there can be no return to it; it was replaced because it was useless for anything but light, and a greater light has arrived. What this means is that the proper pursuit of righteousness is forevermore removed from the realm of laws, and centered in the only place from which personal righteousness can originate — from within the redeemed and sanctified heart wherein the Spirit of God dwells and performs his work. Those who wish to return to the Law in order to bring about righteousness fail to understand the true nature of the task before us; it is not the mere regulation of behavior, it is the transformation of soul and spirit by the power of the gospel, a task that can only be accomplished through faith.

The superiority of grace to law argued from Romans 3:21-10:15

Paul fought a running battle with legalistic thinking within the early church; they too had those within their number who thought that righteousness could be produced through the keeping of the Law, and this conflict shows through clearly in his epistle to the Romans. Because of his teaching regarding law and grace Paul was, in so many words, accused of being an antinomian (cf. 3:8). Let's see how Paul deals with this subject in this letter to the Roman Christians.

He begins his letter by arguing that all men in their natural (unsaved) state stand condemned before God. In Romans 1:16-2:16 he argues that those who are without the Law are condemned because they have not yielded themselves to the knowledge of God in creation (1:18-19). Beginning in 2:17-29 he argues that those who do have the Law, referring to the Jews, are also condemned because they have not kept it. In 3:1-20 he addresses the question sure to arise in the minds of his listeners: If the Jews stand condemned too, what is the advantage in being a Jew? His answer is simple: The Jews were entrusted with the promises of God; promises which God fully intends to keep, even though the Jews, as a people, have thus far failed to respond in faith (2:2-4). The great advantage of being a Jew is not as some might suppose, that they are the inheritors of the Law, but rather that they are the inheritors of the promises of God (3:3-4). It is important to recognize that Paul's teaching on this subject comes some twenty-five years after the Jewish nation rejected Jesus as their Messiah, signifying that their rejection had not nullified the unconditional promises of God. (Paul will return to this topic in chapter 11.) The advantage of being a Jew is that God has made special promises uniquely to them, promises he fully intends to keep in spite of the unbelief of some Jews (3:3-4). So, of what advantage is the Law? Actually none, insofar as producing true righteousness. Its only real benefit is that through men's failure to keep it, the righteousness of God is demonstrated; that is to say, it shows man how unholy he really is. The one who does not have the Law is condemned apart from the Law (by his conscience), and the one who has the Law is condemned by the Law, but in both cases the end result is the same (3:9-20). How so? — Because the Law is powerless to transform sinners into saints, and we are all sinners (3:23). So, what is the solution to this problem? That's the question Paul hopes all who read this letter will ask, and his answer is given in 3:21-8:30.

Romans 3:21-31

Paul began by pointing out that there is a kind of righteousness available to man that cannot be obtained by means of the Law. It is the righteousness of God granted to man upon the exercise of genuine faith (v. 21). Paul wants his readers to be assured that this is not some novel idea; it was a truth clearly set forth in the Old Testament (*i.e.*, "being witnessed by the Law and the

Prophets"), and in the next chapter he will develop the Old Testament roots of this truth further, but first he wants to fully develop his explanation of the kind of faith that leads to righteousness (3:21-31). The faith that results in divine righteousness is faith in Christ, regardless of one's status as a Jew or non-Jew (v. 22). All men are sinners (v. 23), and any who are to be saved must be justified as a free gift from God. This righteousness cannot be purchased or earned; it can only be received as a gift, by faith (v. 24), possible only because of Christ's sacrifice on the cross (v. 25). Christ's sacrifice demonstrates God's righteousness, because God "passed over" the sins of believers in the Old Testament era (*i.e.*, in view of what Christ would do on the cross; God did not carry out the judgment for their sins, but instead passed over those sins, suspending judgment until the time that Christ dealt with those sins on the cross, cf. vv. 25-26).

Given the fact that all men, regardless of when or where they live, or their genealogical heritage, must be reconciled to God by faith apart from the works of the Law, all boasting is excluded (vv. 27-28). No one will ever contribute any righteousness, not even a speck, to that needed for his or her salvation. Does this concept in any way disparage the Law? Certainly not, because the Law was never intended for any purpose other than leading men and women to acknowledge this very fact, and to repent of their sins and turn to God for mercy and grace. Paul now returns to an earlier thread in the discussion and seeks to establish the fact that grace through faith is a concept that preceded the giving of the Law, and therefore the application of law is subordinate to justification by faith.

Romans 4:1-25

Paul began by asking, what was Abraham's experience regarding justification? His answer is that Abraham has nothing about which to boast, because he too received righteousness by faith (vv. 1-3). Paul anticipated that some of his readers might confuse the relationship of this righteousness to the right of circumcision (and thus to works), so he made the observation that

Abraham was declared righteous before his circumcision (vv. 9-12). In fact, circumcision had nothing to do with the obtaining of righteousness as far as Abraham was concerned. Paul contends that the promise made to Abraham and to his descendants was not to be realized through the Law, but through faith. If fulfillment were to come through the Law, then the promise would be nullified (v. 14-15). When we understand the nature of the Law, as condemnatory, then we can see why the promise (both the kingdom, and the righteousness to enter it) must be based on faith, for the Law has no power to produce righteousness, only the power to condemn (vv. 16-17).

Paul continues in chapter 5 to discuss the nature of grace through faith and its superiority to the Law. It ought to be obvious, but perhaps we should reiterate the observation that Paul's entire treatise in this section, as in others, is occasioned by a flood of externalism into the church. Given the amount of space devoted to the correction of this error, it is apparent that legalism was a nearly universal problem that had to be dealt with in almost every church.

Romans 5:1-11

Paul says we are justified by faith; the result is peace with God. Whereas the natural man in his unsaved state is at war with God (8:7-8), the justified man is at peace with God, and anticipates sharing in God's glory to be manifested when his promises are fulfilled (v. 2). Though we enter into that hope through various difficulties, the result will be perseverance (v. 3), proven character (v. 4), and a hope that does not disappoint (v. 4), because it is in a God who does not break his promises. Christ died for us even while we were yet sinners. He didn't wait for the Jews (or Gentiles for that matter) to become suitable objects for salvation, or to commend themselves to him through works of righteousness, for they (and we) were incapable of producing such works (v. 8). It is a hard truth to accept, but the fact is that God simply does not need our help to save us, nor do we have any help to offer, though we can gratefully receive his love and forgiveness, and respond with a thankful heart filled with praise.

Romans 5:12-21

When Adam fell, the entire human race fell. How this can be is difficult to understand; yet it is true. When Adam sinned, the entire human race died spiritually and the natural world was deeply impacted in ways we are still struggling to comprehend. Even before the giving of the Law, all men eventually died, evidencing the universality of the effects of sin throughout the human race. Adam's sin was different from any other sin prior to the giving of the Law, for Adam broke a commandment given by God, and until the giving of the Law there were no other commandments to be broken. Prior to the Law all men and women died because they were sinners, having inherited both their guilt and their nature from Adam. After the Law there was a set of commandments that could be broken; now man could be "doubly dead," dead because of his connection to Adam, and dead because of his own personal disobedience. The Law was like a blanket smothering man in condemnation; for no sinner could keep it, not even the smallest part of it, at least inwardly. Man is sinful through to the core, and every level of his being, body, soul, and spirit, is under the influence of evil, selfish motives. Why did God give the Law? It was a light intended not to correct man's problem, but to expose it so the solution could be applied. That solution is grace, the grace of God manifested in Christ and his sacrifice on the cross; for just as through Adam's sin death spread to all men, so in Christ's one act of obedience on the cross there resulted justification of life to all who would accept it by faith (vv. 15-21, cf. 3:21-22). The question sure to arise is this: If the Law was useful in the past to show men their sinfulness, and thus their need of grace, could it not be useful for that purpose today? Certainly, the Law has been exposing sin all down through history, even though its covenant force ceased at the cross. This is one of the great benefits of the reading and preaching of the Old Testament, but we don't have to return to slavery to learn that we don't want to be slaves. We have the record of life under the Law in holy writ so we can learn from the experiences of others. The fact is, if men refuse to learn these lessons from scripture under the convicting power of the Holy Spirit, they wouldn't learn them under the Law either. We don't need to return to the Law, what we need is the powerful proclamation of the whole truth of scripture.

Paul now turns his attention to the more practical matter of life under grace, and he answers questions sure to arise in the minds of his readers.

Romans 6:1-14

Undoubtedly Paul was aware of the accusations that had been made against him concerning his teaching of grace. And he now proceeds to answer the questions of those who might innocently misunderstand, or others who might intentionally distort his position. The first question Paul addressed was this: Does the teaching of grace imply that believers should not be concerned about sin (v. 1)? The logic Paul is addressing runs like this: The more one sins, the more grace God bestows; therefore, sin is good because it promotes grace. Paul's answer is firm: "Absolutely not!" Such thinking is a complete misunderstanding of grace (v. 2). Grace is not freedom to sin, it is freedom from sin (vv. 5-7) and its terrible effects. That release is first from sin's power (death), then from sin's perversion of the human nature (at the completion of our redemption, the redemption of the body), and finally from sin's presence (in God's eternal kingdom). What possible motivation could a regenerated person have for returning to that which killed him? Paul puts it this way: "You have died with Christ and have been raised up with Him for this purpose — that you might walk in newness of life"(vv. 3-5). The one who has faith in Christ has, in God's manner of reckoning, been crucified with Christ in order that they should no longer be slaves to sin. How does this work? Before faith a man or woman is a slave to sin; every part of their nature is under sin (body, soul, and spirit), but when faith comes (as a gift of God, cf. Eph. 2:8-9) Christ's death, with all of its sufficiency and efficacy, becomes theirs. The application of the atonement accomplished by Christ's sacrifice is wrought in stages. First, the spirit is immediately cleansed of sin (Rom. 8:10), and the Spirit of God takes up residence within the believer infusing him with spiritual life (regeneration); then the Spirit of God works progressively to sanctify the soul (the seat of the heart and mind); finally, God will redeem the bodies of his saints when Christ comes to resurrect them. Notice the character of this work: It is a work of redemption from the power, perversion, and presence of sin (*i.e.,* separating the believer from sin). In light of this, who would suggest that further entanglement with sin could be good? There is nothing in the redemptive work of Christ that leads one toward sin. Of course, there will always be those who use grace as an excuse to sin, just as there were those in Jesus' day who distorted the intent of the Law to justify their sin. Such people are always with us, but their distortion of the truth is not an argument against the truth; it is only an indication of their own foolishness and self-deception. Believers under grace are going to sin because they are not yet perfect (experientially); but grace, properly understood, promotes holiness and imparts the power through the regenerating and indwelling Holy Spirit to produce works consistent with righteousness (Rom. 8:3-17), something the Law could never do. How is the power of sin broken? It is broken not by the Law, but by grace (vv. 12-14). Paul was so burdened to emphasize this truth that he repeated essentially the same arguments again in verses 15-23.

Romans 7:1-6

Paul continues his argument by drawing upon a concept with which his readers were already familiar — that the law of marriage is binding until death (vv. 1-3). He then takes them to the next level of the argument by explaining that their participation by faith in Christ's death had caused them to die to the Law that they might be married to another, to Christ (v. 4). This transfer from bondage to Law, to being joined to Christ, is the only way believers can bear spiritual fruit. In fact, Paul points out that the Law actually arouses sinful passions (v. 5). How so? It is a simple truth that when a sinner is told not to do something, he or she wants to do it all the more! (Parents of small children will relate to this, but the principle holds true of adults as well.) True righteousness cannot be produced by the prescription of external regulations; righteousness is the product of a transformed life (v. 6); Paul called it "newness of spirit" (not "Spirit" as the NASB has it, but "spirit," *i.e.*, the renewed, regenerated spirit within the believer). It has been said previously, but is worth repeating, that the Law cannot produce righteousness; even acts of outward obedience to the Law must be distinguished from righteousness. Righteousness is more than outward obedience; it is obedience from the heart, an obedience that exalts God and responds to his sovereignty over one's life. Thus true righteousness is obedience that is borne out of the love of God, just as sin is borne out of the love of self. Such acts of righteousness only come forth from one who is being led and empowered (filled) by the Holy Spirit.

Romans 7:7-12

If the Law arouses sinful passions (v. 5), is it then sinful in some way? Paul's answer is an absolute "No!" It is not the fault of the Law that we are sinners incited by the words, "Thou shalt not!" On the contrary, apart from the Law we would not know what sin is (v. 7). Unfortunately, the more a sinner discovers about sin, the more he is drawn to it (v. 8); this is not the fault of the Law, but the perverseness of our fallen nature. The principle we have to take away from this discussion is that by the Law is the knowledge of sin; that knowledge revealed to a sinner does not produce righteousness, but a downward spiral of condemnation and more sin. The Law can be useful in the hands of the Holy Spirit to draw God's elect unto himself, but it can never produce righteousness, nor can it bring about God's kingdom. Nevertheless, the Law does still serve an instructive purpose: to show man his sin. Paul next focuses on the heart of the problem. There is nothing wrong with the Law; it is just that our problem can't be solved from the outside; it can only be solved through a process of sanctification that begins within man's innermost being.

Romans 7:13-25

Paul describes the perplexing situation in which he found himself, and which is true of everyone who has begun the process of sanctification; he found that he was not doing the good he desired in the inner man, but the very thing he did not desire — sin (v. 15). In so saying, he was not disparaging the Law; rather he was acknowledging his sin, as evidenced by the fact that he agreed with the Law, that his sin was, in fact, sin (v. 16). Contrary to this, antinomianism denies either the reality of, or responsibility for sin; thus Paul's statement can never properly be labeled as antinomian. By acknowledging his sin for what it was, Paul confessed agreement with the Law, not that he was under the Law, but that sin is always sin, even for a person under grace. Being under grace doesn't change the nature of sin, but it does change how that sin is dealt with. Under the Law there were legal prescriptions for dealing with sin (albeit symbolic rather than efficacious). Under the Law, Paul would have observed these outward legal prescriptions (which would have had no efficacy, but would have reminded him of the redemption to come in the work of Messiah); however, under grace Paul experienced conviction wrought by the indwelling Spirit of God and the recognition that his only acceptability before God was based upon God's gift of righteousness through faith in Christ. Would Paul have been better off under the Law? Would he have been less likely to sin? Of course not, sin is a universal problem whether under Law or grace. For anyone who is tempted to think that the application of Old Testament Law would make an individual, or a society more righteous (I speak here to the theonomists), they should carefully study the history of ancient Israel; that history is filled with idolatry, social injustice, and personal and national sin of every sort (Acts 7:1-53).

Paul made a very interesting statement in verse 17. He said, in essence, "I'm not the one doing these things, but the sin dwelling in me is doing them." Was Paul attempting to sidestep responsibility for his sins? Absolutely not, he had already acknowledged responsibility (v. 15), but he was revealing a profound insight into the nature of salvation, of which one of the components is sanctification (separation from sin). He revealed here that sanctification is a progressive work. When he came to faith in Christ, something happened within him, he became a new creature (2 Cor. 5:17), his inner man (*i.e.*, his spirit, 7:22 cf. 8:10) was sanctified. Now that inner man, living in continual union (fellowship) with the Holy Spirit desires only to please God. So why did Paul as a believer continue to struggle with sin? Because only part of his nature, his spirit, was sanctified; his flesh (a euphemism for the body and mind) was still unsanctified, and will not experience complete sanctification until he is transformed in Christ's presence (1 Thess. 5:23). Until that time, Paul and all believers struggle with sin (vv. 21-25). Why did Paul share his deeply personal struggle? —Because he knew it to be a universal struggle, one every believer has to own up to.

Having addressed the universality of the struggle with sin, Paul is now ready to deal with the question of how the believer is to live in light of this struggle, not through the application of legal prescriptions, but through inner transformation by the Spirit of God.

Romans 8:1-11

For the sinner, and we are all sinners, there is no greater truth than that expressed in Romans 8:1. We may be sinners, yet for those in Christ there is no condemnation. Paul tells us why in the next three verses: because Christ has fulfilled the Law for us (v. 4), that is, for those who are not seeking to be justified by the deeds of the flesh (*i.e.*, by works). The Christian life is a Spirit-led life. We are saved by faith, and we are transformed into Christ's image by faith, as we walk by the Spirit. God knows that changing a man's outer behavior only produces a legalist who begins to compare himself to everyone else, but changing a man or a woman from within produces the kind of true humility and bro-kenness over sin that we see evidenced in Paul's own experience, a brokenness that exalts only God and refuses to gauge itself by what others do, or don't do. Do you see why the principle of law doesn't mix with grace? We cannot operate by both principles. If we choose to be governed by law we will either experience condemnation and shame, or we will convince ourselves that we can meet the requirements, in which case we become a self-deluded legalist. On the other hand, if we choose to be governed by grace, we acknowledge that we are needy sinners able to please God only through the power of the indwelling Holy Spirit, and though we might fail a thousand, or a million times, God still loves us and is there to move us forward no matter what circumstance we may have created for ourselves. Those who claim that teaching grace is to give license to sin evidence in their thinking that they have already become legalists, for they have bought into the belief that external regulations can produce righteousness, but they are wrong. It is the uniform testimony of scripture that only the work of the Spirit within the heart of man can produce true works of righteousness.

Romans 8:12-17

Does grace mean that the believer simply gives up on living righteously? Certainly not! We are under obligation, but it is not an obligation to the flesh, nor is it an obligation to the Law, but to the one who has loved us. In fact, Paul goes so far as to say that it is those who are being led by the Spirit who are the sons of God (v. 14). Does this sound like an abandonment to sin? Those who know Christ as Savior do not serve him out of the fear of retribution (the principle of law), but because they have been adopted into a new family, and God has become their Father (v. 15), and the Holy Spirit has taken up residence within (vv. 14,16).

Romans 8:18-30

God cursed the world when man fell; he did that in order to make redemption possible (vv. 19-22); in the meantime life is difficult, but God is at work doing what man cannot do for himself. God gives those who place their faith in Christ his Spirit, that is to say, he implants the Holy Spirit within them, both as a guarantee of the completed redemption to come (Eph. 1:13-14) and as a help at the present time (Rom. 8:26). Ultimately, it is God who sees the believer through this process (vv. 28-30). It isn't up to the believer to save himself, or to sanctify himself, or to glorify himself; all of this is God's work.

Paul isn't quite finished with the conflict between law and grace. He points out the reason for Israel's failure (9:30-10:21), and their ultimate conversion through the triumph of faith (11:1-32).

Romans 9:30-10:15

Paul begins with this enigma: How is it that the Gentiles who were not pursuing righteousness attained righteousness, while the Jews, who were pursuing righteousness, failed to obtain it? The answer, Paul says, is because the Jews were pursuing righteousness through works of the Law rather than by faith; and since the Law is powerless to produce righteousness, the Jews failed (though a few, like Paul, did obtain righteousness by faith). While the Jews were seeking their own righteousness, in accordance with the Law, they failed to subject themselves to the righteousness of God that is by faith (10:1-3). Why? — Because faith and Law are mutually exclusive. The Law does not lead one to Christ until he or she gives up and confesses that they are unable to keep the Law. As long as one thinks he can keep it, he is under the delusion of self-righteousness. This is why in verse 4 Paul says, "For Christ is the end of the Law to everyone who believes." How many times must he repeat this? Faith can only begin when a person realizes they cannot keep the Law, and that is just as true of a saved sinner as it is of an unsaved sinner!

Attempting to keep the law is the ultimate self-deception. In order to think we can, we have to be under the assumption that we can do what only God can do, that is, to ascend into Heaven (v. 6), or descend into Hell and rise again (v. 7). In essence, when we seek to obtain our perfection by the Law, we make ourselves out to be God! Paul seems to be implying that legalism is actually a form of idolatry. The key to righteousness is not the Law, but faith in Christ (vv. 9-12). Can the Law transform a believer into a more spiritual person? According to Paul the answer is "No." As we have seen, the Apostle repeatedly refutes the notion that the Law plays any part in our perfection. The Law is powerless to bring about anything but condemnation and death, and it is incompatible with the concept of inner transformation by the power of the Spirit on the basis of grace through faith. Do we need to know about the Law and man's failure under law historically? Of course we do. The Holy Spirit can use that as he can all other scripture to our benefit, but that is not the same as being subject to the Law.

Conclusions on grace vs. law

From the passages we have surveyed one thing is clear: The New Testament provides no support for legalism. The New Testament is emphatic in stating that the promises made to Abraham, which include both eternal salvation and the kingdom, can be obtained only through faith, and they are equally emphatic that faith and Law cannot co-exist. This does not deny the goodness of the Law (when properly understood for what it was intended), nor does it result in antinomianism, as is sometimes charged; rather, it leads to the recognition of a higher law, the law of the Spirit of life in Christ Jesus, a different kind of law with transforming power.

There is a reason the word "gospel" was chosen to describe the message of Christ's atoning work. The word "gospel" means "good news." Before the cross, the message received from the Law was bad news, news of death and condemnation (Rom. 7:9-10). The gospel of Christ is the good news of freedom, life, and righteousness provided on the basis of grace through faith in Christ plus nothing. The voice of legalism is not the voice of the New Testament gospel (Gal. 1:6-8); it is the voice of slavery, death, and despair. It is, as Paul pronounced, a tainted and "accursed gospel," which proceeds from the rationalizing mind that has yet to comprehend the transforming power of the true gospel of grace through faith alone.

Personal apostasy

Personal apostasy refers to an individual falling away from their profession of faith. The key question concerning these individuals is whether they were genuinely saved. Since many passages tell us that apostasy inevitably results in eternal damnation, this question is of considerable importance with respect to the permanence of salvation. The doctrine of personal apostasy is a prominent teaching in the New Testament, discussed or alluded to in almost every book. In fact, an understanding of this doctrine is essential to the interpretation of many New Testament passages, as well as to an understanding of the New Testament's general teaching regarding salvation.

Apostasy defined

The word "apostasy" is derived indirectly from a Greek word that appears in 1 Timothy 4:1. The word *aphistemi* (translated "fall away" in the NASB) is the verb form of *"apostasia"* from which we transliterate the English term "apostasy." The idea is to make a break or departure from something. The significance of a departure is, of course, determined by the context—i.e., what one is departing from. In 2 Timothy 2:19 Paul uses this word to encourage Christians to depart from evil (the NASB says, "abstain"), whereas in Hebrews 3:12 the author uses it to warn people not to fall away from the living God. Obviously, departing from sin and departing from God are actions that would result in different consequences. It is important to recognize that the occurrence of the word *apostasia* (or other related terms) doesn't necessarily indicate that a passage is referring to personal apostasy; likewise apostasy is very frequently described in passages where this term is not used. Some of the key passages in the New Testament dealing with personal apostasy are: 1 Timothy 4:1-3, Hebrews 3:1-19; 6:4-8, 10:26-31, 12:14-29, 2 Peter 2, 1 John 1-3, and Jude 5-16.

Description of personal apostasy

The description of an apostate given in the New Testament is of an individual who, while fully understanding the truth of the gospel and having professed faith in Christ, ultimately falls away (or "departs") from their profession of faith. This happens because they were never genuinely saved. We have to be careful not to confuse "the faith" (the gospel) with personal faith (a choice to yield to the demands of the gospel). Apostates defect from "the faith," because they have no personal faith.

The Greek and Roman world was not a friendly place prior to the influence of Christianity. The heathen world could be very cruel, and the social effects were everywhere to be seen, from the exposure of unwanted infants and the elderly, to rampant moral degradation even under the guise of religious worship. Where Christianity penetrated this darkness there were people who were attracted to the life of local churches and the care that Christians showed to one another; there were also those who saw the church as an institution to be exploited. Whatever the case, many people came into the orbit of Christianity who had not genuinely yielded themselves to Christ resulting in regeneration and true conversion. (Christ foretold this gradual infiltration by unbelievers in his parables recorded in Matthew 13.) Some of these eventually returned to their former religion, or went on to the next religion. This phenomenon was both perplexing and distressing to the churches. As a result, there are numerous references and explanations, as well as warnings about apostasy throughout the New Testament. Unfortunately, the modern church has largely lost sight of this teaching, and the result has been confusion and incorrect interpretation of many New Testament passages, principally the passages discussed below. Lack of clarity about the nature of personal apostasy is also at the heart of much of the argumentation between Arminians and Calvinists, though there are other important differences. Let us look at each of the major New Testament passages describing, or serving as warnings against personal apostasy.

1 Timothy 4:1-3

In this passage Paul describes an apostate as one who departs from "the faith" (v. 1). Some have mistakenly taken Paul's statement to mean that these individuals were previously saved. However, this is a reference to a departure from the gospel itself, not from personal saving faith. We must not confuse "the faith" with personal faith in Christ (cf. Jude 3); "the faith" refers to the body of truth (inclusive of the gospel) that defines Christianity; personal faith (*i.e.*, "saving faith") is submission to the gospel (cf. 1 Pt. 1:22; 2:8; 3:1; 4:17). Of course, in order for someone to depart from the faith, they must at one time have professed to believe the faith. In other words, an apostate is one who professes to believe the truth for a while, but later turns from that profession. There is simply no way to tell from a profession if the faith professed is genuine. True faith can only be seen through a transformed life consistent with belief in the truth, over a period of time. The fact that Paul indicates it was from "the faith" that these departed, rather than from "faith" (*i.e.*, personal faith) lends no support to the contention that these individuals were previously saved.

2 Peter 2:1-22

Peter describes the same type of person that Paul described in 1 Timothy 4:1-3. Notice the linkage: 1) In verse 15, he "forsakes" (relinquishes) the right way. 2) In verse 20, after escaping the defilements of the world by the knowledge (*epignosis*) of the Lord and Savior, he reverts back to those defilements. The question we have to answer is this: Is there any indication from this passage that the apostates described here were saved? The answer is "No," and that answer is supported from three lines of evidence.

The first line of evidence is found in 2 Peter 2:20. Peter says, "...the last state has become worse for them than the first." Verse 21 defines the two states to which verse 20 refers; the first state is: "...not to have known the way of righteousness." The second state is: "...having known it, to turn away." If we took this statement to refer to saved people, that would put Peter in the position of saying that these people were better off before they were saved—an absurdity, which makes it obvious that this passage cannot be referring to saved people. No matter what kind of

Christian one might be, it could never be properly said that they were better off before they were saved. The Arminian view of this passage is that the people described were saved and then lost their salvation, in which case they certainly would be worse off, but not worse off than they were before they knew the gospel as this passage says, only worse off than they were before they lost their salvation. But that's not what the passage actually says; the passage says that they are worse off than before they knew the gospel. The idea is that these individuals were better off before they turned away from the truth, because up to that point they could have yielded themselves in faith and been saved, but now they have determined to reject the truth, and in so doing they have rendered themselves with no further recourse since there is no other means of salvation than faith in Christ. If a person rejects the truth with full knowledge (*i.e.*, the *epignosis*) of what he is doing, what hope is there? Such a person has understood the truth of the gospel and with sufficient knowledge and due consideration rejected it.

The second line of evidence is found in verse 22. What does the proverb of the dog returning to its vomit mean? A dog returns to its vomit because that's a dog's nature. Why does a pig wallow in the mud? —Because that's a pig's nature. Giving a pig a bath doesn't change its nature. This proverb simply illustrates the difference between reformation and transformation. Even having experienced a measure of personal reformation, an apostate turns away from the faith because he or she was never transformed through personal faith in the truth. Personal reformation may involve both attitudes and actions (soul and body) but does not originate from a renewed spirit, as does transformation. When such a one departs from the faith and denies the Savior, they are simply doing what is in accordance with their untransformed nature; they may have appeared to be a saved person from what could be seen externally, but their nature was never changed, and eventually some of them overtly return to their old ways (cf. Luke 11:24-28), while others covertly remain as "hidden reefs" within the local church (Jude 12). (While apostasy may be perplexing and disheartening, it is the "hidden reefs" who never overtly apostatize that are the greater danger to the local church, especially if they serve in positions of leadership.)

The third line of evidence indicating that the individuals described in 2 Peter 2:1-22 were never saved is that, as we have seen, a saved person cannot lose their salvation, and these individuals are certainly unsaved. Verse 1 says that apostates will be "destroyed" (Gr. *apollumi,* which means, "to destroy utterly," a total and final destruction). This is the same term that is translated "perish" in John 3:16; there the ones perishing are set in bold contrast to the saved. (In Matthew 15:24 *apollumi* is translated "lost"; the idea is that to be lost indicates a future of eternal destruction in Hell.) In 2 Peter 2:9, Peter indicates that these individuals will be kept under punishment "for the day of judgment." In 2:17 he says, "the black darkness has been reserved" for them. This phrase, composed of six Greek words, is repeated in only one other place in the New Testament: Jude 13. A comparison of Jude 5-13 clearly establishes that Jude was speaking in reference to the same people Peter had in mind (apostates). Note that Jude adds the word "forever" in the phrase; doubtless, this is eternal judgment. Consequently, we see that apostates are lost and there is no indication they were ever saved.

Hebrews 3:1-14

There are three major views on the meaning of this and the other related passages in Hebrews (6:4-14; 10:26-31; 12:14-29). The first view is that these passages are warnings to Christians not to live carnally. According to this view the "rest" referred to in Hebrews 3:18-4:13 does not illustrate salvation, but rather the rest a believer enters into when they learn to trust and obey God; thus it denotes a level of spiritual attainment. Proponents of this view argue that if the rest mentioned here, which Israel failed to enter, represents salvation, then that would imply that even Moses was not saved, since he did not enter the promised land. This objection fails to take into account the fact that Israel in the wilderness is used here analogically (as an illustration), thus Israel's failure is not an example of personal apostasy, but an analogy. There is a difference in saying that something is analogous to a particular thing, and in saying that it is an example (*i.e.,* the very thing itself). The second view is an Arminian view that says that these passages are warnings to Christians not to apostatize and thus forfeit their salvation. The case will be made here that the correct view is that these passages are warnings to people in the church about the danger of failing to take possession of salvation (*i.e.,* the failure to exercise saving faith), thus falling beyond hope into apostasy. When we come to Hebrews 6:4-8, we will note an additional view, the hypothetical view, with respect to that passage.

The major problem we must deal with in Hebrews 3:1-14 is determining who is addressed. In verse 1 the address is clearly to "holy brethren, partakers of a heavenly calling" and in verse 6 to the house of God (in so many words). Again, in verse 12 they are referred to as "brethren." There can be no doubt that these are all references to a group of saved people. However, each time the readers are addressed as "brethren," or some other term indicative of genuine faith (cf. vv. 1-6a, 12), the address is qualified. The identification as saved people established in verses 1-6a is qualified in verse 6b (where "if" is the third class conditional — "*ean*" {the subjunctive mood — implying that the conditional state is uncertain}; in other words, they may or may not actually be of God's house). What the writer is saying is this: You are what I have called you (in verses 1-6a), assuming you hold fast (v. 6b). What is the opposite of holding fast? Verse 12 defines it as "falling away" (*apostasia*). Again, the identification as saved people established in verse 12 is qualified in verse 14 (once again "if" is the third class conditional, subjunctive mood). In other words, the author courteously addresses his audience according to their profession since he does not know their hearts, but he does so with clear qualification. His form of address contains the cordial assumption that they are what they claim to be, though he clearly has concerns that some may eventually prove to be apostates, as have others that have already departed. There is a parallel to this form of address in Paul's letter to the Corinthians. Three times in 2 Corinthians Paul refers to his readers as "brethren," twice as "beloved" and in the first verse he addresses the letter to "saints"; but in 13:5 he warns that some might not be saved. Clearly his appellations were conditioned upon true faith in Christ. Even though Paul addressed the readers as "saints" and "brethren," he knew the likelihood that in any church there are some who, though they fully understand the gospel, have yet to act on it. The writer of the letter to the Hebrews does the same thing; he writes to a local congregation warning them about the possibility of apostasy even though he is convinced that most of them are truly saved (cf. 6:9). After all, how else could such a letter have been addressed? We could hardly expect him to have said: "To the saints and potential apostates," such would have been offensive, not fitting the desired tone of the letter. While the passage is addressed to those professing faith in Christ, it is a warning of the danger of failing to take possession of salvation through faith in Christ.

The presence of these conditions is clear evidence that the author was concerned about the salvation of some in the local church. His assertion is that those who are truly saved are those who "hold fast the beginning...firm until the end," (*i.e.*, they are not of those who "fall away"). One ought not to construe this to imply works salvation. The idea is not that one is saved because he or she holds fast, but rather that holding fast is an invariable characteristic of true faith. So much so that falling away indicates that there was never saving faith. One is not saved because they hold fast, they hold fast because they are saved. Failure to make this distinction is the basis of much confusion. This agrees with the message of 1 John 2:18-19. Therefore, we should understand the "rest" referred to in 3:15-4:13 as illustrating salvation through means of faith. Those who have placed their faith in Christ have entered that rest; all who have not entered are strongly exhorted to do so before it is too late. Again, there is no indication from this passage that a saved person can be lost. The message is this: It is those who hold fast to the end that are truly saved. It is simply the nature of saving faith to be persistent to the end.

Hebrews 6:4-12

The three basic interpretations of the Hebrews apostasy passages were given above; however, we need to mention one additional interpretation given to 6:4-12, which we will refer to as "the hypothetical interpretation." It asserts that this passage describes what would happen if a saved person could apostatize (which proponents view to be impossible); thus, according to this view we have a hypothetical postulated to make a point. Although this interpretation is certainly incorrect, it is appealing in that it holds that saved people cannot apostatize since that would (hypothetically) lead to the loss of their salvation. Thus, this interpretation argues against a saved person being able to apostatize, but fails to recognize that apostasy, as described in the New Testament, is an actual condition for some.

The fact that this passage is addressed to a believing audience has been a stumbling block to some who fail to see that the key is being able to distinguish between who is being addressed (a mixed group that is presumptively Christian) and who is being referred to. Whoever they are, they are described by five statements: 1) they have been enlightened; 2) they have tasted of the heavenly gift; 3) they have been made partakers of the Holy Spirit; 4) they have tasted the good word of God and the powers of the age to come; and, 5) they have fallen away. How do we know that apostasy (as defined) is in view in this passage? First, because of the description; the individual described is one who has "fallen away." The word *parapipto* is a strong term; it means, "to defect." [Although *parapipto* is used only here in the New Testament, we can get some feel for the term by observing the usage of *pipto* in Romans 11:11 where it is translated "fall" and refers to a complete and irrecoverable fall. *Parapipto* (*pipto* with a prepositional prefix) is an intensified form of *pipto*.] The nature and the magnitude of this defection can be seen in the last half of verse 6, "…since they are re-crucifying the Son of God for themselves and putting him to public ridicule" [author's translation]. Note the following: We are told that they "re-crucify" the Son of God (*i.e.*, they display in their own hearts and minds the same hostility and rejection toward Christ as did those who crucified him. This rejection is both personal and public; they re-crucify him "to," or "for" themselves (middle voice) and put him to "open shame" (ridicule). This is clearly the same description given of apostasy elsewhere (cf. 1 Tim. 4:1; 2 Pt. 2:1; 1 Jn. 2:18-19.). While some imply that carnality in the life of a believer is figuratively a re-crucifixion of Christ, such a thought is completely foreign to the book of Hebrews (cf. Heb. 10:10-14). Re-crucifixion of Christ in the heart and mind of an individual can only be taken as rejection of his messiahship; it is a "falling away" which, as we have seen from Hebrews chapter 3 disqualifies one from the title of "brethren," and being "partakers of a heavenly calling." The second reason we know this passage is describing apostasy is because of the nature of the examples given. In verses 7 and 8 the two types of ground represent two types of people. There are those that respond with fruit and those that respond with thorns and thistles (cf. Jesus' parable of the sower in Matthew 13:1-23). The ground described in verse 8 is clearly representative of the person described in verse 6 who "falls away." Notice the description of this ground: "... it is rejected and a curse is at hand (impending), of which the end is unto burning" [author's translation]. The word "curse" is *katara*, which refers to condemnation. Of course, it would be impossible for a saved person to suffer the condemnation of God. Otherwise, what is he or she saved from, if not condemnation? Some find what they suppose to be a loophole in the word "nigh" (AV) or "close" (NASB). The argument given is that this can describe saved people because it does not say that they are cursed, only that they are "close" to being cursed. But, if as has been established, a saved person cannot be lost, how close can one get to something that is absolutely impossible? It is as ridiculous to think that a saved person could be close to condemnation as it is to think that such a one could be condemned. The word translated "close" is *eggus*. Its usage here has the sense of that which is impending (cf. 2 Pt. 2:3b). The idea is that the judgment of the apostate has not been carried out, but that it will be carried out when he faces the Lord whom he has persistently denied with full knowledge. The third reason for believing that the person described in Hebrews 6:4-12 is an apostate (as defined) is that apostasy is indicated by way of contrast with true faith. Verse 9 says, "But, beloved, we are convinced of better things concerning you, and things that accompany salvation, though we are speaking in this way" (NASB). The word translated "accompany" is *echomena*, which in the middle voice, as here, means, "to seize" or "to possess for one's self." Notice that the writer distinguishes his readers in general from those people he has just described in particular: They (the believers) had taken possession of salvation, clearly implying that those described earlier (vv. 4-8) had not. There are two responses to the gospel: one is to take possession of salvation; the other is to turn from it, or passively ignore it. The people described in verses 4-8 are those who having received the gospel message and perhaps at some superficial level having embraced it, have ultimately turned away. Is there any indication that those who apostatized were ever true believers? The answer, as before, is "No." However, the descriptive clauses in this passage present us with more problems than the previous passages because they contain some descriptions that are easily mistaken for genuine faith.

The first clause occurs in verse 4, and describes the subjects as "...those who were once enlightened." The word "enlightened" is *photizo*, and its use here is figurative. The idea is of a person coming to understand truth. The question is: "Does enlightenment come before or after saving faith?" The answer is, "Both." One certainly comes to understand some things only after coming to faith in Christ, but they must understand the gospel before they can make the decision to come. So, enlightenment both precedes and follows saving faith. The point with respect to the passage at hand is whether this reference to the subjects having been previously enlightened indicates faith on their part. Since one can be enlightened without responding in faith, we must conclude that there is nothing in this description that indicates these individuals possessed saving faith. We should also note from John 1:6-13 that although every man is enlightened at some time, not all are saved.

The second clause (also in verse 4) describes the subjects as ones who "...have tasted of the heavenly gift." While there is some uncertainty as to what the heavenly gift refers, the key to unraveling this statement lies in the word "tasted." Obviously this is a metaphorical use of the word, since the heavenly gift is not something that could be literally (physically) tasted. The word *geuomai,* when used metaphorically means, "to perceive," as in, "a taste of reality." It is not necessary for a person to be saved to perceive the gift of God. The reason is simple: Perceiving salvation through the illuminating and convicting work of the Holy Spirit is an integral part of the *epignosis* (sure knowledge) of the truth that one must possess before they can accept Christ. When a person comes to the sure knowledge of the truth (the truth being the gospel), they have perceived (*i.e.,* metaphorically "tasted") the gift of salvation, even if they eventually reject it. [Partaking of the Holy Spirit should not be confused with partaking of Christ {3:14}. In order to partake of the Holy Spirit, one merely needs to be confronted with the reality of the gospel through the illuminating and convicting work of the Holy Spirit. However, to be a partaker of Christ, one must receive the witness of the Spirit. So, while "partaker" in one context implies salvation, in the other it does not. Here, as elsewhere, context is critical.]

The third clause also occurs in verse 4, and describes the subjects as having been made "partakers of the Holy Spirit." There is general agreement that no one could be saved unless they first become a recipient of the work of the Holy Spirit. That work includes illumination, conviction, and calling. Actually, apart from the work of the Holy Spirit there would be no call to refuse. Because we normally regard "partaking" as active (*i.e.,* the result of active volitional choice on the part of the subject), it is easy to misunderstand what is being said in this clause. No such choice is indicated here since "partake" is in the passive voice. In other words, these are not individuals who chose to partake (by an act of faith), but people who were only passive recipients of the illumination, conviction, and general calling of the Spirit. To put it another way, we could say that they were made partakers of the Spirit in the same way that a person is made a partaker of the judicial system when he or she receives a speeding ticket.

The fourth descriptive clause is in verse 5 and pictures the subjects as those who "have tasted the good word of God and the powers of the age to come." Again we have the word "tasted" (*geuomai*), and as before it is here used metaphorically (since one cannot literally taste the scripture or future realities). These individuals are said to have perceived the good word of God and the powers of the age to come (possibly a reference to the ministry of the Spirit in signs and wonders as manifested in the early churches). But this could be said of anyone within the church, whether saved or lost, so again, there is no implication that these individuals were saved.

The fifth descriptive clause occurs in verse 6 and pictures the subjects as having received all of the aforementioned benefits "and then have fallen away." The question is: "What did they fall away from?" The answer is that they fell away from what they had — the opportunity (by virtue of knowledge and conviction) to respond to the gospel. Here we encounter a hard concept, hard in the sense that it is not pleasant to consider, but there comes a time in the life of every person who persists in refusing the gospel when their refusal becomes permanent by their own choice. There is a time in the life of every person when they are at the closest point they will ever be to coming to Christ — maximum light, conviction, persuasion, etc. If they refuse at that point they will never come. Since no unsaved person knows when he or she is at their closest point, refusing to place one's faith in Christ could, potentially, render them beyond hope. The writer of Hebrews is delivering a poignant warning to those within the church who had come out of the world and into the church, but who had failed, as of yet, to enter into salvation, hence the strong parallel to Israel's wandering in the wilderness described in Hebrews 3:7-4:11. There is nothing in this last clause that indicates that these individuals were true believers.

Hebrews 10:26-31

We need to preface our examination of this text with a brief orientation. Verse 26 begins with the word "for." When we examine verses 26-31, which describe the path to apostasy, what we find is that this section stands in contrast to verses 19-25, which describes true belief. Note also the parallel between 10:19-25 and 3:1-6, and between 10:19-25 and 3:12-14. What we have is a recurring warning against apostasy.

Here we see six reasons why the people described in verses 26-31 are apostates (as defined). The first reason is given in verse 26 where the text says, "For if we go on sinning willfully after receiving the knowledge of the truth, there no longer remains a sacrifice for sins." We know from our previous remarks on 2 Peter 2 that "the knowledge of the truth" refers to an understanding of the gospel (this identification is consistent throughout Peter's writings, see 1 Peter 1:22). So, we recognize here that we have a person who "sins willfully" (*i.e.,* makes a conscious choice of sin over Christ) after receiving the sure knowledge of the gospel (the *epignosis*). What we must understand is the nature of this state (the word "sinning" in the original is a present participle and indicates a continuing condition, or state). The word "willful" is *ekousios,* which means "voluntary." In other words, the description is of a person who has abandoned himself or herself to a state of sin. In light of 1 John 3:6-10 this cannot describe a Christian who is merely struggling with sin. This is the description of a person who has voluntarily abandoned himself to sin and does not know Christ, regardless of what he or she might claim. (Virtually the whole Book of 1 John is devoted to this theme.) The second reason why this passage must be describing apostasy (as defined) is found in verse 26b, which reads, "...there no longer remains a sacrifice for sins." The word *apoleipetai,* translated "remains," means "to be left." We could say, "...there is left no sacrifice for sins." The reason why there is no sacrifice for sin is because the person described in this passage has, with full knowledge, rejected the only sufficient sacrifice for sin, which is Christ. The third reason this passage is describing apostasy (as defined) is found in verse 26. Here we are told what this person does not have—a sacrifice for sins. In verse 27 we are told what he does have: the prospect of a terrifying future. Note this very important fact given in verse 27: These people are classed as "adversaries" of

God. They are adversaries whom God is going to judge with a consuming fire. The NIV reads: "...but only a fearful expectation of judgment and of raging fire that will consume the enemies of God." The fourth reason why this passage must be describing apostasy (as defined) is found in verse 29. Here we encounter three parallel statements; they all indicate a rejection of the gospel, but they express it in different words. The first statement says that they have "trampled under foot the Son of God." *Katapateo*, which is translated "trample" means "to spurn" (when used figuratively, as here). The idea is an outright rejection of Christ. In other words, the person in view considers the Son of God as "worthless," like dirt beneath his feet. The second statement says that he "regarded as unclean the blood of the covenant by which he was sanctified." "Unclean" (*koinos*) means "common." The idea is that this person has no appreciation for the sanctity of Christ's death, it evokes no positive response from within. The third statement says they have "insulted the Spirit of grace" (the Holy Spirit). Our English word "insult" doesn't carry the depth of force that *enubrizo* indicates. The idea is an arrogant, insolent, scornful, even blasphemous disregard of the Spirit's work in calling men to salvation. In these three statements, we have three pictures of the rejection of the gospel. The fifth reason why this passage describes apostasy (as defined) is seen in verses 30-31. *Ekdikesis*, translated "vengeance," refers to retributive justice; the idea is punishment in the strictest sense of the word. The sixth reason why this passage describes apostasy (as defined) is in verse 39, where the author reflects back on what he has said in verses 19-38. Two words in the first part of this verse are key to understanding who and what is being described here. "Shrink back" (*hupostoles*) means, "to turn back"; the idea is equivalent to *apostasia* ("to fall away"), "destruction" (*apoleia*) means "perdition." Perdition is lostness. Also, note the contrast presented in verse 39b. There can be no doubt that verse 39 identifies the people described in verses 26-31 as apostates.

Is there anything in this description that would lead us to believe these individuals were saved? Arminians point out that there are a few reasons for thinking that this is the case. First, since the writer includes himself in the group he refers to by the pronoun "we" (v. 26), some assume that he must be referring to saved people. However, the verse itself defines who is included within the scope of this pronoun; it is everyone who has "received the knowledge of the truth," which encompasses both those who have responded positively (unto salvation) and those who have responded negatively (remaining unsaved). There is no grammatical or contextual reason for restricting this pronoun to refer only to saved people. [The scope of a pronoun must be determined by the context. For instance, the pronoun "we" in verse 39 is clearly restricted to saved people because the context limits the reference to saved people. In verse 26 the reference clearly includes unsaved people.] The second reason offered is that in verse 26 the subjects are said to have "received the knowledge of the truth." As we have noted above, one must receive the knowledge of the truth in order to make a decision to come to Christ; thus such knowledge precedes salvation and in no way indicates that these individuals were saved. In 2 Peter 2:20 Peter describes people who receive the knowledge of the Lord and Savior, but remain unsaved. We should not confuse "receiving the knowledge of the Lord" with "receiving the Lord." These are entirely distinct. Receiving the knowledge of the Lord does not imply any decision on the part of the recipient. All that is indicated is that these individuals came to understand the truth of the gospel; it indicates nothing in the way of a positive response. The third reason offered is based on verse 29: The people in question are said to have been "sanctified" by the blood of the covenant (*i.e.,* by Christ's blood), which some take as an indication that the writer is referring to believers. The answer to this objection is somewhat more involved than the others for this reason: When we hear the word "sanctify" (*hagiazo*) we tend to associate it with sanctification in regard to salvation. However, *hagiazo* is capable of a much broader use; in 1 Corinthians 7:14 it is specifically applied to the unsaved spouses of believers. *Hagiazo* carries the idea of placing something into a privileged position. It might be a position of grace, or of righteousness, or of consecration, or of opportunity. So, in what sense is it appropriate to refer to a lost person as sanctified by the blood of Christ? The answer is that the death of Christ sanctifies every man and woman in that it puts them into a position of opportunity to be saved (*i.e.,* it makes them "savable"). This clause has probably been the greatest sticking point for many, but it is important to recognize that this is due to reading a very narrow concept of sanctification into the passage rather than recognizing the broader biblical usage of the terminology. Just as there is a special sense in which only true believers are sanctified, so there is another sense in which all men, especially those that are exposed to the gospel, are sanctified.

As we have seen, there is nothing in this passage that indicates these individuals were once saved; they are simply people who having come to understand the gospel said "No" (or "Maybe" — which is the same thing), instead of "Yes." The underlying message of the passage is this: Today is the day of salvation; don't put it off. Whatever a person may think, they are without excuse and without remedy if they fail to respond to the gospel (cf. Heb. 3:7-19).

Hebrews 12:14-29

In these sixteen verses there are five statements that indicate this passage is a warning against personal apostasy (as defined). The first is in verse 14b. What the writer is saying is simply this: Pursue salvation; don't stop short only to be lost. There are two contrasting responses to the gospel. One response is to take possession of salvation (cf. Heb. 6:9, the NASB rendering, "accompany" is *echomena* — middle voice, which means, "to possess for one's self"). The other response is to turn away from salvation. Here the writer is clearly concerned that some may not press forward and obtain (by faith) that sanctification (salvation) without which they are lost. The second statement is in verse 15a. This statement might be somewhat difficult to interpret, if not for the context of verses 14-16; however, given the context, it is apparent that coming "short of the grace of God" means failure to enter into salvation. The third statement is in verse 16. Here "godless" (*bebelos*) means "irreligious." The writer is clearly describing apostasy. Even the illustration of Esau is of one who had something within reach, but turned from it. (This should not be construed to imply that Esau was not saved; the reference to Esau is purely analogical.) The fourth statement occurs in verse 25a, and is an admonition about refusing him who warns from Heaven. *Paraitesesthe* (translated, "refuse") indicates a decisive rejection of God's warning of judgment. The fifth statement, which is found in verse 25b, describes those who "turn away from" God. Unlike some of the other apostasy passages in Hebrews, this one contains no statements that might easily be misconstrued to refer to true believers. It is simply a sobering message: Don't be like Esau and trade your opportunity for a bowl of soup; if you do, you'll be sorry!

1 John 1:1-3:12

Virtually the entire book of 1 John comprises an extended contrast of vain profession versus true faith, and demonstrates that disingenuous faith sometimes manifests its true nature in open defection. For the sake of brevity we will focus primarily on the first three chapters of the book. In these chapters John discussed the problem of those within the local church who claimed to know God, but their lives evidenced a different reality. The opening verses seem to indicate that this church had become infected with an incipient form of gnosticism. We know that regardless of whether these individuals were connected with gnostic belief or not, they are clearly identified as those who deny that God came in the flesh (cf. 4:2); they professed to be in right relation to God but were characterized by corrupt living (1:5; 3:4-10), denial of sin (1:8-10), disobedience to the commands of God (2:3-4), hatred (or at least a lack of love) toward the brethren (2:9-11; 3:11-18; 4:20), love of the world (2:15-17), in some cases open defection (2:18-19), denial that Jesus was the Messiah (2:22-23; 3:14-15), and denial of the hypostatic (personal) union of the divine and human natures of Christ (4:1-6). John makes the point early on that such individuals are excluded from the fellowship of God. He does this by way of contrast, stating that it is those who "walk in the light," not those who merely profess, who have fellowship with God.

It is a tragedy that the concept of fellowship has been so misconstrued. Perhaps the most prevalent view of fellowship is that Christians who obey God and "walk in the light" are in fellowship with God, and those Christians who sin and do not confess their sins are "out of fellowship"; hence, the misconception that confession restores broken fellowship. Such a view is completely at odds with the message of 1 John. John clearly contrasts two kinds of people: the children of God (true believers, whose life is characterized by walking in light), and children of the Devil (whose lives are characterized by walking in darkness and denying the faith), cf. 3:10. True believers have fellowship with God; everyone else is in darkness. This does not mean that believers do not sin, they do. But when they sin, truly saved people confess their sin and move forward. In fact, verse 7 clearly demonstrates than sin does not interrupt a believer's fellowship with God. John says "...but if we walk in the light (*peripatomen* — present continual action) as He Himself is in the light, we have fellowship (*koinonian* — present continual action) with one another, and the blood of Jesus His Son cleanses us from all sin (*kathapizei* — present continual action)." [NASB] Notice that these three actions occur simultaneously: walking in the light, having fellowship, and being cleansed from all sin. John doesn't say that if one walks in the light but falls into sin and loses his or her fellowship, that when they confess their sin fellowship is restored; he says this: If one is walking in the light, they are (at the very same time) experiencing fellowship with God and being cleansed from all sin. It should be apparent that John was not teaching that sin breaks fellowship, or that confession restores it. (This is not intended to minimize the importance of confession, which is a necessary component in experiential sanctification.) The fact is that Christians can no more lose their fellowship with God than they can lose their salvation. While this discussion may seem to be unrelated to the topic at hand, it is important to understand the subject with which John is dealing. According to John, there are two basic categories of people associated with the church: those who claim to be in right relation to God, and are; and those who claim to be in right relation to God, and aren't. Those who claim to be in right relation to God, but who do not know him, are the same people described in the previous passages who ultimately (if they persist in their unbelief) fall beyond hope (cf. 2:18-19). For the remainder of this survey we will proceed in the same manner as with the other passages — to demonstrate that the individuals described are set in contrast to those who are saved.

In 1:5-2:2 John's argument proceeds from the nature of God. God is light without the slightest hint of darkness (v. 5), so God's children, who are in him, are children of light and walk in the light (vv. 6-7). This does not mean that they are completely without sin, for as verse 7 clearly says, their lives are characterized by three activities all occurring continuously: they walk in the light, they have fellowship with God and with their brethren, and as they walk in the light they are being continually cleansed of sin. Of course, this is a very verbose statement, but John wanted to be certain his readers understood what he meant. Stated succinctly, what John said is this: If a person knows God, his life may not be perfect but one thing is certain, his life will reflect that he is a child of light rather than darkness. In essence, John said that it is possible to see the evidence of true faith from the outside. This is an important truth that has been largely obscured in modern Christianity as we have lost our grip on the doctrine of conversion. Why did John make such a statement? — Because the church was experiencing the destructive effects of those within that claimed to be right with God (i.e., in the light) who were not what they professed to be. The only practical means of identifying true faith in another is conversion — the outward change that manifests inner transformation, a change that can only be observed over time (cf. Mt. 13:19-23, esp. vv.20-21). [We must be careful in view of Christ's teaching in Matthew 13 that some seeds sprout quickly, but die. In this parable only those plants yielding fruit (evidencing the works of the Holy Spirit) represent saved people. We must not be fooled by those who readily respond to the gospel and seem to grow for a while. They may yet prove to be unfruitful; only time will tell. We are not thus judging the new believer, but suspending judgment until the evidence is in.]

Apparently the particular form of unbelief that John was confronting had the characteristic of denying personal responsibility for sin. This makes a strong case that it might have been an early form of gnosticism, since that was a feature that is known to have been associated with gnostic beliefs. John's retort is clear and direct: If anyone says he has no sin, he is deceiving himself (v. 8), and calling God a liar, since God has declared all men to be sinners (Ps. 53:1-3). Confession of sin, that is, coming to grips with what we are, is one of the core characteristics of true faith, it is called "repentance," and it is one of the reasons many people refuse to come, because they cannot bring themselves to admit what they are. Repentance isn't just something one does in order to obtain salvation, it is an integral part of faith, the turning from sin in order to turn to God for help, and it doesn't cease after a person is initially saved, it continues to be a part of faith as one progresses through the Christian life. The person who doesn't manifest repentance, or as John says, "confession," only evidences that true faith is not present.

In 1 John 2:3-11 John emphasizes that the reality of true conversion (knowing God) will manifest itself not only in the inner life of the believer, but in the outer life as well. James also deals with this subject (Jam. 2:14-26), but John takes it a step further; he not only asserts that the true knowledge of God is evidenced by obedience (vv. 3,5,6) and love of the brethren (vv. 7-11), but he states categorically that where there is a lack of these (as a general characterization) the claim to know God is invalidated; such people live in the darkness, not in the light, and thus do not know God. This is tough language that the church today needs to hear.

In 2:12-18 notice how John continues his contrast of true faith and false profession. In verses 12-14 he reasserts the position of the truly converted: Their sins are forgiven (v. 12), they know God (vv. 13-14), they have overcome the Evil One ("overcome" is *nenikekate*—perfect active, *i.e.*, they now stand as victors based on the triumph of their exercise of faith in Christ when they first believed in him) cf. vv. 13-14, they are strong spiritually (v. 14), and the word of God abides (continually) in them (v. 14). The love of the world is inconsistent with Christian faith. (John is not referring to the people of the world, but to worldliness, *i.e.*, the espousal of the world's values.) Anyone who loves the world does not love the Father (v. 15), because the character of the world (that is, fleshly lust, material lust, and pride—or what today might be called "me-ism") do not come from the Father; they are the product of the darkness that is in the world. The world is destined to perish, but not so the one who does the will of the Father (*i.e.*, the one who truly knows God).

In 2:19-27, having laid the foundational truth that there are two kinds of people within the visible church (those who truly know God, and those who merely profess to know him), John now embarks upon his explanation of the apostasy of individuals within the local congregation. He reminds the believers that they are living in the last hour (*i.e.*, "the last time"—the *eschaton*, which from the Old Testament perspective began with the advent of the Messiah). They had been taught that in the *eschaton* false Christs (antichrists) would come. [Jesus is the source of this information. It originates from his Olivet Discourse, cf. Mt. 24:24. Whether these believers had access to Matthew's gospel is unknown, but they certainly had access to apostolic teaching, which would have included this important information.] In verse 19, which is undoubtedly one of the most important explanatory passages in the New Testament, John makes the profound assertion that those who have departed (implying a complete departure from the faith) have done so because they were never "of us" (*i.e.*, of the children who dwell in light, that is, those who know God). In light of the reiteration in the second half of the verse, it is quite impossible to misunderstand his meaning. He says that we know they were not of us because (*ei gar*, "for if," giving the reason) "if" they had been of us they would have remained with us (*i.e.*, they would not have apostatized). John states that the departure of these apostates happened for a purpose (*all' hina* – "hina" being a purposive particle), "in order that it might be shown that they all are not of us"; the sense is that not everyone who professes to be right with God is truly saved. This verse establishes two critical points with respect to the theme of the book and New Testament soteriology: 1) the theme of this book is the contrast of true belief with mere profession; and, 2) it establishes the doctrine of the permanence of salvation, since is clearly states that anyone who departs from the faith they once professed was never genuinely saved. (See the previous discussion on the permanence of salvation.)

John did not want his letter to sound as if the believers could not have figured this out for themselves (vv. 20-21). After all, they did have the Holy Spirit (v. 20). We may assume that John was prompted by the Spirit to write these things as a matter of record for the church at large. In verse 22 John returns to his discourse reiterating that the one who denies that Jesus is the Christ (the Messiah, God's Son in the flesh) speaks in the spirit of antichrist, which denies both Father and Son (v. 22). The denial of Christ is also a denial of the Father (v. 23), which answers the question some have posed, "Is it possible that some Jews who rejected Christ as Messiah were sincere worshipers of God?" Obviously, in light of John's statement there can be no doubt that those who rejected Jesus, as the Christ, could not have been sincere worshipers of the Father. (This has implications for the dual covenant theory.)

In 2:28-3:12 John continues his contrast with the admonition to abide in Christ, but adds an additional motivation: that we might have confidence and not shrink away from him (as will those who dwell in darkness) at his coming (v. 28). Again, he reinforces his previous statements to the effect that it is those who practice righteousness that are born of God ("practice" = *poion*, present active participle, signifying to practice as an ongoing manner of living). The one who practices sin (again, *poion* as before) also practices lawlessness, because sin is lawlessness. The ones who walk in darkness not only sin, they blatantly disobey God's explicit commands (v. 4). Christ did not come to save men so that they would be free to sin, but so they could be free from sin (v. 5). He repeats what he has said before: "No one who abides in Him sins," not a reference to individual sins, everyone sins, but to the giving of one's self to live under the dominion of sin. He admonishes the brethren not to be deceived; true belief manifests itself in righteousness (v. 7). Where righteousness is absent, it is to be assumed that saving faith is also absent, and the subject is a child of the Devil (v. 8). John says that the Devil has sinned from the beginning and Christ came to destroy the works of the Devil (v. 8); so by implication, the one who sins (continually, as a life-style) is not in Christ. Notice the strong dichotomy. John leaves no room for misunderstanding. He is not merely contrasting spiritual believers with carnal believers as some suppose; he is contrasting the saved with the lost. Not only does the one who is born of God not practice sin, he cannot, because God's seed (the indwelling Holy Spirit) abides in him. As if he had not stated this truth robustly enough already, John now connects all the dots so that no one has any reason to misunderstand what he is saying. He vigorously maintains that it is possible to tell who are children of God and who are children of the Devil by their lifestyles (v. 10). In an age of private religion and tolerance, this is not a popular text; and if strictly applied, which it should be, we would have to confess that there are probably far fewer saved people than the number professing faith would suggest.

There are other passages in 1 John where we see the same contrast between the truly saved and the professing but unsaved (3:14-15; 4:1-6, 7-10, 11-21; 5:1-12); nevertheless, the point is sufficiently made that there are two kinds of people within the professing church: those that know God, and those who say they know God, but don't.

The path to apostasy

In understanding the path to apostasy it would be helpful if we could get a clear picture of what is involved in a person coming to faith in Christ. Probably the best and most succinct statement is that faith is simply the exercising of positive volition (choice) with respect to the gospel (the truth about who Christ is and what he accomplished on the cross, and of course, his resurrection, cf. 1 Cor. 15:1-8). Thus faith is obedience to the truth of the gospel. The absence of either core ingredient (truth in the form of the gospel, or yieldedness of the will, *i.e.,* yielding to that truth with all of its implications) would preclude true faith. Consequently, from the human perspective, there are basically two areas in which a failure can occur such that a person does not come to have saving faith: failure to understand the truth of the gospel, and failure to act on that truth.

We know from several passages discussed already that an apostate has at one time known and professed belief in the truth (cf. 2 Pt. 2:20; Heb. 10:26, both employ the term *epignosis* referring to sure or certain knowledge). Once a person comes to have the *epignosis* there are two things that can occur to lead him or her to apostasy. The most obvious fault is an immediate and final refusal to yield one's self to the truth of the gospel. The other, and perhaps not so obvious failure, is that in the absence of a positive choice to accept Christ, the person may simply drift away from the truth with which they have been confronted. In either case the result is the same: a failure to exercise faith.

Paul says in 1 Timothy 4:1-3 that one avenue of apostasy is that people are led astray into demonic doctrine. It is instructive to note that these doctrines are most often communicated through the vehicle of religion. If that is surprising, we should note what Christ said about the religious system of his day (Mt. 23:1-36, cf. 7:21-23). Undoubtedly many fall into apostasy after coming to understand the gospel because they simply delay in responding and are diverted by false religion under the guise of truth.

In Hebrews 3:13 the writer says, "lest any one of you be hardened by the deceitfulness of sin." What is meant by "the deceitfulness of sin"? Simply that sin promises fulfillment, but it delivers death. Sin is a lie (Heb. 10:26-27). Once a person has come to the sure knowledge of the truth, the choice to remain in a state of sin is inherently a rejection of Christ (cf. v. 29), which in some cases results in a final decision from which a person will never turn. Whether the failure is an immediate rejection, or simply a delay in acting on the gospel, the one common thread is that the decision to yield one's self to the demands of the gospel is not made promptly upon coming to the knowledge of the truth. The most dangerous position that any person could be in is having come to a knowledge of the truth, to delay in responding, for each moment that "Yes" is withheld is another "No!" One can quickly find himself or herself on an exponentially downward curve away from God and the opportunity of salvation.

The characteristics of an apostate

The purpose in exploring the characteristics of apostasy is not judgmental, but preventative; if we do not know what apostasy is and what it looks like, we will be ill prepared to warn the church of what could happen. Just as some physical agents can be silent killers if we ignore proper warnings, so apostasy is a silent killer within every local church, and every congregation should be warned, lest anyone fall victim. What does apostasy look like? An apostate no longer holds to the truth of the gospel. (1 Timothy 4:1 and Hebrews 6:6 — they fall away from the faith; Hebrews 3:6,14 — they do not hold fast; Hebrews 10:39 — they shrink back to destruction; Hebrews 12:14 — they do not pursue sanctification (the sanctification acquired by faith that is required for acceptance before God); Hebrews 12:25 — they turn away from God (by turning away from the truth); 2 Peter 2:15 — they forsake (relinquish) the right way. Apostates are often individuals who have permitted themselves to be deceived by false religion (2 Tim. 4:1-3). The heart of the apostate is an evil, unbelieving heart (Heb. 3:12). When an apostate chooses to remain in the church, they do so out of improper motivation. They do not remain in the church to worship and serve God. A person cannot reject Christ and love God (Jn. 5:23, cf. vv. 37-38). Their motivation is clearly indicated in 2 Peter 2:3 and Jude 12. Apostates are people who have been hardened by the deceitfulness of sin (Heb. 3:13; 10:26; 2 Pt. 2:9-15). An apostate's attitude toward Christ is one of absolute rejection (Heb. 6:6; 10:29; 12:25; 1 Pt. 2:1 "deny" = *arneomai,* meaning, "to renounce," or "disclaim"). Apostates by their own choice are hopelessly lost individuals (Heb. 6:6). Their hopeless condition is not due to the fact that God has cut them off, but because they have cut themselves off from God. If a person rejects Christ as Savior at the highest level of revelation, conviction, and calling after coming to the full knowledge of the truth, they will never receive him. It is not for us to classify individuals; God knows the heart and future of each man and woman. However, it is important for us to know that apostasy is possible so that men and women might be warned of the potential risk of failing to act promptly on the gospel, and thus ultimately falling beyond hope.

Review Questions

1. Describe substitutionary atonement.

2. Explain what is meant by the statement, "Christ's death is sufficient for all, but efficient only for those who respond in faith."

3. How does Christ's death impact a person who does not accept him?

4. Explain the biblical support for the sufficiency of Christ's death for the sin of all men (unlimited atonement).

5. Are all sins (of all men) actually forgiven in the death of Christ? Explain your answer.

6. Describe conditional election.

7. Describe unconditional election.

8. How does the doctrine of total depravity relate to one's view of election?

9. Distinguish between the general calling of God and the effectual calling of God.

10. Define "repentance" and "faith," and discuss the relationship between them.

11. Is it possible to have true faith without repentance? Explain.

12. Discuss the ingredients of faith.

13. Discuss the relationship of trials to faith.

14. Define "forgiveness," and describe the two kinds of forgiveness.

15. Explain what is involved in justification, using scripture to support your answer.

16. What is regeneration, and what is the relationship between regeneration and indwelling?

17. What does it mean to be sealed by the Holy Spirit? What benefit does sealing convey?

18. What is adoption as used by Paul in the New Testament?

19. Explain "Spirit baptism" and what it accomplishes.

20. Explain why only Church-age believers experience Spirit baptism.

21. Explain the meaning of sanctification and discuss the three aspects of sanctification.

22. What is "glorification"?

23. Give an argument for the perseverance (eternal security) of those genuinely saved.

24. How does God ensure that the saved will not be lost?

25. What is an apostate?

26. Why is the biblical discussion of apostasy sometimes a problem for interpreters?

27. What are two problems that can lead to misinterpreting a passage to mean that believers can lose their salvation?

Creation

Creation

A brief history of biblical cosmology

In the past, creation was not a "hot topic," but in modern history several things have happened to bring this issue to the forefront. Years ago, prior to the emergence of biological evolution and modern atheism, most people in western culture believed in God. Naturally, they assumed that God made the world. The biblical account was simply taken at face value and little attention was devoted to the analysis of the Bible's account of creation. (It is unfortunate that in the absence of controversy some biblical truths are neglected.) The pre-scientific Christian conception of the origin of the universe was very simplistic: Most people just believed that God had created the universe a few thousand years before their time. Bishop James Ussher calculated the date of creation at 4004 B.C. (that date appeared in many Bibles until the mid-twentieth century). The emergence of the theory of biological evolution challenged the assumption that the world was recently created. After all, if evolution were true it would have taken long ages for life to evolve from simpler organisms, and longer for the first life forms to have emerged in the first place. With the growing popularity of evolution people began to look for evidence of the antiquity of the earth. In this regard, geology and biology developed together. The ages of various rock formations were dated based on the assumed amount of time that would be necessary for their evolution (or the evolution of the creatures embedded within them). Evolutionary biologists then used the "findings" of geology to support biological evolution.

Though conservatives — those who tend to understand the Bible literally — rejected evolution as incompatible with the Bible, most eventually accepted the proposition that the earth might not be as young as Christians had previously assumed. In an effort to square this emerging realization with the Bible various theories were put forth. One was the "gap theory." The gap theory proposed that God created the earth (Gen. 1:1), and at Satan's fall God judged the earth and that it lay in ruins for a very long time (Gen. 1:2) until God renovated it. According to the gap theory the six-day account in Genesis 1:3-31 is the account of the earth's renovation (Gen 1:3-2:3) along with the creation of plants, animals, and man. According to this theory the earth could be any age, since no one knows how long the gap between Genesis 1:1 and 1:2 might have been. This seemed to square the Bible with modern thinking about the age of the earth, while at the same time clearly rejecting biological evolution. This view came to be one of the dominant views among biblical conservatives and remained so until fairly recently, about the 1960s. Many of the leading Bible expositors of the early twentieth century held to one form or another of this theory.

Other ideas designed to reconcile the Bible and scientific observations about the age of the earth were also suggested. One theory proposed that God created the materials of the universe and then waited, possibility a very long time, before forming them into their present arrangement. Theistic evolution was also proposed by those who took a less-than-literal view of Genesis. This theory not only attempted to square the Bible with the presumed antiquity of the earth, but went a step further and attempted to reconcile the Bible with biological evolution. Theistic evolutionists proposed that God used evolution as the means of creation, at least partially. Another view called "progressive creationism" suggested that the days of Genesis chapter 1 were actually long geologic ages in which God performed his work of creation in bursts. This view was essentially non-evolutionary in that it did not account for the rise of the various species through evolution; it simply sought to square the Bible with current thinking about geology and paleontology.

More recently, since the mid-1960s the trend among some biblical conservatives has been back to the original conception of a young universe and earth (in the range of eight to ten thousand years old). Recent creationism began to gain ground in the 1970s.

There were several reasons for this. The gap theory was in serious trouble with proponents beginning to notice flaws in the theory. Biblical conservatives found their backs to the wall with the explosion of evolution in schools, colleges, and universities, and they desperately needed to mount a serious challenge. Finding support for a recent creation would be the surest antidote for evolution. Time is to evolution what fuel is to a fire, take away the fuel and the fire dies; take away time and evolution dies. Other theories seemed to have fallen by the wayside, or clearly had problems. Perhaps because of its adversarial relation to evolution, recent creationism quickly coalesced into a highly focused and organized movement. Organizations like the Institute for Creation Research have been prolific producers of educational materials, most of which have been distributed in churches, Christian colleges, and seminaries, where they have had a significant impact. Part of the appeal of recent creationism is that it seems to bring together a literal and non-evolutionary interpretation of the Genesis account, and to harmonize the Bible with the complexities of modern science. According to recent creationism God created the universe in a mature state perhaps eight to ten thousand years ago; the universe appears old not because it is old, but because it was created mature, imparting to it the appearance of great age.

Of course recent creationism has serious flaws of its own. Although the early geological evidence offered for the age of the earth was largely suspect due to its evolutionary bias, in recent years (since the mid-1900s) a growing body of evidence suggests that the universe is much older than the eight to ten thousand years allowed by recent creationism. Also, recent creationism hinges on the ability of a mature creation to fully account for the universe's appearance of age, but this explanation is seriously flawed, as will be explained further along. Before proceeding, we need to understand three key terms that will be used throughout this discussion; they are: "creation *ex nihilo*," "immediate creation," and "mediate creation."

Creation *ex nihilo*: The terms *"ex"* and *"nihilo"* when put together mean, "out of nothing." Creation *ex nihilo* refers to the original creation of time, matter, energy, space, *etc.* It does not refer to the subsequent forming or shaping of matter after its original creation.

Immediate creation: Immediate creation is simply another term for creation *ex nihilo*, and the two terms are completely interchangeable. Immediate creation signifies that God brought something into existence directly, as opposed to forming something that already existed.

Mediate creation: Mediate creation refers to forming (or fashioning) something out of existing materials. The creation of Adam and Eve are examples of mediate creation, since God did not produce man out of nothing, but out of the dust of the earth (which he had previously created), and woman out of man.

The early Christian view of creation

The pre-scientific view of creation held prior to the modern scientific period is that the world was created out of nothing approximately six thousand years ago. The nice thing about this view was that it did not require any elaborate explanations to account for why the universe and the earth appear to be old. To the pre-scientific mind the universe looked to be about six thousand years old, and as they say, "that was that," neat and simple.

Factors giving rise to the pre-scientific view

The pre-scientific view was based on a simplistic reading of the Old Testament that gave no consideration to the problem of the apparent age of the universe. By adding up the genealogies and reigns of the Old Testament kings and any other available chronological data, some biblical scholars thought they could arrive at a fairly accurate date for creation. Using this method, Bishop James Ussher (1581-1656) dated creation at 4004 B.C. (or more precisely, the evening prior to October 23, 4004 B.C.). Bishop Ussher's chronology was so widely accepted that his dates appeared in the margins of many Bibles until very recently. While this chronology is no longer considered to be valid, primarily because of problems with the pre-flood portion of the chronology, it was still an amazing piece of work for its time.

Problems with the pre-scientific view

Of course, there were problems with the pre-scientific view. First, it didn't entirely fit with the biblical text. The creation account in Genesis does not make the claim that everything recorded from Genesis 1:1 to 1:31 occurred in a six-day period (literal, or otherwise). As we will see when we look at what Genesis actually says, it is virtually certain that the *ex nihilo* creation (*i.e.*, the original creation out of nothing) occurred sometime before the first of the six formative days of Genesis 1. Second, the pre-scientific view does not account for the apparent age of the universe. The universe clearly appears to be older, much older than six thousand years. (We will discuss the apparent age of the universe further along.)

Reconciliation theories

Only in the modern period have we become aware of the fact that the universe appears to be much older than a few thousand years. In fact, current estimates of the age of the universe now extend from about thirteen to fifteen billion years. Prior to the modern period there was no need to reconcile the Genesis account with scientific observations. However, with new evidence of the age of the universe, it became necessary to speculate as to how the truth of Genesis and science might be squared. This need gave rise to numerous reconciliation theories. A reconciliation theory is a speculative understanding of the Genesis account and how it might fit with modern science. While many Christians are convinced that there is adequate scientific evidence that the universe is old, most conservative Christians reject biological evolution as both incompatible with the Bible and unsupported by the scientific evidence. Nevertheless, there have been those within Christendom who have embraced biological evolution, and that is reflected in at least one of the theories we will examine. Naturally, the degree to which each theory reconciles Genesis and modern science varies. Some of these theories provide for reconciliation between Genesis and science both in regard to the age of the universe (cosmology) and biological evolution. Other theories reject biological evolution, at least at the macroevolutionary level, and simply attempt to reconcile Genesis with the apparent antiquity of the universe. It is important for the student of the Bible to understand that all of these theories are, to varying degrees, speculative. It is essential to make a distinction between what the Bible actually says and reasonably implies, and a theory that attempts to show how that information relates to modern science. A particular reconciliation theory may prove to be untrue, but just because a particular theory proves untrue does not mean that the Bible is wrong. Reconciliation theories are simply speculations about how Genesis might fit with modern science. It is also worth pointing out that these theories come and go in popularity. From the early nineteen hundreds to the nineteen-sixties, the chaos (preformative) theory and the gap theory were predominate among biblical conservatives, whereas since the nineteen-sixties recent creationism has become very popular. Just as there was a paradigm shift among biblical conservatives in the nineteen-sixties and seventies, we are now on the verge of another shift as flaws inherent in recent creationism are becoming apparent. For those who might have been taught a reconciliation theory as if it were biblical fact, such a paradigm shift can be disconcerting. It is important to keep in mind that Christian teaching on the subject of creation contains two distinct streams of information. One stream is what the Bible actually says (primarily the Genesis text); the other stream is what we think that biblical information means in light of our present understanding of the universe. Often both streams are combined and presented as an interpretation of Genesis; that's unfortunate because such a procedure does not distinguish the biblical facts from the theoretical component. Most of the theories we will look at have significant problems, yet it is not difficult to find individuals who subscribe to each of these theories. In fact, there are, no doubt, some whose view of Genesis has not progressed beyond the pre-scientific view. While such laxity is not fatal to our faith, it may be fatal to our witness. If we refuse to acknowledge what others see clearly, we can hardly expect our message to be taken seriously.

Day-age theories

Day-age theories state that the days of Genesis 1 were not literal twenty-four hour days, but long geologic ages—millions, or billions of years in length. There are two forms of the day-age theory: theistic evolution and progressive creation. These differ in that while theistic evolution accepts macroevolution, progressive creation attributes the origin of species to creative bursts spaced out over long geologic ages. Interestingly, much of the current paleontological evidence and much of the modern radiometric dating is consistent with progressive creationism, except for dates for humans extending beyond the range of biblical history.

Theistic evolution

Theistic evolutionists speculate that God created the materials of the universe and the physical laws, and then used evolution (chance interaction, mutation, and natural selection) to complete the process. They offer basically the same evidence for theistic evolution that is offered by atheistic evolutionists. There are varieties of theistic evolution. Some proponents suggest that God created the first life and allowed evolution to run its course; others hold that life arose as a result of natural processes from the materials that God created.

Problems with theistic evolution

From the biblical point of view there are two major problems with theistic evolution. First, it isn't compatible with a normal/objective understanding of the account of creation given in Genesis 1-2. Genesis states that man is a direct creation of God. Genesis also states that God created all of the animals "after their kind" (Gen. 1:24,25). This statement precludes the idea that all life has arisen from simpler forms. Secondly, the account of man's fall into sin and the plan of redemption, of which the rest of the Bible is largely occupied, are based upon a normal/objective under-standing of the first few chapters of Genesis. If the creation ac-count were to be regarded as mythical, or even allegorical, then the entire message of the Bible would be questionable. Third, there are fundamental scientific problems with the theory of evo-lution itself, for example: abiogenesis (life from non-life), the problem of irreducibly complex systems, the apparent design of organisms, the problem of how non-intelligence produced the in-formation necessary for the pattern of living things, and the lack of evidence from the fossil record and nature for the existence of species intermediates.

Progressive creationism

Progressive creationism states that God's creative activity extended over long ages. This non-evolutionary view regards each of the days of the Genesis account as representing an era of inde-terminate, and possibly variable length, during which God progressively created living things in bursts. According to this theory the species arose in the time frame that modern science claims is indicated in the fossil record, but not as a result of evo-lution. Consequently, the days of Genesis are understood as a lit-erary structure representing the creative epochs. In the past, some proponents of day-age theories used 2 Peter 3:8 as support. (In 2 Peter 3:8, Peter indicated that with the Lord a thousand years is "as one day.") However, as we will see, 2 Peter 3:8 does not sup-port this use.

Problems with progressive creationism

There are several difficulties associated with progressive creationism. First, it isn't compatible with a normal understanding of Genesis. However, the theory cannot be ruled out on that basis, because it is possible that the days of Genesis 1 were intended simply to represent indefinite time periods, not 24-hour days. There are numerous instances in the Bible where the term "day" represents a time period other than a 24-hour day; for example, the frequently used expression, "the day of the LORD." In this case, the reference to "evening" and "morning" would simply form a kind of literary inclusio for each metaphorical day. Second, as to the use of 2 Peter 3:8 where Peter said, "...one day is with the Lord as a thousand years, and a thousand years as one day," this statement does not mean that when scripture indicates a day we are at liberty to interpret that to mean an indefinite amount of time. Peter was simply saying that God is unaffected by time. He was not saying that when scripture indicates a time relationship we are at liberty to take that figuratively. It is odd that 2 Peter 3:8 would be chosen to support the idea that time references in the Bible are somewhat elastic. Actually, this passage indicates quite the opposite. If a day in this passage were not literally a day, and a thousand years were not literally a thousand years, this passage would make no sense, since the meaning only comes into sharp focus when we understand that Peter is saying that a literal twenty-four hour day and a literal thousand years are all the same to a timeless God. However, having said that, the fact that 2 Peter 3:8 does not support the day-age concept is not a negative for this view; it is more the lack of positive biblical evidence. Third, progressive creationism would need to be able to explain how the creation of plants (Gen. 1:11-13) preceded the formation of the sun (Gen. 1:14-19). Fourth, it is sometimes suggested that Exodus 20:11 seems to preclude this view by stating that everything was created in six days. Of course, if Exodus 20:11 simply reflects the Genesis account, then whatever "day" means in Genesis is also meant in Exodus 20:11. Progressive creationism still does not solve all the scientific problems, since there are incompatibilities between the record of biblical history and modern science in the area of scientific dating, especially the dates of human existence. Unfortunately, the scientific dating process is itself theory-bound. Until far more information is available on the validity of proposed scientific dates, it would be ill advised to try to construct a biblical view based on that information.

Several interesting books have been written in the last few years promoting one version or another of the day-age theory; see: *The Finger Print of God* (Promise Publishing Co.) and *The Creator and the Cosmos* (NavPress) both by Hugh Ross, and *A New Look at an Old Earth* (Schroeder Publishing) by Don Stoner, and *The Science of God* (Broadway Books) by Gerald L. Schroeder. Unfortunately, while these books correctly point out some of the flaws in recent creationism's young earth view, they incorrectly assume that the only alternative is some form of day-age view.

Literary theories

Various literary theories claim that the days in Genesis chapter 1 are only some sort of literary structure in which the creation story is either told or set. According to one of these views the six days of Genesis were not six days in which creation took place, but six movements in the creation story. A variation on the literary framework theory is that God revealed the account of creation in six days, and that Genesis contains a synopsis of what was revealed each day. In either case, the six days are not viewed as a time frame for the work of creation, but simply a literary structure for telling the story of creation. These theories do not speak directly to the issues of the age of the universe or evolution. The literary framework theory can stand alone as an extremely vague general theory, or as a complement to another more detailed theory, such as progressive creationism or theistic evolution.

The gap theory

Once very popular among biblical conservatives, this theory proposed that God created the world, which was subsequently judged with devastating effect when Lucifer fell. This theory proposes that the six-day account in Genesis 1 is the account of the earth's reconstruction after its judgment. According to this theory the original creation is mentioned only in Genesis 1:1. Genesis 1:2 describes the condition of the earth after its judgment, and Genesis 1:3-31 describes the earth's subsequent re-creation.

Several arguments have been offered in support of the gap theory. First, it is assumed that it would have been out of character for God to create the earth "formless" and "void" (Gen. 1:2); therefore, something must have happened to cause the earth to become formless and void. Second, the terms *"tohu"* ("formless") and *"bohu"* ("void," or "empty") are used together in only one other instance in the Bible, where they clearly indicate judgment (Jer. 4:23). Third, the idea that the original creation was judged by God could fit with the biblical description of the fall of Lucifer, presumably recorded in Ezekiel 28:11-19 and Isaiah 14:12-21. (Although the name "Lucifer" is used of Satan in this volume, it is not likely a personal name as the AV indicates in Isaiah 14:12, but should be translated "morning star," or "bright one.") Fourth, the gap theory appears to reconcile the Genesis account with the apparent age of the universe. (A variation that subscribes to a pre-Genesis 1:3 plant and animal kingdom also attempts to square Genesis with modern fossil dating.)

There are three principal problems with the gap theory. First, the grammar of Genesis 1:1-2 does not allow for a gap between verses 1 and 2. Quite interestingly, this fact was first brought to light in the 1950's by one of the foremost gap theorists of the time, Dr. Merrill F. Unger, in an article that appeared in the theological journal *Bibliotheca Sacra*, in January 1958, titled: "Rethinking the Genesis Account of Creation." The reason, as Dr. Unger pointed out, is that "In the original language [Hebrew] Genesis 1:2 consists of three circumstantial clauses, all describing conditions or circumstances existing at the time of the principal action indicated in verse 1, or giving a reason for that action." To put it simply, what Dr. Unger pointed out was that the timing of the main verb of the sentence (v. 1, "created") controls all the circumstantial clauses describing the conditions in verse 2. (Verses 1 and 2 are one sentence in the Hebrew.) This means that at the time God created the heavens and the earth, <clause #1:> "the earth was [at the time of its creation] without form, and void;" <clause #2:> "and [at the time of creation] darkness was upon the face of the deep;" <clause #3:> "and [at the time of creation] the Spirit of God moved upon (or better, "was moving upon" {participle}) the face of the waters." When read this way, as indicated by the grammar, there is simply no way that verse 2 can be a description of the earth having been judged subsequent to its creation in verse 1, because verse 2 describes the conditions of the earth at the time of its original creation in verse 1. This interpretation completely rules out any notion of a gap between verses 1 and 2. Interestingly, Dr. Unger remained committed to the gap theory, albeit a modified version. His solution to the problem was to assert that the creation referenced in verse one was not, after all, the original creation, but the re-creation of the earth after its original creation and judgment (which must have occurred prior to Genesis 1:1), thus placing the original creation, the earth's judgment, and the gap prior to Genesis 1:1. While this was a highly creative solution, it had the unfortunate effect of making the gap theory an extra-biblical theory, since it pushed the gap right out of the Bible! It took about twenty years for Dr. Unger's observations to take hold, but the shot had been fired, and ultimately the gap theory died, a victim of friendly fire. The second problem is that the gap theory was never well supported biblically. The creation passage (Genesis 1:1-31) says nothing about the fall of Lucifer, or the earth being judged. All of that material has to be transplanted into the story. The third problem is that a great deal of weight is placed on identifying the terms *tohu* (formless) and *bohu* (empty) with judgment. While it is true that the only other place these terms are used together in scripture is a picture of divine judgment (Jer. 4:23), it is also true that one example does not establish a pattern. There simply isn't enough biblical evidence to conclude that these terms must refer to judgment when used together.

Recent creationism

Recent creationism claims that the universe was created within the last eight to ten thousand years. There are two forms of recent creationism: classic recent creationism, which makes use of the mature creation argument to account for the apparent age of the universe; and relativistic recent creationism, which depends upon relativity to account for the apparent age of the universe. In some respects recent creationism is similar to the original pre-scientific view, in that it subscribes to a young creation, with the *ex nihilo* (original) creation occurring on the first of the six days of

Genesis chapter 1. In other ways it is very different from the pre-scientific view. It recognizes the discrepancy between the apparent age of the universe and the age limit allowed by the recent creation theory, and it seeks to reconcile the difference. Recent creationists make extensive use (and misuse) of scientific information in seeking to establish that the universe is young.

Classic recent creationism

According to classic recent creationism, God made the world in a mature (fully developed) form approximately eight to ten thousand years ago. According to this view, since the world was created in a mature state, it appears older than it's actual age. Recent creationists claim that either Genesis 1:1-2 is included as part of the first day of creation, or that these verses are either a title or summary introduction to the creation account. In other words, they dismiss the idea that Genesis 1:1-2 could be referring to an original *ex nihilo* creation that occurred prior to the first day. They also see support for recent creation in Exodus 20:11, which seems to suggest that nothing was created prior to the first day of Genesis. Exodus 20:11 says, "For in six days the LORD made the heavens and the earth, the sea, and all that is in them...." Accordingly, since the first day of Genesis would have been fairly recent (eight to ten thousand years ago, based on Old Testament chronology), neither the universe nor anything in the universe could be older than eight to ten thousand years.

While recent creationism claims to be a biblical view, its support is almost entirely from "creation science" observations. The following are some examples of the kind of scientific information used to support this view. 1) Decay of the earth's magnetic field indicates it is less than ten thousand years old. 2) The amount of helium in the atmosphere (given that it is generated at a constant rate) indicates that the earth could not be more than about ten thousand years old. 3) The presence of oil under pressure creating oil gushers indicates a recent creation, since otherwise the pressure would have been relaxed over long ages through dissipation of pressure in permeable rock. 4) The amount of dust found on the moon suggests that the moon is seven to eight thousand years old (based on assumed levels of annual deposit). Also, the amount of cosmic dust deposited on the earth indicates an age less than ten thousand years. 5) The earth's rotational velocity indicates that the earth could not be old. Given a constant rate of decline in velocity, if the earth were billions of years old, the original high rotational velocity would have produced a very different looking planet (land masses would have formed primarily around the equator). 6) The existence of comets indicates a young universe. Since comets give off particles as they travel through space, if the universe were billions of years old, the comets would already be completely spent. 7) Diamonds have been found that have measurable amounts of carbon-14, which should be undetectable if they were more than 100,000 years old.

The difficulty with using the above, and similar observations, as evidence of recent creation is this: Even if we were to assume that the above observations are valid, they still would not prove a recent *ex nihilo* creation. All of these factors can be fully accounted for by a recent mediate creation (a rearrangement of existing materials), as suggested by the preformative view. In other words, all of the scientific factors that recent creationists point to can be accounted for even if the universe were old, as long as the six formative days of Genesis were fairly recent. Thus, the same observations can be used to support an alternate theory that recent creationists have not ruled out, and which fits with the first chapter of Genesis better than the recent creation theory. This illustrates a key methodological flaw in recent creationism. Since recent creationists assume that all creation, including the creation *ex nihilo*, occurred within the six days of Genesis, they therefore conclude that any evidence of recent creative activity, whether *ex nihilo* or formative, is evidence of a young universe. However, this reasoning is unsound because the Genesis account clearly places the *ex nihilo* creation prior to the first day of Genesis, meaning that the *ex nihilo* and *mediate* aspects of creation may have been widely separated in time. Also, recent creationism fails to consider the possibility that a remote *ex nihilo* creation in the distant past combined with a recent mediate (formative) creation eight to ten thousand years ago could fit the same data, as well as biblical history.

Problems with classic recent creationism

There are three fundamental problems with classic recent creationism: an observational problem, a logical problem, and an ethical problem. (Relativistic recent creationism is discussed separately.)

The unique qualities of light are very helpful in understanding the size and age of the observed (currently visible) universe. The current scientific estimate of the size of the observed universe puts it at a radius of about 13.8 billion light-years. [The "observed universe" should not be confused with the "observable universe." Since the furthest galaxies that can now be seen have moved since the light left them, the size of the potentially observable universe has increased, and is estimated to be about 46 billion light-years in radius.] If, as astronomers estimate, we are seeing light from galaxies 13.8 billion light-years distant, this would lead to the conclusion that the universe could not be just a few thousand years old. We have to be very cautious with these numbers; nevertheless, even most knowledgeable recent creationists generally accept the current estimate of the size of the universe, and even if these figures were off by ninety-nine percent (which no cosmologist, Christian or non-Christian, believes), the indicated age of the universe would still be far older than the eight to ten thousand years estimated by recent creationists. Some have suggested that perhaps the solution to this problem is that the speed of light was faster in the past than it is now; While that theory cannot be entirely discounted, any theory that requires a large-scale change in one of the fundamental constants of the universe should be viewed with caution, and, as we will mention further along, changes in the speed of light would not solve some of the problems created by the apparent history of events in the universe, such as partially or completely merged galaxies.

Another problem is that recent creationism depends upon creation with maturity to account for the apparent age of the universe; this relationship can be expressed as:

$$\text{Appearance of Age} = \text{Maturity}.$$

When recent creationists look at the universe and see features that appear to be millions or billions of years old, they account for the apparent age by virtue of the universe's maturity at creation. So recent creationists, in effect, take the position that one cannot distinguish between an object appearing to have age and a newly created, mature object. The problem is that this line of reasoning is easily demonstrated to be false. Let's imagine an experiment that demonstrates that mature creation and appearance of age are not the same. If maturity fully accounts for the appearance of age, it should be impossible to distinguish between an object created mature and an object reaching a mature state through time. However, objects that reach maturity through time not only appear mature, they also exhibit the accumulated effects of events having taken place in time. For example, suppose we had the newly created Adam stand beside a man that had reached the same level of maturity through the passage of time. Would we be able to tell them apart? Certainly an examination of growth plates, scars, worn teeth, broken bones having healed, stretch marks, skin damage due to sun exposure, *etc.*, would make such an identification easy. Why? — Because maturity and the appearance of age are not equivalent. The same is true in regard to the universe. The universe exhibits not only maturity, but also the scars of great age. When we look at the universe, we see that it is covered in scars, scars demonstrating great age: galaxies having collided and merged, stars having spent their fuel and having exploded across thousands of light-years of space, gravitational interference between galaxies, light streams in space containing billions of years of history in light images streaming back to their sources. So, if what we see when we look at the universe cannot be fully explained by a mature creation, and it cannot, the recent creationist is left without any explanation of why the universe appears old.

Finally, there is the ethical problem. This problem is more difficult to explain. Let's begin with a question: Does God lie? Obviously the answer is "No"; yet recent creationism implies (unintentionally, of course) that God has lied about the fundamental nature of creation. How so? Astronomers estimate that we are seeing light from distant galaxies billions of light-years away. If that is true, the natural assumption should be that the universe could not be any younger than the amount of time it would have taken that light to traverse the distance from its origin to earth. (Actually it would have to be a good bit older than that.) Of course this implies a not-so-recently-created universe. At this point some recent creationists suggest a possible solution: that God simply created the light stream in place, *i.e., in situ.* (This is sometimes referred to as the "creation in transit theory.") If this were true, then any image we see through a telescope of an object greater than eight to ten thousand light-years distance never originated at the source it appears to have come from. (The epistemological implications of this would be staggering.) Such an explanation plants doubt as to the true nature of the universe and what can be known by observation; that's highly problematic since God clearly intended that our observation of both nature and the universe should lead us to him (Psa. 8:3; 50:6; 97:6) and to a correct, though incomplete, view of his nature and power (Rom. 1:19-20). However, we have not yet come to the ethical problem posed by this theory. If the foregoing explanation were true, then for a galaxy five billion light-years distant from earth, the light stream at the moment of creation would have been five billion light-years (assuming it reached all the way to the earth) So, what's in a light stream five billion light-years long? The answer is: five billion years of history recorded in images. Yet that's five billion years more history than is possible. Taking this one step further, this would imply one of two things: Either the universe is discontinuous (*i.e.,* more like a stage prop, in which case observations mean nothing), or God has recorded a history in starlight of events that never happened. Either of these explanations would be disturbing because they imply that God has intentionally misled man about the nature of the universe and its creation.

If that were not enough of a problem, it gets worse. We have images of large nebulas, galaxies in collision (some even completely assimilated), and large intergalactic gravitational effects for which only an older universe (*i.e.,* older than ten thousand years) can account. Take the merger of two galaxies as an example: two galaxies, each with a breadth of about a hundred thousand light-years could hardly merge in the space of ten thousand years. Even if God created them such that their outer edges were already in contact (odd), and even if they were moving toward one another at the speed of light (not really feasible), the minimum time required for a complete merger would be fifty thousand years (one moves fifty thousand light-years to the left while the other simultaneously moves fifty thousand light-years to the right). Add to that the amount of time required for the images to arrive on earth, and we can see that ten thousand years doesn't begin to be enough time, even in this greatly oversimplified example. Thus, recent creationists are forced to suggest that the universe was created with all of these scars — scars depicting a history that never was. And to make it all look very realistic, those events that never happened appear to have obeyed the general laws of motion and gravitation. Astronomers have observed that when two galaxies have merged, or are in the process, their angular momentums and gravity merge according to the general laws of motion and gravity, causing the new galaxy to form a shape predictable by the classical laws of physics. In some cases nearby galaxies have simply brushed, scattering stars in their spirals across tens of thousands of light-years of space. In the case of the Cartwheel Galaxy one galaxy has passed completely through another, blowing out a huge ring of gas over a hundred and fifty thousand light-years in diameter that is now condensing into new stars. It is impossible that such structures could have been formed in the time allowed under recent creationism. If God put his omniscience to work to devise a plan to thoroughly deceive man about the origin of the universe, he couldn't have devised a better plan than what the recent creationist proposes.

Relativistic recent creationism

   In view of the problems associated with classic recent creationism, Dr. Donald Humphreys proposed a relativistic solution in which the universe could have aged billions of years while only six days passed on earth (Donald Humphreys, *Starlight and Time: Solving the Puzzle of Distant Starlight in a Young Universe*, Master Books, 1998). The theory is complex and based on the fact that gravity distorts time. Dr. Humphreys' theory, which could be termed "white hole cosmology," postulates that the universe expanded out of a white hole (a hole with a gravitational event horizon, but from which matter and light can escape, but not re-enter (essentially a black hole in reverse). According to this theory the earth is at the center of the universe, and since an event horizon affects time (making it run incredibly fast), as the universe expanded and the event horizon shrank, the entire universe (with the exception of the earth) eventually passed through the event horizon. Since the event horizon would weaken as it shrank, the greatest aging effects would be seen in the galaxies furthest from earth (since they passed through the event horizon first, while it was still strong). On the surface, white hole cosmology seems to provide an explanation of the age differential between the earth and more distant parts of the universe; however, the specifics, as proposed by Humphreys, face enormous problems both with the text of Genesis 1:1-31 and science, especially since the existence of white holes is purely speculative. (Unlike black holes, no evidence of the existence of white holes has ever been found.) In proposing such a cosmology, it is possible that Dr. Humpreys has unintentionally sown the seeds for the destruction of recent creationism. According to this theory, ninety-nine percent of the universe is much older (point of presence) than even the maximum figure generally allowed by recent creationism (ten thousand years). In other words, this view acknowledges that the bulk of the universe was not created recently. And if it is acknowledged that the universe does, in fact, appear to be old, not just mature, why postulate such an unlikely theory just so one can contend that the earth is young — a claim the Bible never makes.

The preformative theory

This view is generally called the "chaos view" in the theologies; however, the term "preformative" is preferable because it more accurately describes the view. This view proposes that God created the universe *ex nihilo* sometime prior to the first formative day of Genesis. The six days of Genesis describe God's subsequent activity in preparing the earth as a home for man. According to this view, all of the work done by God during the six days of Genesis was formative (mediate) creation, not *ex nihilo* creation.

The preformative theory is based upon a literal understanding of the Genesis account, and it does not impose any age assumptions on creation (whether young or old), nor does it require any corollary theories, as is the case with recent creationism. It simply claims that God created the materials *ex nihilo* in verses 1-2, and then, subsequently formed those materials. This should not be confused with the gap theory, which proposes a gap between Genesis 1:1 and 1:2 (where no gap is allowed by the grammar). The preformative theory allows for an unspecified time between Genesis 1:2 and 1:3 where the grammar presents no problem, but unlike the gap theory the preformative view does not suggest any particular events relating to that time period. The preformative theory can be held in combination with other compatible theories.

Historically, the main objection to this view has been to pose the question: "Why would God create the universe and then allow a period of time to pass before filling it with living things?" The answer to the question is: "We don't know." "Why" questions involving God are very difficult to answer unless the answer is revealed in scripture. However, it is possible to venture a response: Maybe the "cake" wasn't ready to be iced immediately. At this point someone might say, "But why would God need to wait for the completion of physical processes before forming and filling his creation?" Couldn't God simply command everything to be instantly ready? The answer is "Yes, he could," but that does not mean that he did, and there is no reason why he should have done so. God is the one who ordained the physical processes at the *ex nihilo* creation, and God, being timeless, would not be the least inconvenienced by the passage of any length of time in creation. It has also been suggested that Isaiah 45:18 implies that the six-day forming and filling activity of God had to be closely associated in time with the *ex nihilo* creation. However, there is nothing in Isaiah 45:18 that implies the forming and filling of the six days of Genesis had to occur immediately after the *ex nihilo* creation, only that the forming and filling had to occur at some point, because that was God's ultimate purpose in creation.

Occasionally one sees this objection: If this view were correct, it would mean that God, contrary to his nature, created the world in a chaotic (disordered) state. The flaw in this objection is fairly obvious. Even though the original creation was as yet unformed, or we might say that it was in a preformed state, it was far from chaotic, for all of the ingredients of creation (time, matter, energy, space, and the physical laws governing them) were present. It certainly may be characterized as incomplete, but not chaotic. Suppose I went into your kitchen while you were making a cake and saw only a bowl full of gooey batter and said to you, "You can't make a cake that way, why that's beneath your dignity; don't you know that cakes have layers with icing?" You would probably suggest that if I would leave you alone for a while you would produce just such a cake. The same is true in regard to creation. The fact that all of the creative work was not done instantly does not imply that the job was inferior, chaotic, or in any way beneath the majesty of God.

The biblical account of creation

The real test of any view is how well it reflects what the Bible actually says. The Genesis record (1:1-2:3) gives the most extensive account of creation contained within the pages of scripture. It tells of the creation of the raw materials of which everything is made, and how those materials were fashioned to make heavenly bodies, plants, animals, and finally man. Since we are approaching this topic from a Christian perspective, we must acknowledge that the Genesis account is factually true in every respect when understood as it was intended. The most prominent feature of the account is the arrangement of creation according to six formative days. (I say "formative" because there does not seem to be any indication of *ex nihilo* creation within the six-day period.)

Another feature that should be apparent even to the casual reader is that the first two verses of the passage are not part of the first day. This is clear from the fact that each formative day begins with the phrase, "And God said. . ." and ends with, "And there was evening, and there was morning — the {nth} day." This familiar structure is an inclusio marking where a segment of the account begins and ends. When repeated, as they are here, these inclusios form a symmetry that makes the story easy to remember. These highly visible structures can also help us to see the natural breaks in the passage, and what they indicate is that the account of the first day does not begin until verse three; this means that the first two verses should not be grouped with the first formative day. This leads to an important question: Since verses 1-2 (which comprise one sentence) are not part of the first day, in what way do they relate to the six days that follow? There are essentially two possibilities. Either these verses describe events that precede the first day or they do not, in which case they would likely be a title or summary introduction to the section that follows (1:3-2:3).

There is general agreement among interpreters that Genesis 1:1 refers to the original creation *ex nihilo*. If these two verses refer to activity prior to the first day, then the original *ex nihilo* creation (which is not referred to in the remainder of the story) must have occurred prior to the first formative day. The implications of this are of enormous importance, because this would mean that the original creation of the universe could have predated the six days of Genesis chapter one by a very long period of time. Some recent creationists group Genesis 1:1-2 with the first day and others view these verses as a descriptive title to the creation story. However, neither of these views is correct. As we have already observed, the literary structure clearly indicates that Genesis 1:1-2 is not part of the first day. That leaves two options: Either these two verses are simply a descriptive title to the creation account, or they describe events prior to the first formative day. Can we determine with any degree of confidence which of these two alternatives is correct? The answer is a definite "Yes." If these verses are a summary title to the six days, they ought to summarize the activities recorded for those days. On the other hand, if they refer to events that took place prior to the first day, it should be possible to detect a sequence or progression from the description in verses 1-2 to what follows. Genesis 1:1-2 says, "In the beginning God created the heavens and the earth. Now the earth was formless and empty, darkness was over the surface of the deep, and the Spirit of God was hovering over the waters." In order to determine if this is a summary title we need to ask: Does "formless," "empty," and "dark" summarize the activity of the six days (vv. 3-31)? The answer is obviously "No." In fact, it describes the opposite. Can we see a sequential or progressive relationship between these first two verses and the rest of the creation story? "Yes" — what is "dark" in verse 2 is illuminated in verse 3; what is "formless" in verse 2 is formed and fashioned in verses 3-31; what is "empty" in verse 2 is filled with living things in verses 11-31. This progression plainly indicates that Genesis 1:1-2 describes activity (v. 1) and a state (v. 2) prior to the first formative day. Thus, we can say with confidence that the original creation *ex nihilo* (recorded in verse 1) took place before the first of the six formative days began. This is confirmed by the fact that there is no indication of *ex nihilo* creation during the six-day period. Light was the first thing produced during the six days, but we know that the existence of light presumes the existence of space, time, energy and matter ($E=mc^2$). Likewise the separating of the terrestrial and atmospheric waters, and the gathering of the terrestrial waters into oceans was a rearrangement of existing matter and space. The stars were "made" (Heb. *'asah*, "formed," this term is never used for creation *ex nihilo*), and the living plants and animals were made from the pre-existing materials of the earth.

A common objection to the position just given is that according to Exodus 20:11, all of God's creative activity, including the creation *ex nihilo*, was performed within the six-day period. Exodus 20:11 says, "For in six days the LORD made the heavens and the earth, the sea, and all that is in them...." However, when we examine Exodus 20:11 we find that the word "made" is the Hebrew term *'asah*, meaning, "to form," a term used only for mediate creation (*i.e.,* formation of existing material). Hence, the correct understanding of this passage is that the formative activity was six days in duration; however, it says nothing about the original *ex nihilo* creation being part of the six days; in fact, Exodus 20:11 says nothing about the *ex nihilo* creation at all.

The words translated "made" and "created" were carefully chosen when this account was recorded. *Bara'* is usually translated "create" and has a broad range of meaning. Just like the English "create," *bara'* can be used of *ex nihilo* creation, or the forming of existing material into a new arrangement. In the Genesis account of creation *bara'* occurs in 1:1,21,27 (twice) and in 2:3 (to summarize the entire process). *'Asah* is usually translated to "make," or "create," but has a much more narrow meaning than *bara'*; it is only used of forming existing materials. In the Genesis account of creation *'asah* occurs in 1:7,16,25,26, and 31. The usage and relationship of these two words is similar to the relationship between the English words "create" and "make." The thing to remember is that whereas *bara'* can be used to substitute for *'asah* (since *bara'* is a more comprehensive term), *'asah* can only be used where *ex nihilo* creation is not in view. Therefore, there is a very limited interchangeability between these words. This explains why several occurrences of *bara'* (vv. 21 and 27 [2 times]) and every occurrence of *'asah* in this passage refers to *mediate* creation, even though *bara'* in 1:1 clearly refers to the *ex nihilo* creation. Needless to say, an unclear understanding of this relationship can result in a great deal of confusion over what the first chapter of Genesis actually says.

In summarizing the account of creation from Genesis 1:1-31, we should note the following: 1) The original creation of the heavens and earth (*ex nihilo*) is stated to have occurred prior to the beginning of the first formative day. We have absolutely no way of knowing, from the Bible, how much time might have lapsed between the original creation (1:1-2) and the beginning of the first day (1:3). Hence, we cannot know, from the Bible, the age or even the approximate age of creation. 2) The activity recorded during the six days of Genesis was formative in nature rather than creation *ex nihilo*. 3) Even though the original creation of the universe might have occurred long before the six days of Genesis, formative activity would have occurred within eight to ten thousand years ago in order to mesh with biblical history. 4) Scientific estimates of the age of the universe in billions of years are not averse to a literal understanding of the Bible. However, estimates that place life prior to the limits of biblical history are not consistent with a normal understanding of the Bible. Obviously a great deal hinges on how much weight one is willing to place on modern scientific dating, which is mostly radiometric or other methods correlated to evolutionary assumptions.

The history of modern scientific cosmology

While the discussion has been principally concerned with what the Bible says about the origin of the universe, it is important to know how this information fits with modern theoretical (scientific) cosmology, since any biblical theory that is seriously at odds with sound scientific observation would likely be problematic.

From the time of Aristotle (c. 300 B.C.) to the early 19th century the secular view of the universe was that it is infinite and eternal. This was very convenient, since an eternal universe requires no explanation of its origin. However, this theory posed problems. If the universe were infinite in all directions there should be stars visible at every point in the sky (at some distance), and if it were eternal, there would have been time for the light from all those stars to reach the earth. Therefore, if the universe were infinite and eternal, the night sky should be bright. Since the night sky is not bright, it is apparent that the universe could not be infinite and eternal. This realization in the early 1900s led to another view called "the steady state theory." The steady state theory said that the universe is eternal but stars are being born and dying in a perpetual cycle. This theory accounted for why the night sky is not bright, since stars eventually die out, and it required no Creator and thus fit with purely naturalistic assumptions. The problem with this theory turned out to be the second law of thermodynamics, which implies that over time in any physical system there is an increase of entropy (spent, or dissipated energy, which has no potential to do useful work). If the universe were eternal, then it would have had eternity for the useful energy level to reach zero; thus, the universe would be cold and completely dark, which is not the case. In spite of this difficulty, most physicists subscribed to some form of the steady state theory well into the 1950s and '60s, because this best fit with naturalistic (monistic, or antisupernatural) assumptions shared by most physicists at the time. In the early 1900s a growing body of evidence had begun to point to an expanding universe, but this evidence was largely ignored by science. In 1914 Vesto Slipher presented evidence that several nebulae were receding from the earth. In 1915 Einstein's General Theory of Relativity predicted an expanding universe. However, Einstein simply zeroed out this expansion with a purely arbitrary "cosmological constant." In 1922 Alexander Friedman, a Russian mathematician, predicted the expansion of the universe, and in 1929 Edwin Hubble proposed the law of red shifts, based on the observation that the light spectrum of a galaxy is more shifted toward the red (long wavelength) end of the spectrum the further that it is from the earth. The problem with an expanding universe is that it implied a definite age limit, since it could not have been expanding forever. (To see the problem, simply imagine a film of the universe's history run backwards; it could only shrink until its volume reached zero, which would be the point of its beginning.) Of course if the universe is not eternal, then it must have had a beginning. This is precisely what was penned in the opening verses of the book of Genesis. Scientists and natural philosophers recognized that a universe with a beginning was problematic for naturalism, scientism, and atheism. Obviously, if the universe had a beginning, it could not have created itself. So, the implication is clearly that something, or someone, outside of the universe, something eternal, must be responsible for the existence of the universe. Of course, the implications of an absolute beginning to the natural realm would be a stunning defeat for naturalism, a defeat that the naturalistic scientific community absolutely could not allow to happen. In fact, one of the classic arguments for the existence of God, the cosmological argument, said just that, that the existence of the universe implies the existence of something, or someone eternal, since something cannot come from nothing. As best they could, scientists tried to avoid the inflationary big bang view. However, in 1965 two Bell scientists measured a 3 degree Kelvin excess antenna temperature in all directions in which they pointed their microwave antenna. This figure coincided very closely with the predicted residual temperature that would have been left over from a cosmic big bang origin. Later evidence provided by the Cosmic Background Explorer (COBE) satellite in 1990-92, and the Wilkinson Microwave Anistrophy Probe (WMAP) have confirmed even more closely the theoretical predictions of a hot big bang origin of the universe. Since the mid-1960s naturalistic scientists have found themselves in a dilemma. They cannot, under any circumstance, acknowledge an absolute beginning of the universe, yet all the available evidence points to the fact that the universe had a beginning. They have been left with only one alternative: to continue to argue that some natural process is eternal, and therefore no supernatural cause is required. Of course the perceptive reader will recognize that this discussion crossed over from science to philosophy long ago. The fact that scientific cosmology has landed precisely in the same spot as the Bible has indeed been disturbing to naturalistic scientists and philosophers, most of whom are atheists and have an obvious interest in the issue far beyond the bounds of science. Since an absolute origin is highly problematic for purely naturalistic thinkers, a number of theories have been put forth to try to get around the implications of a beginning of the universe. One theory has been the oscillation theory. This theory suggests that the universe has gone through an infinite number of expansions and contractions (crunches), and is, after all, eternal, needing no explanation for its origin. Not surprisingly, the problem with the oscillation theory is the same as with the steady state theory. The second law of thermodynamics implies that no physical process can go on forever; it will eventually "wind down." Two other problems with this theory are that the universe doesn't seem to have enough mass to contract, and if it did, it is believed that its low mechanical efficiency would not likely result in a subsequent re-expansion. More recently the Hartle-Hawking model suggests that some eternal phenomenon was in place prior to the emergence of the present physical laws, and this phenomenon accounts for the origin of the universe. Stephen Hawking calls this phenomenon "imaginary time"; and as we will see, it is quite appropriately named. Given imaginary time, Hawking hypothesizes that the universe could have emerged out of nothing, all by itself, with no need for a Creator. In his book, *The Universe in a Nutshell* (Bantum Books, 2001), Hawking assures his readers that imaginary time does exist (see chapter four). This assertion has confused many people, including some scientists who simply assume that Hawking would not make such a statement if it were not provable, yet that is exactly what he has done. One of the fundamental concepts of big bang physics is that no scientific statements can be made about any-thing prior to time zero. Why? — Because one cannot make any scientific statements about anything prior to the existence of the present physical laws. So, how does Hawking know that imagi-nary time exists? In the first three chapters of *The Universe in a Nutshell* he delicately weaves an assumption into his discussion; that assumption is that science demands a natural (*i.e.,* non-supernatural) explanation for everything. (This is, of course, the bedrock of all natural philosophy.) Given the compelling evidence for an inflationary big bang origin of the universe, any natural explanation would require a quantum event, since the universe would have been very small when it emerged from nothing, and since quantum events require time, Hawking hypothesizes that some kind of time must have existed (*i.e.,* imaginary time) before the emergence of real time (which began at creation). With this, Hawking proceeds to explain how the universe might have emerged out of nothing (that is, nothing other than imaginary time and quantum mechanics). The problem with this explanation is that this isn't science at all; it's just naturalistic philosophy in the guise of science. Hawking has done nothing more than a clever job of concealing his naturalistic assumptions and hoping the readers would get lost in so many details of post time-zero physics that they wouldn't notice it was all based upon a mere unproven, indeed unprovable assumption.

The present state of scientific cosmology is this: The universe, as we know it, as described by the laws of physics, had a beginning. That beginning encompasses everything we know, including: time, matter, energy, space, and the properties we call physical laws (which includes quantum mechanics and relativity, and any as yet undiscovered unification principles). Science can make no authoritative statements about what might have preceded the universe's creation, since such statements would have no basis in physical law. As far as theoretical cosmology is concerned, we have finally reached the end of the road. While scientists will undoubtedly continue to suggest what might have happened "if such and such were true," they cannot go back further than the moment of creation, actually a few moments after the creation when the properties we call physical laws originated. Therefore, science will never know any more about conditions prior to creation than it knows right now—which is absolutely nothing. This is a permanent limitation. Needless to say, some will undoubtedly claim to find a way to ascertain the unknowable starting conditions of the big bang, but such attempts must always be based upon assumptions, no matter how cleverly hidden. Science is simply at the end of the road, it can do no more than theorize, and confirm or deny, what might have happened after the moment of creation; any claim beyond that can only be an intellectual hoax in scientific garb. Having already seen that many in the scientific community have shown themselves willing to disregard fundamental physical laws in order to maintain their naturalistic assumptions, as is the case with both the steady state theory and later the oscillation theory, we shouldn't be surprised to hear assurances that they now know the initial starting conditions of the big bang—and that those initial conditions do not require anything supernatural (*i.e.*, God).

Review Questions

1. Define the following terms: creation *ex nihilo*, immediate creation, mediate creation.

2. Describe the pre-scientific view of creation.

3. What is a "reconciliation theory"?

4. Describe theistic evolution and discuss any biblical or theological problems.

5. What are the two forms of the day-age theory?

6. Describe progressive creationism and discuss any problems with that view.

7. Describe the literary view(s) of the creation story.

8. Describe the gap theory.

9. Discuss any problems with the gap theory.

10. Describe the recent creation theory and discuss the evidence used to support the view.

11. Describe the three basic problems with recent creationism.

12 Describe the preformative view of creation and discuss any problems associated with the view.

13. Explain the usage and relationship between the Hebrew words *bara'* and `*asah*

14. What do we learn about ultimate origins (*ex nihilo* creation) from an examination of the creation account in the first chapter of Genesis?

15. Has modern science been able to explain creation without the need for a Creator? Explain.

Angels

Angels

The word "angel" appears over two hundred and eighty times in the English Bible (AV). The principal words from which it is translated are: *malak* (Hebrew), and *angelos* (Greek) — both meaning, "messenger." While it can refer to any messenger, it is most frequently used of spirit beings of various classes who are intelligent and powerful non-human creatures (Heb. 1:13-14), some of which inhabit Heaven, the place of God's throne, and others of which inhabit the physical universe (Rev. 12:12). They are referred to as: "sons of God" (Job 1:6 cf. 38:7), "watchers" (Dan. 4:13,17,23), "holy ones" (Ps. 89:7), "sons of the mighty" (Ps. 89:6), God's "host" (Gen. 32:1-2), "ministering spirits" (Heb. 1:14), "princes" (Dan. 10:13), "principalities and powers" (Eph. 6:12), and by individual names (Dan. 9:21; 10:21; 12:1).

The nature and appearance of angels

Angels are created beings (Ps. 148:1-5) that were present before the earth was formed (Job 38:1-7); however, they do not predate the original creation *ex nihilo*, since they are not eternal. Like us, they are personal beings. They are intelligent, they engage in worship, and they rejoice and praise God. They are wholly distinct from men (Heb. 2:6-7; 12:22-23). Angels are not born, and do not marry or procreate (Mt. 22:30), neither are they subject to death (Lk. 20:35-36). When appearing to men, they usually appear in human form (Gen. 18:2; Rev. 21:17 cf. Deut. 2:11). However, in Heaven they may appear differently (Rev. 4:6-9). In the Bible angels always appear in masculine form, and sometimes (if not always) are youthful in appearance (Rev. 16:5). On occasion they appear in such a way as to indicate their supernatural status (Mt. 28:3-4; Acts 6:12). Angels are highly intelligent (2 Sam. 14:17,20) and possess supernatural power, though both their power and intelligence is finite (Mt. 24:36; 2 Pt. 2:11). They are able to transport themselves quickly (Dan. 9:21), though they can be hindered (Dan. 10:1-21, esp. v.13), and they have the ability to appear suddenly (Lk. 2:13-14; Acts 1:10).

The moral character of angels

The Bible refers to both elect (holy) angels (Mk. 8:38; 1 Tim. 5:21), and to fallen angels, or "angels that sinned" (2 Pt. 2:4). It is often stated that the angels were created holy, and that some sinned. However, that view is problematic, since holiness is a positive quality rather than the mere absence of sin. Adam was not created holy, but he was created without sin. Had he obeyed God, he would have become holy, but instead he disobeyed and became sinful. Given that angels as well as men are free moral agents responsible for their choices, it is apparent that angels, like Adam, were created sinless and became either holy or unholy by virtue of their choice of obedience or disobedience to God (2 Pt. 2:4). Angels, having been individually created, do not comprise a race; therefore there is no transmission of sin from one angel to another. The only way that one angel's sin could affect another is through influence.

The classes, number, and organization of angels

The Bible refers to only two classes of angels: seraphim (Isa. 6:2, mentioned only in this passage) and cherubim (Gen. 3:24; Ezek. 10:1-22; 28:14). However, we are unable to determine from scripture what this distinction means, and there is no particular reason why there could not be any number of classes of angels, all or some with distinct attributes and functions. The angels are virtually innumerable (Rev. 5:11), and both the holy and the unholy angels are organized into hierarchies (Rev. 9:11; 12:7; Eph. 6:11-12). The Bible refers to "archangels" (*i.e.*, chief angels, cf. 1 Thess. 4:16; Jude 9) and to "chief princes" (Dan. 10:13), and indicates that some are closer to the throne of God (Lk. 1:19); there are also differences of rank among fallen angels (Jude 8-9).

The function of holy angels

Angels are engaged in various ministries both to God and man. They praise God (Ps. 148:1-2; Rev. 5:11-14) and serve him (Ps. 103:20), and at least some appear before him at certain times (Job 1:6; 2:1). The angels observe earthly affairs (Dan. 4:13; 1 Cor. 4:9) and serve as ministering spirits to the elect (Heb. 1:13-14). On occasion they bring answers to prayer (Dan. 9:21-23; Acts 12:5-7), aid believers in their ministries (Acts 8:26), offer encouragement in times of danger (Acts 27:22-24), protect and preserve the saints (Acts 5:19; 12:7-10), transport believers after death (Lk. 16:22), and they will gather the saints at the second coming (Mt. 24:31), and presumably they will be involved in gathering the saints at the rapture of the Church (1 Thess. 4:13-18, note v.16). With respect to the unrighteous, angels inflict judgment (Acts 12:23; Rev. 16:1-22), they will gather the unrighteous for punishment at the second coming of Christ (Mt. 13:39-40), and they will bind Satan and confine him in the Abyss at the close of the present age (Rev. 20:1-2).

The function of unholy angels

Unholy angels oppose the work of God, God's holy angels (Dan. 10:13), and his people (Eph. 6:12), and they support the work of Satan (Rev. 12:7). Demons appear to be a subgroup of fallen angels that at times possess (take control) of men and animals.

Satan

The existence of Satan, God's chief opponent, is taught in the Old Testament (Genesis, 1 Chronicles, Job, Psalms, Isaiah, Ezekiel, and Zechariah), and by every New Testament writer. Jesus referred to Satan on numerous occasions. He is called by various names, including: "Satan," meaning "adversary" (52 times), "the Devil," meaning "slanderer" (35 times), "the Evil One" (Eph. 6:12), "the Serpent" (Rev. 12:9), "the Dragon" (Rev. 12:9,12), "the Tempter" (Mt. 4:3), "Beelzebub," and "the Prince of Demons" (Mt. 12:24 cf. v.26). The name "Lucifer" found in the AV at Isaiah 14:12 is unlikely to be a personal name and should be translated "morning star," or "bright one." Nonetheless, students of the Bible find it convenient to refer to Satan by this name, especially when making reference to him prior to his fall.

If Ezekiel 28:14 refers to Satan, as seems to be the case, he is there classified as "the anointed cherub that covers," and possibly of greater rank than any of the other angels. He fell through pride (Isa. 14:12-14; 1 Tim. 3:6), and thus sin entered into the creation. As a result, he became the enemy of God and the adversary of God's people (Mt. 13:24-43; 1 Pt. 5:8). Jesus characterized Satan as "a murderer" and "a liar" (Jn. 8:44), and the Apostle John referred to him as a confirmed sinner (1 Jn. 3:8, cf. Jn. 8:44). Satan's life can be divided into six periods: on the "holy mountain" in the angelic governance of the creation (Ezek. 28:14); in the heavenlies, *i.e.*, in the physical universe (from his fall to his imprisonment at Christ's return, Eph. 6:11-12); confinement to the earth (during the second half of the tribulation period, cf. Rev. 12:9); confinement in the Abyss (during most of the millennial portion of the kingdom of Christ on earth, cf. Rev. 20:1-3); a brief period on earth near the close of the millennium (Rev. 20:1-3); and finally, eternity in the Lake of Fire (Rev. 20:10). As a creature Satan is a finite being. Though he is powerful, his power is limited by the cooperation given to him (Jam. 4:7), and by God (Job 1:12; 2 Cor. 12:7; 2 Tim. 2:26). Thus, as seen in the case of Job, there are some things that Satan can only do by divine permission.

Demons and demon possession

In the "enlightened" modern age in which we live, demonism is often dismissed as primitive religious belief, and thus there are three theories in addition to the biblical view that need to be considered.

The mythical theory

The mythical theory claims that accounts of demon possession in the Bible are symbolic (not literally true), and that they depict in symbolic terms our Lord's triumph over evil. Obviously such an explanation is not consistent with the verbal inspiration of scripture, or its normal/objective interpretation.

The accommodation theory

The accommodation theory suggests that when Christ and the disciples referred to demons it was not because they believed that such things really existed, but because their contemporaries believed in demons, and thus they accommodated their language to those beliefs. (The swine in the story of Matthew 8:28-34 must have been very accommodating too!)

The psychological theory

According to the psychological theory, emotionally unstable people who believed in demons fancied that they were demon possessed and acted accordingly. Then, believing that Jesus had power over demons, they believed that they were delivered at his command. (Need we mention the swine again?)

The biblical view

Obviously all three of the views above are inconsistent with the verbal inspiration of scripture. The biblical view is that demons are real, personal, malevolent spirit beings. Though it does not seem to be their chief work, demons do have the power to control people, either partially or completely eclipsing the human will under certain circumstances. The reason for the onset of demon possession is not stated in scripture, but it is at least possible that some individuals have opened the door to demon possession by their personal choices, or interest in the occult or false religion (which the Bible views as demonic, cf. 1 Cor. 10:20-21; 1 Tim. 4:1; Rev. 9:20). While it is difficult to know how much of this description might be characteristic of demon possession in general, the demon possessed man of Gadara (Mt. 8:28-34, cf. Mk. 5:1-20 and Lk 8:26-40) displayed these qualities: 1) wildness, violence, and persistent antisocial behavior (Mt. 8:28; Mk. 5:4); 2) a preference for nudity (Lk. 8:27); 3) avoidance of community

(Lk. 8:27, 29); 4) possibly a preoccupation with death (Lk. 8:27); and, 5) self-mutilation (Mk. 5:5).

It is important to recognize that Jesus did not "exorcise" demons; he simply commanded them to come out. Exorcism makes use of conjurations, incantations, or religious or magical ceremonies in an effort to expel demons (Merrill Unger, *Biblical Demonology*, Scripture Press, 1963, p.101). In other words, in exorcism the power is assumed to reside in the right formula or ceremony. However, in Jesus' case, and in the case of the apostles, the power was divine authority (Mt. 10:1 — note that the word "power" (AV) is the Greek word *exousia*, which should be translated "authority"). There is no evidence that believers today are given the authority to expel demons, though we can, and should pray for people we believe may be under demonic influence or control.

Review Questions

1. Describe the nature of angels.

2. With respect to moral character, what are the two types of angels?

3. What are the two classes of angels mentioned in scripture?

4. Describe the functions of holy angels.

5. What are some of the names applied to Satan? What do those names tell us about Satan?

6. What are the six periods of Satan's existence?

7. Describe three incorrect theories of demon possession.

8. Discuss the biblical view of demon possession.

The Church

The Church

The word "church" is translated from the Greek word *ekklēsia*, which means "congregation." In the New Testament, this becomes a designation for the invisible, universal "Body of Christ," of which all believers in this age are a part. The term is also used to designate a local congregation. In this volume "Church" (uppercase) refers to the Body of Christ, whereas "church" refers to the visible church.

The universal (invisible) Church

The universal Church is composed of all redeemed people living between Pentecost (A.D. 33) and the removal of the Church from the earth at the rapture (1 Thess. 4:13-17). (Reformed theologians differ on the definition of the Church; they view the Church as all redeemed people.) The Church is simply another name for "the Body of Christ" (Col. 1:18,24), and Spirit baptism is the operation that places a believer into that body (1 Cor. 12:13). Since Spirit baptism did not begin until Pentecost, A.D. 33, the Church could not have existed prior to that time. There are numerous reasons for believing that Pentecost A.D. 33 marks the beginning of the Church.

1) The disciples recognized that Pentecost marked the beginning of the Church (Acts 11:15-16).

2) Jesus indicated that the Church was a future reality from the standpoint of his earthly ministry (Mt. 16:18, note the future tense, "I *will build* my Church").

3) The Church age is parenthetical to God's program for Israel. This can be seen from the complete absence of any mention of the Church, or the Church age in the Old Tes-

tament. Looking from the Old Testament perspective, one would never know that the Church (or the Church age) would exist. The Old Testament discusses in great detail the coming of Messiah, the day of the LORD, and the establishment of the kingdom of God, without so much as a hint of the future existence of the Church age (Eph. 3:1-10). For example, consider Isaiah 61:1-3, where Isaiah prophesied elements of the first advent of Christ (vv. 1-2a) and of the second advent (vv. 2b-3) in the same sentence, without so much as a hint of the intervening Church age. Consider also Daniel 9:24-27, in which the angel Gabriel revealed to Daniel the outline of God's prophetic program for Israel from the decree to restore Jerusalem in 444 B.C. to the end of the tribulation period, with no hint of the Church or the Church age. Israel and the Church are distinct entities, and this is seen nowhere more clearly than in Paul's discussion of this subject in Romans 11:11-32. Sadly, Paul's warning to the church at Rome not to become haughty in thinking that the Church has replaced Israel in the divine program has gone unheeded, and this is precisely what has happened. In the second century the church had become predominately Gentile, Jerusalem had been destroyed in A.D. 70 and the Jewish people scattered. To many Christians it no longer seemed feasible that God would fulfill his promises to Israel since Israel had ceased to exist as a nation; therefore, ignoring the clear revelation of God in scripture, they reasoned that it must be God's intention to fulfill those promises to the Church. Of course, many of the promises God made to Israel are ethnic and geopolitical in nature, and could not be fulfilled to the Church in a literal fashion; thus, interpreters began to spiritualize (allegorize) those promises; that is to say, they began interpreting the promises non-literally, applying them to the Church. This resulted in a great distortion of scripture and a redefining of the Church as a continuation of the one people of God, rather than as a parenthetic entity, as indicated by Paul (Rom. 11:11-32). This shift in the defining of the Church as a continuation of Israel in spiritual form has resulted in great theological error. For example, viewing the Church as a continuation of, or replacement for Israel is the basis for replacement theology, realized eschatology, covenant theology, infant baptism, and many other errors.

It is of paramount importance for the student of the Bible to know that Israel and the Church are distinct entities, and that the Church does not predate Pentecost, A.D. 33. Just as membership in the Church had a beginning at Pentecost, that membership will be closed at the rapture when Christ comes to claim his bride, the Church (Mt. 24:36-25:30; I Cor. 15:51-53; 1 Thess. 4:13-17). Thus, the extent of the Church age is from Pentecost A.D. 33 to the rapture. (See the next chapter for a discussion of the rapture of the Church.)

The local (visible) church

Local churches are visible manifestations of the one universal Church. Of course, it is always the case that unsaved people will attach themselves to the local church, and it is also true that local churches have a tendency to apostatize over time (usually within a few generations); thus we can expect in any local church to have a mixture of saved and lost people. In cases where the local church apostasy is fairly complete, there may be few, if any, saved people.

The mission of the local church

The mission of the local church is the same as that of the universal Church: the twofold purpose of evangelism and discipleship (edification) of believers. That purpose was clearly stated by Christ in the great commission he gave prior to his departure (Mt. 28:19-20).

The resources of the local church

God has given the local church resources by which to accomplish its mission. Those resources include: the scriptures, leadership, spiritual gifts, and discipline.

Local church leadership

Biblically, local church leadership is to be exercised through three primary avenues: elders, deacons, and the congregational body. An imbalance or failure in any one of these areas results in dysfunction within the local church. In the discussion that follows we are not defining the roles in accordance with the practices of any particular denomination, but as defined in scripture.

a. Elders (the presbytery)

With respect to the local church, the highest spiritual authority outside of Christ and his apostles resides in the elders of the local congregations. In the beginning, an apostle or the representative of an apostle often appointed elders. However, apostolic appointment was a practical consideration, not a requirement. There were occasions where churches sprang up apart from apostolic ministry and appointed their own leadership, and there is no indication from the New Testament that the apostles challenged the validity of such churches or their leadership. Thus, we do not find the Bible teaching either apostolic succession or any form of succession of spiritual authority, though under ordinary circumstances it is obvious why that would be the best method. We must bear in mind that Paul's direction to Timothy that he appoint elders in the churches under his charge should not be taken as normative, for these were newly planted churches which in their infancy lacked the ability to select qualified leaders. Much has been made over ordination in the past nineteen hundred years, both Roman Catholic and Protestant, and while the commissioning of leaders is vitally important, from a biblical perspective ordination conveys no powers or prerogatives not vested within the local body. Additionally, in the early churches the eldership in each congregation was to be constituted by multiple elders of equal authority, though perhaps not of equal giftedness or influence.

Paul laid out the qualifications for elders to Timothy (1 Tim. 3:1-7) and to Titus (Tit. 1:5-9). We must be careful not to confuse elders with deacons, as these are distinct offices, each with its own qualifications. Elders occupy the highest office in the local church, and deacons serve as ministry extenders under the general oversight of the elders.

Qualifications of elders

Paul gives the following qualifications for elders (also called "bishops," or "overseers ").

1. It should be observed that the New Testament makes no provision for the appointment of female elders. This is not simply a first century cultural phenomenon as is sometimes suggested. Paul stated in 1 Timothy 2:9-15 that the woman is not to exercise authority over the man because of the dignity imparted to the man by virtue of the order of creation (*i.e.*, that man as the head of the race was created first, and hence that the woman was created to serve in a support capacity, rather than a leadership capacity over the man). The fact that Paul points to the order of the creation of the first man and woman makes it clear that his reason is universal and transcultural, and thus binding in every culture and time. (Note also that having just made that point, Paul, in giving the qualifications of elders, uses only the masculine pronouns, cf. 1 Tim. 3:1-7.)

2. They are to be monogamous (1 Tim. 3:2).

3. They are to be temperate (not given to drunkenness), prudent, respectable, and hospitable (1 Tim. 3:2).

4. They must hold fast to the word in their own personal lives, and be able to teach and exhort in sound doctrine, and to refute error (1 Tim. 3:2; Tit. 1:9).

5. They should not have an addiction to alcohol (1 Tim. 3:3). (We may assume this would apply to other addictions as well.)

The Church 329

6. They are not to be quarrelsome, and self-willed, but gentle and uncontentious (1 Tim. 3:3; Tit. 1:7).

7. They are not to be materialistic (1Tim 3:3).

8. They must be good managers of their own households, with believing children. (1 Tim. 3:4; Titus 1:6).

9. They should not be new to the faith (1 Tim. 3:6).

10. They must have a good reputation outside the church (1 Tim. 3:7).

b. Deacons (and deaconesses)

The word "deacon" comes from the Greek *diakonos*, meaning, "servant." This office was introduced into the early church in order to free the elders from more mundane tasks that did not require a high level of spiritual knowledge and insight or teaching ability. That is not to say that individual deacons did not possess those abilities, only that such was not a requirement for this office. Many vocations benefit from partnerships between those who are highly qualified and helpers with lesser qualifications so that services can be extended to a larger group of people. The deacons were, in a sense, "leadership extenders," in that their service to the local church allowed the limited number of elders to serve a larger congregation than would otherwise be possible. This was a very broad category of service, and how, and at what level an individual deacon might be used would vary according to the needs of the church, the nature of the ministry, and the deacon's individual capability. Stephen is an example of a high-functioning deacon in the Jerusalem Church (Acts. 6:1-15, esp. vv.5, 8-15).

Qualifications of deacons

1. 1 Timothy 3:11 seems to allow for women to serve in this role, though in view of Paul's prior teaching regarding women not exercising authority over men in the church

(1 Tim. 2:9-15), it seems likely the role of deaconess would be focused on either service in general to the local body, or ministry to and discipleship of other women.

2. They must be dignified and forthright, not "double tongued" (1 Tim. 3:8).

3. They must not be addicted to wine, or materialistic (1 Tim. 3:8).

4. They must hold fast to the faith, not only outwardly, but also inwardly, *i.e.*, "with a clear conscience" (1 Tim. 3:9).

5. They should be proven first, by serving on a trial basis (1 Tim. 3:10).

6. They should be above reproach, *i.e.*, of good reputation (1 Tim. 3:10).

7. Women who serve should be dignified, not gossips, temperate, and faithful in all things (1 Tim. 3:11).

8. Men should be monogamous, and good managers of their households and children (1 Tim. 3:12).

In comparing the qualifications of elders and deacons, it is apparent that both offices have the same personal and moral qualifications. The difference is that an elder must be able to teach, exhort, and to refute error; and that is no small distinction, since it presumes considerable spiritual development, knowledge of the truth, and wisdom on the part of the candidate for elder, which can only be acquired over time. Thus, it is evident why an elder should not be a new Christian.

Spiritual gifts

Spiritual gifts were discussed under the work of the Holy Spirit. However, it should be noted that the gifts given by the Holy Spirit in this age (beginning at Pentecost), although exercised by individuals, are actually gifts to the Church as a whole (1 Cor. 12:1-31, esp. v. 28); they are given for the Church's edification (1 Cor. 12:4-27). Although similar abilities were occasionally given in the Old Testament, such manifestations of the Spirit of God there were highly selective, not universal as in the Church where every believer possesses some gift; and unlike gifts in the present age, special supernatural endowments of ability in the Old Testament were not permanent.

Ordinances

Ordinances refer to commands that the Church is to carry out. In the broader sense we could view evangelism, edification, and protection of the Body of Christ (including discipline) and symbolic observances (water baptism and the Lord's supper) as ordinances. The two symbolic observances that Christ commanded the Church to keep are: the Lord's supper (Mt. 26:17-30; Mk. 14:22-25; Lk. 22:14-22 cf. 1 Cor. 11:17-34), and water baptism (Mt. 28:19-20). In these observances Christ's sacrifice is remembered (the Lord's supper); and identification with him in his death, burial, and resurrection are acknowledged publicly (water baptism). It is important to understand that these observances are purely symbolic; they neither convey grace, nor do they change the participant in any way other than to provide an opportunity for obedience. Water baptism, though an important act of obedience (both on the part of the church and the new believer) is not a requirement for salvation. [1 Peter 3:21 refers not to the efficacy of water baptism but the work of Christ, of which baptism is symbolic. Acts 2:38 does not imply that baptism results in the forgiveness of sins, but rather in this case repentance and baptism are euphemistic for "faith." Note that the repentant thief on the cross was assured of his salvation even though he had no opportunity to be baptized (Lk. 23:39-43).]

Discipline

The local church in the New Testament was a body under discipline. Being under discipline is the essence of discipleship. In associating with a local church, an individual placed himself or herself under the authority of that local body, to be guided and discipled. Obviously such power can, and undoubtedly was abused. Nevertheless, without discipline the local church could not carry out the great commission of making disciples (Mt. 28:19-20); and as an institution, it could not have survived. The New Testament churches exercised discipline at several levels. The primary level of discipline was instruction (1 Tim. 4:1-16; 6:2; 2 Tim. 4:2). At this level the local church was responsible for imparting the fundamental truths of the faith, and exhorting its members to adhere to truth, both in principle and in practice. When instruction with exhortation failed, the next level of discipline was rebuke. Rebuke involved a verbal warning to a member, or group, that they were not adhering to the faith. Although there is little information on how this was actually practiced, it seems safe to assume that there were also levels of rebuke befitting the circumstances. Paul directed Timothy to use rebuke judiciously in accordance with the circumstances (1 Tim. 5:1-2,20; 2 Tim. 4:2). The highest level of discipline in the local church was excommunication (Mt. 18:15-17). This level of discipline was reserved only for serious offenses where lesser forms of discipline had failed. Of course excommunication has no bearing on a person's salvation, only on their participation in the fellowship and function of the local church (2 Thess. 3:6-7,14). Those excluded were not only cut off from the fellowship of the local congregation and regarded as unbelievers (for so they acted), they were also severed from the close personal fellowship of individual believers. It is important to understand that this most extreme level of church discipline was not intended as punishment, for punishment is not a legitimate function of the local church; rather, it was intended to prompt repentance and restoration of the offender to the fellowship of the local church (1 Cor. 5:1-13 cf. 2 Cor. 2:1-11).

The Church in prophecy

The Church, which began at Pentecost, is composed of both Jews and Gentiles, but it should not be confused with Israel, nor should the promises God made to the Church be confused with the promises previously made to Israel. The promises God made to the Jewish nation included a land and nation forever, with Messiah, David's Son, ruling on the throne, *i.e.,* a theocratic kingdom on earth (Ps. 89:19-37, esp. vv. 34-37; Isa. 9:6-7). God also promised Israel spiritual redemption and regeneration, both individually and nationally. The fountainhead of those promises is the Abrahamic covenant (Gen. 12:1-3,6-7; 13:14-17; 15:1-21; 17:1-14; 22:15-18); and those promises were further expanded in the Palestinian covenant (Deut. 29:1-30:20), the Davidic covenant (2 Sam. 7:12-17), and the New covenant (Jer. 31:31-34), as well as numerous other prophetic passages in the Old Testament (Ps. 98:1-9; Isa. 11:1-12:6; 25:1-12; 32:1-8; 35:1-10; 40:3-11; 66:1-24; Jer. 33:10-26). Paul stated quite emphatically in Romans 11:11-32 that God still intends to fulfill those promises, for as Paul said concerning those promises, "...the gifts and the calling of God are irrevocable" (v.29, NASB). Thus, it should be apparent that Israel and the Church are distinct entities. The Church's expectation concerning the future is that the redeemed of the Church age will be raptured (caught away) from the earth prior to the day of God's wrath (the day of the LORD) which is to come upon the earth prior to Christ's second coming (1 Thess. 4:13-17; 1 Cor. 15:51-53); and the Church-age saints will be taken to Heaven (Jn.14:1-3) to stand before the judgment seat of Christ (1 Cor. 3:10-15) from which they will return with Christ (at the conclusion of the tribulation period) as his bride, to enter the millennial kingdom on earth in which God will begin to fulfill all of the promises made to a purified and redeemed nation of Israel (Rev. 20:4-6). At the conclusion of the millennium, the present heavens and earth will be destroyed and the lost of all the ages will receive their final judgment (Rev. 20:10-15). After that judgment the new heavens and earth will appear, and the New Jerusalem, the heavenly city, will descend to the earth (Rev. 21:1-22:5); this marks the beginning of the eternal phase of the kingdom. In God's eternal kingdom, all of the promises he made to both Israel and the Church will be fulfilled.

Review Questions

1. What is another name for the universal Church?

2. When did the Church begin?

3. At what point will the Church age come to a conclusion?

4. What is the mission of the local church?

5. What are resources of the local church?

6. Describe the New Testament pattern of local church leadership.

7. Discuss the differences in the functions of elders and deacons.

8. Briefly discuss discipline in the local church.

9. Briefly discuss the distinction between the Church and Israel, and why this distinction is important.

10. What events await the Church in the future?

11. In what role(s) could you see yourself functioning in a local church? For example: as a pastor, youth leader, group teacher, specialized ministry, support role, administration, *etc.*

The Future

The Future

General introduction

From what we know of the apostles' teaching from the New Testament, they accepted at face value the Old Testament promises of a coming theocratic kingdom on earth, ruled by Messiah. It will be through the Messiah and his kingdom that God will fulfill the promises he made to Abraham and to Abraham's descendants. In the gospels Jesus taught that the kingdom was "at hand" and "in your midst" (Mt. 4:17; 10:7; Lk. 17:20-21); when debating with the Pharisees, he told them that the kingdom of God had overtaken them (Mt. 12:28). Although such statements indicated only the nearness (imminence) of the kingdom, not its actual inauguration (with the King seated upon the throne), some misinterpret them to mean that the theocratic kingdom promised in the Old Testament is not to be a physical kingdom, but a spiritual (immaterial) kingdom. However, this view would place the New Testament into the position of contradicting the clear teaching of a large part of the Old Testament, and as a result it does great damage to both the Old and New Testaments. Those who hold to such a view are then forced, for consistency's sake, to revise the teaching of the Old Testament (*via* allegorization) in order to reconcile it with what they misunderstand Jesus' statements in the New Testament to mean. But, Jesus never said that the kingdom would not be a literal, physical kingdom; he simply said that the work of spiritual renewal (a prerequisite necessary for the manifestation of the visible kingdom) had already begun with his own ministry; hence, the only thing that hindered the kingdom program was the response of those who heard the message of the gospel. That being the case, the kingdom was, quite literally, "at hand," or "upon them." Obviously unregenerated people could not inherit the kingdom of God, so it was necessary for a preparatory work of reconciliation to precede its inauguration. This initial preparatory work was predicted in the Old Testament (Isa.

44:1-5, 21-23; Jer. 3:15; 23:14-18; 31:1, 27-34; Ezek. 11:19-20; 20:1-44; 36:25-32; 37:11-14, 21-28; Hos. 6:1-3; 14:4-8; Joel 2:12-17, 28-32; Mic. 7:18-20; Zech. 13:7-9); thus, there is no inconsistency between what the Old and New Testaments actually (literally) say about the nature of the kingdom. Misunderstanding what Jesus meant in saying that the kingdom is "at hand" has resulted in a great deal of confusion about the nature of the kingdom. The mistake made by some seems to be in confusing "the part" (the initial preparatory spiritual basis—which is what Christ's ministry accomplished), with "the whole" (the full expression of the kingdom in its outward visible and material form when Christ returns). While some might reason that a spiritual kingdom would be superior, that is simply not true. First, such a view is clearly anti-cosmic (viewing the material creation as inferior to the spiritual) and this doesn't fit with the biblical view of the material world. Second, since the visible manifestation of the kingdom is linked to the progress of redemption, the final physical expression of the kingdom represents nothing less than the zenith of God's work of redemption and renewal (both of mankind and of creation). Christian theology has long suffered under the false notion that the material creation is inferior to the spiritual realm. This concept, which was derived from Greek philosophy (primarily Platonism), has hampered biblical interpretation for almost nineteen hundred years, and although it has been massaged into the theology of virtually every commentary ever written, it is long past time to recognize this for what it is: pagan thought in Christian garb. While the Bible recognizes that the world has been under the curse of sin since the time of the fall, the world as it came from the hands of the Creator was pronounced by him to be "very good" (Gen. 1:31); and it will be so again once the work of redemption is completed (Rom. 8:18-25). We must not forget that sin and evil have affected the spiritual realm as well as the material realm (Satan and the fallen angels are evil, spirit beings; and fallen men have as part of their nature a fallen immaterial nature). Since it is only in the material realm that we can see the effects of evil, there is a tendency to assume that the material realm is morally inferior to the spiritual; but the Bible does not support an anticosmic worldview. The failure of many of the church's leading thinkers down through history in assuming the moral inferiority of the material creation is the single greatest source of confusion over the meaning of future prophecy. An anti-cosmic presupposition leads invariably to the denial of the Bible's clear teaching of a future, visible kingdom of God on earth, and in turn has resulted in the allegorization of major portions of the Bible, obscuring biblical truth in other areas as well.

Jesus did say that the kingdom was "at hand," but he also confirmed the Old Testament understanding that the full expression of the kingdom is to be a literal kingdom as prophesied in the Old Testament (Mt. 25:31-46). Consequently, since Jesus did not begin his reign during the time of his first advent, the apostles and the early church expected him to return and inaugurate his kingdom rule at some time in the future. Even the prayer Jesus taught his disciples to pray viewed the kingdom not as present, but as a future reality (Mt. 6:10). The book of Revelation, the final word of the New Testament, confirms that the concept of the kingdom presented in the New Testament is the same as that prophesied in the Old Testament. Thus, while the details concerning the kingdom were progressively revealed as scripture was recorded, the basic concept of a literal, visible kingdom is uniformly taught from Genesis to Revelation. This view, that Christ will return to establish a visible, physical kingdom, is called "premillennialism."

The rise of allegorical eschatology

By the early second century A.D. it became popular to deny the normal/objective meaning of the Old and New Testament promises of a visible kingdom. There were several reasons for this. First, by the early second century the church and its leadership had come to be overwhelmingly Gentile. The late first century transition from a Jewish church to an overwhelmingly Gentile church had a profound impact on how Christians viewed their place in God's revealed plan, and indeed how they viewed the plan itself. The Old Testament writers, Christ, and the apostles, all taught that the coming kingdom was to center on a redeemed nation of Jews (Israel), with the Gentiles being blessed too, but as secondary rather than primary beneficiaries of the promises of God to Abraham (Rom. 11:11-32). However, as the Church became almost entirely Gentile, it became unpopular for Gentile Christians to think of the Jews as the primary beneficiaries of the promises of God. After all, hadn't the Jews rejected their Messiah? And didn't God allow the Jewish nation to be destroyed by the Romans in A.D. 70? And weren't the Jews, for the most part, hostile to the gospel? Surely, they reasoned, God did not still intend to fulfill his promises to the Jews. This rationalization resulted in an error that has dogged the church even to the present day. It is the error of "replacement theology." Replacement theology views the Church as having replaced Israel in the kingdom program. Of course the Bible nowhere teaches that the Church replaces Israel. Quite the contrary, the Church is viewed as a distinct instrument that God will use to provoke Israel to faith in their Messiah and bring about Israel's conversion so that the promises to them can be fulfilled (Rom. 11:1-31). Nevertheless, we have been saddled with this erroneous teaching for almost nineteen hundred years. Replacement theology has been the view of the Greek Orthodox Church since the second century, and the view of the Roman Catholic Church since the fifth century, and from them it was passed to the reformation churches and into the mainstream of protestant Christianity where it remains to this day. Replacement theology sees no place for national Israel (in the form of a messianic Jewish kingdom) in the plan of God. Those who accept replacement theology generally interpret the Old Testament prophecies of future blessings to Israel as applying to the Church (spiritually). Thus, Catholic and Reformed Christianity routinely engages in the practice of allegorical interpretation (actually, interpolation) in which the promises made to Israel are interpreted to represent spiritual blessings to the Church.

Second, also coinciding with the rise of replacement theology in the early second century was a widespread heresy called "gnosticism." The gnostics believed that Jehovah ("Yahweh") is not the true, eternal God, but a created being who because of his ignorance of the true God, thinks himself to be God. The gnostics viewed the Old Testament as the record of a false religion (since it came from a false "God"); they also viewed the material world as an inferior realm to be escaped from, rather than the object of redemption as taught by Paul in Romans 8:18-21. (Some gnostics viewed the physical not only as inferior, but as intrinsically evil.) With such a view of the material world and of the Old Testament promises to Abraham and Israel, they naturally rejected the Bible's teaching of a future earthly kingdom of God. It appears that the gnostics were among the first (possibly the very first) within Christendom to hold to an entirely spiritual view of the kingdom of God. This view has come to be called "realized eschatology" (today it is generally referred to as "amillennialism," since it denies that there is to be a literal millennial kingdom). While the early church rejected most of the beliefs of the gnostics as heresy, the idea of a spiritualized kingdom gained considerable following in the early church. It was first adopted in the second century in the eastern (Greek Orthodox) churches where gnosticism was strongest. For a short time this resulted in the removal of the book of Revelation from the New Testament canon, since Revelation clearly presents the picture of an earthly, physical, premillennial kingdom. The Roman Catholic Church continued to be premillennial through the fourth century (albeit mostly a replacement form of premillennialism in which the kingdom promises are fulfilled to the Church). Replacement premillennialism can be seen as early as the writings of Justin Martyr, c. A.D. 140. It was Augustine (354-430 A.D.) who influenced the Roman Catholic Church to abandon premillennialism for an entirely spiritual view of the kingdom. Of course the Bible does not teach the amillennial view of the kingdom; so it became necessary for Augustine to revise the Bible's message in order to conform it to a spiritualized view of the kingdom, a task that he accomplished through the allegorical interpretation of future prophecy. The big problem for Augustine, and for all non-premillennialists, was (and still is) the book of Revelation. Both Revelation's message, and its place as the final word of the New Testament make it problematic for any non-premillennial view. Revelation was the last message of the New Testament to be written (c. A.D. 87-93), and when taken at face value it unequivocally communicates the same premillennial view of the kingdom as the Old Testament. It became obvious that in order to sustain amillennialism Revelation's premillennialism would have to be muted. After all, if the literal kingdom promised in the Old Testament somehow mutated into a spiritual kingdom in the gospels (as amillennialists suppose), one would have a difficult time explaining why Revelation, written long after Jesus' death (and by one of the gospel writers) unquestionably presents a premillennial view of the kingdom. To deal with this problem Augustine adopted an entirely allegorical view of Revelation. Largely as a result of Augustine's influence amillennialism took root in the Roman Catholic Church, and continues to be the predominate view of the modern-day church, both Catholic and Reformed. More recently, since the sixteenth century, an entire hermeneutical and theological system called "covenant theology" has evolved in order to bolster support for the allegorical view of future prophecy.

Dispensationalism stands in stark contrast to covenant theology in that it represents a return to a pre-replacement worldview and hermeneutic, and therefore accepts the biblical teaching of a literal, visible kingdom built upon a redeemed Israel in the future. The importance of understanding the differences between these views cannot be overstated; these views lead to entirely different understandings of the Church, the meaning of scripture, and the overall plan of God for the future.

Dispensationalists believe that the biblical writers unquestionably present a premillennial picture of the future. Not only does the Bible describe a coming visible kingdom of God on earth, it also describes a number of events that will take place in connection with the unfolding of that kingdom. Some of these events will occur before the rule of Christ is inaugurated, and some will happen afterward. (For a more complete presentation of premillennialism the reader may wish to consult *What the Bible Says About the Future*, by the author, or *Things to Come*, by J. Dwight Pentecost.) Some of the major events we will survey are (in the order they will occur): the regathering of the Jewish people to the land of Israel, the re-emergence of a post-Roman confederation of nations, the rapture of the Church into Heaven, the seven years of tribulation that will precede the inauguration of the kingdom rule of Christ on earth, the second coming of Christ to the earth, the resurrection of the righteous dead, the first phase of the kingdom (the millennium), the dissolution of the present heavens and earth, the resurrection of the unrighteous dead, the judgment of the unholy angels and unredeemed men, the renewal of the physical creation, and the second phase of the kingdom (eternity).

The regathering of Israel

The first major prophetic period of the future is the seven-year tribulation period. The tribulation will prepare the way for the return of Christ and the establishment of the kingdom of God on earth. Since the tribulation will begin with the making of a treaty between national Israel and a coalition of nations having a historic connection to Rome (Dan 9:24-27), it could not begin until Israel was re-established as a nation (which after almost nineteen hundred years, occurred in May of 1948). Naturally this involves at least a partial regathering of the Jewish people to their ancient homeland before the tribulation period begins. Even before the modern Zionist movement began, dispensational premillennialists were looking for the rebirth of Israel in fulfillment of biblical prophecy. Prior to the rebirth of the modern state of Israel, replacement theologians, both amillennial and postmillennial, rejected the idea that Israel would be reborn as literally predicted (cf. Isa. 11:11-16; Hos. 3:4-5; Jer. 31:30-31; Ezek. 37:1-29; Amos 9:8-15; Mic. 4:6-8). However, in 1948 Israel was reborn; this is the only occurrence in history in which a nation dispersed for almost two thousand years has returned to its native land to resume its ancient language and national identity. Amillennialists have claimed that these and other passages predicting a return were fulfilled long ago when the Jews returned from Babylonian captivity (in the sixth century B.C.); however, since many of these passages link the rebirth of Israel with an enduring (eternal) spiritual rebirth and the inauguration of the visible kingdom and personal rule of Messiah, it is apparent that the return from Babylonian captivity could not be the fulfillment of these prophecies. One of the most interesting prophecies of the regathering of Israel is found in Ezekiel 37:1-29. In the first part of this passage Ezekiel prophesied the rebirth of the Jewish nation after a long period of exile. He said that when Israel is regathered, it will no longer be a divided kingdom, as was the case with Israel and Judah; rather, it will be a kingdom united both politically and spiritually, with Jehovah dwelling in the midst of Israel, and his servant David (referring to the Davidic Messiah, *i.e.*, Christ) ruling as King.

The rapture of the Church

Scripture tells us that sometime during the seven years of tribulation preceding the inauguration of the kingdom, God will pour out wrath upon the world for its unbelief and rejection of the truth, and its persecution of the saints. This period of wrath is referred to in both the Old and New Testaments as "the day of the LORD." Since the Church is promised that it will not suffer the wrath of God (1 Thess 5:9), it is apparent that the Church must be removed from the earth prior to the beginning of the day of the LORD (1 Thess. 4:13-18; 1 Cor. 15:35-58). One problem we face in understanding the timing of the rapture is that we do not know at what point during the tribulation the day of the LORD begins. Some view all of the tribulation as the day of the LORD; consequently, they place the rapture of the Church prior to the beginning of the tribulation. This very popular view is called "pretribulationism." Other premillennialists view the day of the LORD as starting sometime during the tribulation period, either at the midpoint or sometime in the second half of the period. Our lack of ability to pinpoint the precise beginning of the day of the LORD has led to several views on the relative timing of the rapture; however, all dispensational (*i.e.*, non-replacement) premillennialists view the rapture as occurring prior to the time of God's wrath. Because of the lack of definitive evidence as to when the day of the LORD begins, we can only say with certainty that whenever the wrath begins, the Church will already be gone. Although it is natural to want to suggest ideas as to when the rapture might occur, we must be careful not to go beyond what the Bible clearly teaches. While the Bible does reveal some facts concerning the nature, and even the timing of the rapture, all views that attempt to place the rapture at a particular point in relation to the tribulation are speculative. Even though we do not know exactly when the rapture will occur, we do know that Christ's coming for the Church is imminent (Mt. 24:36-42); that is to say, it could happen at any time. This leaves a window in which the rapture could occur—anytime from the present, to the time that the day of the LORD begins. Scripture indicates the rapture will happen almost instantly (1 Thess. 4:13-17). It will involve the bodily resurrection of those who have died in Christ and the transformation of living believers. The Old Testament saints and those saved after the Church is removed will be resurrected at the beginning of the millennium (Rev. 20:4). The raptured saints in their glorified, eternal bodies will be taken to Heaven to appear before the judgment seat of Christ. Paul gives a sobering account of this judgment (sometimes referred to as, "the bema seat") in 1 Corinthians 3:10-17. It is not the purpose of this judgment to determine one's eternal destiny; everyone appearing at this judgment is redeemed, since only redeemed people will be raptured. The subject of this judgment is faithfulness, in order than each one might give an account of their stewardship of the grace of God since the time they believed in Christ. Each individual will be rewarded, or not, based upon what is revealed at this judgment. As Paul indicated (1 Cor. 3:10-17), there will be some who merit no reward, though they will be saved. It appears that the marriage of Christ to the Church will take place after this judgment is complete (cf. Rev. 19:7-9).

The tribulation

The tribulation will be a seven-year period of great distress that will precede the inauguration of the kingdom rule of Christ. The tribulation will involve natural disasters, wars, persecutions, and divine judgments. As a result of the distress of this period the Bible indicates that most of earth's population will perish before its conclusion at the second coming. The question arises as to why God would allow such horrible things to happen. The answer is that the tribulation represents the climax of man's rebellion against God, and the things that will happen are the result of that rebellion. During the tribulation God will purge the earth of rebellious men, and purify a people, both Jews and Gentiles, to enter the kingdom when Christ returns (Zech. 13:7-9).

The tribulation will begin with the making of a seven-year treaty between Israel and a Mediterranean confederation of nations having some historic connection to the ancient Roman Empire (Daniel 2 and 7; cf. 9:24-27). A leader will emerge from this confederation who in the book of Daniel is referred to as, "the Prince to come" (Dan. 9:26, AV), and in the writings of the Apostle John as, "the Antichrist" (1 Jn. 2:18,22) and "the Beast" (Rev. 13:1-10). This satanically enabled person will use the first three and a half years of the tribulation to come to power over his empire. The first half of the tribulation will consist of wars, famines, physical disturbances and great loss of life; one quarter of the world's population will perish (Rev. 6:8), yet it will be far less intense than the second half of the period. Since numerous passages indicate that the Jewish temple (the third temple in Israel's history) will be in operation by the midpoint of the tribulation (Dan. 9:27; Mt. 24:15; Rev. 11:1-2; 2 Thess. 2:3-4), the reconstruction of this temple will likely begin early in the first half of the period, though it is certainly possible that construction could begin prior to the period.

Several important events occur at, or near the midpoint of the tribulation period. As a result of angelic conflict in the heavens, Satan and his host of fallen angels will be confined to the earth (Rev. 12:7-17), and God will send two prophets who will prophesy throughout the remainder of the period until they are killed, probably just prior to the second coming (Rev. 11:3-13). At the midpoint of the period, the Antichrist will enter the Jewish temple, proclaiming that he is God, and demanding that all people worship him (Dan. 9:27; Mt. 24:15; 2 Thess. 2:3-4). Satan will raise up a false prophet who will perform great signs so as to deceive the unredeemed into worshiping the Antichrist (Rev. 13:11-18); this will be followed by a great persecution of believers, the most severe persecution of Christians in history (Mt. 24:15; Rev.12:13-14). As the second half of the period progresses spiritual deception will increase (Mt. 24:11; Rev. 13:11-18, cf. 17:1-18;

2 Thess. 2:8-12) and the moral condition of the world will greatly degenerate (Mt. 24:12).

The most severe of the tribulation events will occur in the last half of the period. All of the distress of the first half of the tribulation is described under the first four seals of Revelation 6:1-8. The seals in the book of Revelation are not judgments, though a seal may contain judgments. Rather, the seals represent the major movements of the period. The fifth seal, which allows the Antichrist to persecute and kill a great multitude of Christians, will occur shortly after the midpoint of the period (Rev. 6:9-11 cf. Mt. 24:9,15-22). Well into the second half of the tribulation, the sixth seal, an object from space hitting the earth (Rev. 6:12-17), likely serves as a warning of what is about to take place with the opening of the seventh seal (Rev. 8:1).

We cannot be certain when the day of the LORD begins; however, there is no doubt that the events of the seventh seal are divine wrath (Rev. 6:16-17; 15:1-16:21). During the time of the seventh seal (Rev. 8:1-6) a manifold judgment composed of seven trumpets is unleashed. Under the divine judgment of this period most of the world's remaining population will perish (Rev. 8:7-13). Following the judgments of the first four trumpets, which are cosmic in nature, there will be demonic affliction, war, and another set of judgments referred to as the bowls of God's wrath (the seventh trumpet is comprised of the seven bowls). The first five judgments in the bowl sequence are plagues poured out upon the earth (Rev. 16:1-11). The sixth and seventh bowls involve war, widespread destruction, and preparation for Armageddon, which is the final conflict of the period (Rev. 16:12-21). At the close of the period, the Antichrist will be involved in a conflict to maintain his global dominance (Dan. 11:36-45). The destruction from this warfare will be of a magnitude never before seen in human history. It is only the personal return of Christ in the midst of this conflict that ensures the survival of God's elect (Rev. 16:12-19:21). At his second coming Christ will descend to the Mount of Olives and go forth to defeat the armies of the Antichrist (Zech. 14:1-4). The Antichrist and his false prophet will be thrown into the Lake of Fire

(Hell) and their armies will be destroyed by Christ (Rev. 19:19-21; Zech 14:1-15, esp. v. 12).

The interlude between the tribulation and the millennium

There will be a brief seventy-five day interlude between the conclusion of the tribulation and the beginning of the millennium. Two events take place during this time. The first is the confinement of Satan and his host of angels to the Abyss (Rev. 20:1-3). Little is known of the Abyss; it is distinct from Hades (the interim abode of the dead), and the Lake of Fire (Hell); it appears to be a place of temporary confinement for evil spirits (fallen angels) until they are finally judged and sent into the Lake of Fire (Lk. 8:31; Rev. 9:1-12). The second event that will take place during this interval is the judgment described in Matthew 25:31-46. This judgment is necessary in order to determine who will enter the millennium. Since the redeemed and the unredeemed will be separated into groups by angels at Christ's second coming, it is likely that this judgment will be a summary (group) judgment.

The millennium

The millennial phase of the kingdom is the beginning of the fulfillment of the promises God made to Abraham and to his descendants (Israel). The millennium is the first of two phases in which the visible kingdom of God will unfold. As the name suggests, the millennial phase of the kingdom will last for approximately a thousand years. After the millennium is concluded and all sin is judged, the eternal phase of the kingdom will begin (Rev. 21:1-5). The major difference between these two phases is that the millennium will take place on the present (unrenewed, unpurified) earth, whereas the eternal phase will begin only after the heavens and earth are renewed and purified from the presence and all effects of sin. Although there will be sin and death in the millennium (owing to the presence of unredeemed descendants born to those who entered the kingdom from the tribulation in their natural bodies), there will be no sin or death in the eternal phase. In the eternal phase, Heaven, the New Jerusalem, will descend to rest upon the earth, and the new earth will become the eternal abode of God and his saints. Although the Old Testament does not distinguish between these two phases, they are clearly distinguished in the book of Revelation (Rev. 20:4-22:5, cf. Mic. 4:1-5).

While we know a great deal about the character of the millennium, only a few of the actual events are revealed. One of the first events of the millennium will be the resurrection of the righteous dead (Rev. 20:4-6). Since the Church-age saints will be raised at the rapture, it remains for the Old Testament saints and anyone saved after the rapture who subsequently dies, to be raised. There are four distinct groups that will enter the millennium: 1) the glorified Church saints having been raptured earlier, who will return with Christ at his second coming; 2) those saved after the rapture that survive physically until the second coming; 3) the Old Testament saints, who will be resurrected at the beginning of the millennium; and, 4) those saved after the rapture who do not survive to the second coming (who will be resurrected with the Old Testament saints at the beginning of the millennium). [Some have held that the Old Testament saints will be resurrected at the rapture; however, that seems unlikely since the rapture pertains to "the dead in Christ" {2 Thess. 4:16, cf. v. 14 "in Jesus"}, possibly a technical reference to Church saints. However, we should not be dogmatic on this point.] Of these, only the second group will enter the millennium in natural (untransformed) bodies. Saints of the other three groups will enter the kingdom in glorified (resurrected, or transformed) eternal bodies.

Life in the millennium will be different from previous ages. Christ will be personally present to rule over the earth. There will continue to be governments, but these will be accountable to Christ (Mic. 4:1-8; Zech. 14:17). The curse placed upon the earth at the fall of man will be lifted, at least partly (Isa. 65:17-25). This change in the natural order will affect both animal and plant life, and the earth will become highly productive (Amos 9:13). Nevertheless, the millennium will not be a perfect age. Although only the redeemed enter the millennium, those in their natural bodies will soon propagate children (Isa. 65:19-23), introducing unredeemed sons and daughters. As the period progresses, the population of both saved and lost will soar. As mentioned earlier, because of the presence and effects of sin and death, the millennium will not be a perfect age; rather, it will serve as a transition from the present (imperfect) state to the eternal (perfect) kingdom.

The millennium derives its name from the fact that its duration is approximately one thousand years (Rev. 20:2,7-10). Satan and his host of fallen angels will be confined to the Abyss at Christ's second coming. After he has been in confinement for a thousand years he will be released. At the close of the millennium, God will allow Satan to organize the final rebellion of human history, in order that all who do not love God and his Christ might be manifested and judged (Rev. 20:7-10). This rebellion will have the effect of polarizing humanity into two camps: one belonging to God, and the other to the Devil. Christ's enemies will perish by fire from heaven, and Satan along with the other fallen angels will be cast into the Lake of Fire (Rev. 20:7-10). The final event of the millennium will be the dissolution of the present heavens and earth to prepare the way for the final judgment of the lost and the creation of a new heavens and earth in which will dwell only God, his holy angels, and those made perfect by the blood of Christ.

The interlude between the millennium
and the new creation

At the conclusion of the millennium the present heavens and earth will be dissolved by fire (2 Pt. 3:10-11; Rev. 20:11), and all the unrighteous dead will be resurrected to face judgment. The book of Revelation refers to this as the second resurrection (Rev. 20:11-15). At this judgment (often referred to as "the great white throne judgment") it will be demonstrated to each and every unredeemed person that they are guilty before God and that their name has not been recorded in the Book of Life of the redeemed, and they will be cast into the Lake of Fire, which is the second death (Rev. 20:14).

Eternity

Having finally dealt with evil forever, God will create new heavens and a new earth (Rev. 21:1-5). In this eternal phase of the kingdom, the New Jerusalem, the heavenly city, will descend to rest upon the earth where it will remain forever (Rev. 21:9-22:5). This will be the eternal home of the saints. There will be no one who is unrighteous in this phase of the kingdom. Sin, suffering, sorrow, and death will be no more, and God will dwell forever in the midst of his people. While eternity will certainly be full of new opportunities for the redeemed, the story of biblical prophecy ends here.

Heaven and Hell

The Old Testament conception of eternity is sketchy. While the Old Testament saints did know of the resurrection (cf. Job 19:23-25 and Dan. 12:2), they seem to have had no concept of either Heaven as the eternal abode of the saints, or Hell as a place of torment. Six Hebrew words are translated "heaven" or "heavens" in the AV — *galgal* (1 time), *arabah* (1 time), *aripim* (1 time), *shahaq* (2 times), *shamayim* (419 times), and *shemayin* (32 times); with the exceptions of *arabah* and *aripim*, which should be translated "deserts" and "clouds" respectively, all the others seem to be references to the physical heavens of the universe, either the sky or the heavens beyond. Likewise, there is one Hebrew word that is translated "Hell" in the AV — *Sheol* (31 times). [Prior to the cross, *Sheol* was the interim abode of both the righteous and the unrighteous dead. It is important to note that *Sheol* and Hell (the Lake of Fire) are not the same. When Christ ascended into Heaven he transferred the righteous dead from *Sheol* to Heaven (Eph. 4:8), leaving only the unrighteous in *Sheol*. Since the cross, Sheol contains only the unrighteous dead, who along with the unholy angels, will be cast into Hell at their final judgment.] There is a reference to the new heavens and earth in Isaiah 65:17, though it is not there differentiated from the millennium. It was not until the teaching of Christ that the concepts of Heaven and Hell came into sharp focus (on Heaven cf. Mt. 5:16,20,34; 6:9,20; 7:21; 8:11; 10:32-33; 19:21; 22:30; 23:9; Jn. 3:13,31; 6:33,38,41,42,50,58; 14:1-3; on Hell cf. Mt. 5:22,29-30; 10:28; 18:9; 23:15,33; Lk. 16:23). Not only was Christ the first person in the New Testament to expound the doctrine of Heaven, he is the source of virtually everything revealed about Hell. Hell (Gr., *gehenna*) is equated with the Lake of Fire and should be distinguished from *Hades* (the Greek equivalent of the Hebrew, *Sheol*), which is the interim abode of the dead, though since the cross only the unrighteous dead are in Hades (cf. Rev. 20:13). [The Old Testament believers' sins were not removed until Christ's sacrifice was completed on the cross (Heb. 9:15-17); prior to that time their sins were merely covered (Heb., *kaphar*). Jesus' teaching in Luke 19:19-31 and his conversation with the repentant thief while on the cross (Lk. 23:43) both indicate that the Old Testament saints, as of the time he spoke, had not yet been received into Heaven, but were in a place he termed "Paradise," or "Abraham's bosom." That Paul refers to Heaven as Paradise in 2 Corinthians 12:4 is not an argument that the two are the same, since there is no reason why there could not have been two locations for Paradise, one prior to the cross (*Sheol*) and another afterward (Heaven). Apparently Jesus, at his death, descended into *Hades* (a part of which contained the souls of all the saints who had died prior to the cross) and afterward, when he ascended to the Father, he emptied *Sheol* of the souls of the saints, transferring them to Heaven (Eph. 4:8). This view of Paradise was once commonly taught, but has been largely abandoned due to the influence of covenant theology; nevertheless, it still seems to be the best interpretation of the biblical data.]

The New Testament letters add little new insight concerning either Heaven or Hell, even though Heaven is frequently mentioned. It is not until we come to the book of Revelation that we find additional significant information concerning Heaven and Hell. Throughout the book of Revelation, John describes various scenes in Heaven (4:1-6:17; 7:9-8:6; 10:1-11; 15:1-8; 19:1-10). He also gives a rather detailed description of the holy city, the New Jerusalem, which will descend to the new earth after the millennium (Rev. 21:1-22:5). While the New Jerusalem is not called Heaven, the description given leaves little doubt as to its identification. John also revealed that *Hades*, the interim abode of the unrighteous dead, will be replaced by "the Lake of Fire" (Rev. 20:14-15), which will be the eternal abode of the unrighteous.

Eternal rewards

There are several misconceptions concerning the nature of eternal rewards. 1) Rewards in the kingdom are commonly thought of only as tokens (*e.g.*, crowns, *etc.*). However, Jesus in Matthew 19:27-29, 25:14-30, and 24:35-47 indicates that the actual reward (of which the token is symbolic) is more substantive and practical. One reward Jesus mentioned is responsibility and authority in the kingdom (Mt. 25:14-23 cf. Lk. 19:11-27). 2) It is commonly thought that rewards in Heaven have only temporary significance because the redeemed will return their rewards to God. This is based on a misinterpretation of Revelation 4:1-11. The picture in Revelation 4:1-11 is of worship in Heaven. The four living creatures repeatedly give glory to God, and as often as they do that the twenty-four elders fall down and worship, placing their crowns before the throne. This pattern is repeated again and again. The idea that these elders represent the Church in Heaven is possible, though uncertain; even if so, it does not say that they give up their crowns. How would the pattern be repeated if that were the case? 3) Another misconception is that all believers will have equal status in Christ's kingdom. Jesus taught that some would be honored over others in his kingdom, and that privilege, authority, and honor in the kingdom will be given to those who serve him faithfully in this life. In Matthew 20:17-23 we read that James, John, and their mother came and requested that in the kingdom one son would sit on Jesus' right and one on his left. The gist of this request was that these two be given positions of honor and authority in the kingdom. Jesus did not deny that such positions exist; in fact, he affirmed it to be true when he said that such positions are "for those for whom it has been prepared by my Father" (NASB).

Review Questions

1. What is the first major prophetic time period of the future?

2. Describe the rapture of the Church.

3. Why must the rapture of the Church occur before the day of the LORD begins?

4. Describe the tribulation period.

5. What event begins the tribulation?

6. What events occur at, or near the middle of the tribulation?

7. What happens during the interlude between the tribulation and the millennium?

8. Describe the millennium.

9. What events happen near the beginning of the millennium? What events happen at the end?

10. What events fall into the interlude between the millennium and the new creation?

11. Describe eternity. (Take all the time you like!)

Appendices

Appendix: Radical Higher Criticism of the Bible

Not all Bible scholars believe that the Bible is a book inspired by God. Some believe, and teach, that the Bible is a purely human book, natural rather than supernatural. The seeds of unbelief run all the way back to the early church. There have always been those who refuse the Bible and reject Christ. (These two traits run together.) However, from the seventeenth century to the nineteenth century there was an explosion of unbelief. Christianity was attacked from all sides by men who viewed it as an obstacle to their secular worldview. They knew that as long as the orthodox doctrines of Christianity served as the foundations of society, they could never have a purely secular society. So, they did a very clever thing, they became professors of religion. First they introduced doubts about the authorship and inspiration of the Bible. Having eroded the foundation of Christian belief, every Christian doctrine was then open to contradiction. The simple truth is, without the Bible there is no Christianity. Of course, the church didn't stand by idly while this was happening. Those churches that were not caught up in this unbelief continued to teach the truth such that we now have two divergent streams of Christianity. One stream traces its roots all the way back to the teachings of the Bible. The other stream, which began to diverge in the seventeenth century, has veered more and more into unbelief and the denial of biblical truth.

The good news is that the truth has universally prevailed at both the biblical and intellectual levels. Those who know the truth are on solid ground, and have nothing to fear from those carrying the banner of unbelief. It is mystifying why countless conservative, Bible believing parents, churches, and Christian schools send a fresh crop of young people off each year to theologically liberal, post-Christian colleges and universities, totally unprepared to meet the contradictions of unbelief they will face. Sadly, some of the most virulently antichristian colleges and universities were Christian institutions at one time.

The documentary hypothesis

The documentary hypothesis is a theory which states that the first five books of the Bible (Genesis-Deuteronomy) were written, not as the Bible claims, by Moses (and completed by Joshua, Moses' assistant) in the late fifteenth to early fourteenth centuries B.C., but by various groups of writers (designated as groups "J," "E," "D," and "P") sometime between the eighth and fifth centuries B.C. Now, is this really worth getting into a scrap about? Absolutely! Everything that comes after these first five books presumes their trustworthiness. That means that if these books are not what they purport to be, the Bible is not God's word, and Jesus and all the others who quoted so confidently and authoritatively from these books were ignorant and misguided. The documentary hypothesis is an open attack on the roots of the Christian faith.

It is incredible that a theory that has been so thoroughly discredited on every point is still being taught as fact in institutions of higher learning. Nevertheless, it is being taught, and most students who hear it in college are hearing it for the first time, so naturally they assume that their university professor knows something that their pastor or Sunday school teacher doesn't know, or doesn't want them to know.

History of the documentary hypothesis

The seeds of radical criticism, the denial of the unity and integrity of scripture, can be seen in the writings of H.B. Witter, the first to assert that Genesis 1-2 contains two parallel accounts of creation. Witter suggested that the names applied to God in these accounts could be used to distinguish the underlying source documents from which they originated (assuming such documents existed). However, it was the French physician, Jean Autruc, who formalized the first documentary theory in his book *Conjectures Concerning the Original Memoranda Which it Appears Moses Used to Compose the Book of Genesis*. Autruc suggested there were actually three source documents from which the Genesis material was derived, and that each could be identified through the usage of the names applied to God, since (as he believed) each source document employed a distinct name for God. Autruc did, however, believe that Moses was the complier and editor of the book of Genesis. J. C. Eichhorn introduced Autruc's ideas to Germany with the publication of his introduction to the Old Testament in 1780-83. Eichhorn expanded Autruc's theory on source document identification to include not only the names of God, but other literary considerations as well (style, vocabulary, *etc.*). In 1800 Alexander Geddes, a Scottish Roman Catholic priest dismissed Autruc's theory, suggesting that instead of a few source documents being edited by Moses, the book of Genesis was a collage of many fragments pieced together by a redactor (editor) some five hundred years after Moses' death. Between 1802-05, John Vatter attempted to demonstrate the gradual development of the Pentateuch (the first five books of the OT) from a number of fragments. Although Vatter believed that some of the fragments must have come from Moses' time, the Pentateuch as we know it would not have been compiled until early in the sixth century B.C. Heinrich Ewald disagreed with this fragmentary view and instead proposed that the basis for the first six books of the Bible (he included the book of Joshua) was a writing which he called the "Elohistic writing ("E" document)." He further proposed that a parallel account arose which used the name "Jehovah" instead of "Elohim" ("J" document). Later, Ewald proposed that a subsequent editor took portions from the "J" document and inserted them into the original "E" document. From this point the soup gets very thick, because everyone wanted to get in on the act and invent a theory. However, in 1845 Ewald rejected his own theory, and instead suggested that five narrators wrote the Pentateuch over a period of seven hundred years. The last narrator, living at about 790-740 B.C., completed the work. Ewald held that Deuteronomy was a later addition to the Pentateuch, added around 500 B.C.

In 1853 Herman Hupfeld attempted to show that there were four distinct documents that were combined to form the Pentateuch ("P," a pre-Elohistic source, "E," "J," and "D," the source of Deuteronomy — in that chronological order). In the 1860's Karl Graf reversed Hupfeld's chronological order to "J," "E," "D," "P." Julius Wellhausen took Graf's theory, which had been modified by Abraham Kuenen and formulated what today has become the classic expression of the documentary hypothesis. According to Wellhausen, the earliest portions of the Pentateuch came from the "J" and "E" sources. From these a narrative work was complied with a decidedly "J" flavor. Deuteronomy was compiled in Josiah's time, and Ezra, in the fifth century B.C. added the priestly regulations, referred to as "the priestly document" (not to be confused with Hupfeld's "P" source). Since Wellhausen's time there have been numerous reformulations of the theory, most with more source documents. However, they all rest on the same basic assumptions.

Basic assumptions of the documentary hypothesis

1. The documentary hypothesis depends almost entirely on the highly subjective field of source analysis for its conclusions, while ignoring advancements in the field of ancient near-eastern archaeology. In many cases the presumptions of these radical critics are flatly contradicted by archaeological data.

2. The documentary hypothesis is built squarely upon an evolutionary view of religion, which out of hand dismisses any possibility of the supernatural. In that sense, it is akin to biological evolution — it must be believed, because to the antisupernaturalist there is no alternative.

The documentary hypothesis is built on historical assumptions
that have been proven to be false

The radical criticism of the Pentateuch was originally based on the assertion that these books could not have been written at the time and by the author indicated in the Bible (Moses and Joshua, in the fifteenth century B.C.), because Israel's religion was not as advanced as the theology indicated in these books. (How they determined this we do not know, since the Old Testament is the only source we have of Israel's early religious development.) It is commonly asserted that monotheism did not develop in Israel until the eight century B.C. (a premise now known to be false); therefore the Pentateuch, which is highly monotheistic, could not have been written in the fifteenth century. Contrary to this assertion, W. F. Albright, then chairman of the Department of Ancient Near Eastern Studies and Archaeology at Johns Hopkins University, stated: "It is precisely between 1500 and 1200 B.C., *i.e.* in the Mosaic age, that we find the closest approach to monotheism in the ancient Gentile world before the Persian period." (*Archaeology and the Religion of Israel*, The Johns Hopkins Press, p. 178.)

Another objection offered to Mosaic authorship is that the Pentateuch could not have been written in the fifteenth century B.C. because the Israelites had not yet attained the moral, civil, and legal development reflected in those writings. Archaeology has greatly illuminated our understanding on this issue. Millar Burrows, former professor of biblical theology at Yale University writes, "The standards represented by the ancient law codes of the Babylonians, Assyrians, and Hittites, as well as the high ideals found in the Egyptian book of the dead and the early wisdom literature of the Egyptians, have effectively refuted this assumption." (*What Mean these Stones?* Meridian Books, 1957, p. 46.)

Higher critics have said that the Pentateuch could not have been written in the fifteenth century B.C. because the priestly code was far too advanced for that period. On this subject, Joseph P. Free, Professor of Bible and Archaeology at Wheaton College, and subsequently at Bemidji State College, said: "Archaeological evidence, on the contrary, shows that there is no valid reason for dating the Levitical sacrificial laws late, for they appear in the Ug-aritic material from the fourteenth century B.C." ("Archaeology and Higher Criticism," *Bibliotheca Sacra*, Vol. 114.) In another work, Free has said: "The Code of Hammurabi was written sev-eral hundred years before the time of Moses, and yet it contains some laws which are similar to those recorded by Moses. In light of this, the liberal has no right to say that the laws of Moses are too advanced for his time, and could not have been written by him." (*Archaeology and Bible History*, Scripture Press, p. 161.)

It has been asserted that the Pentateuch could not have been written in Moses' time because writing was virtually un-known in Palestine at that early date. This assertion has been proven time and again to be false. We now possess a vast amount of written material dating from the second millennium before Christ. This includes the Ras Shamra tablets, Egyptian correspon-dence, the Mt. Sinai Inscriptions, and the Gezer Calendar.

British Assyriologist A. H. Sayce says regarding the late dating of Old Testament books: "...this supposed late use of writing for literary purposes was merely an assumption, with nothing more solid to rest upon than the critic's own theories and presuppositions. As soon as it could be tested by solid fact it crumbled into dust. First Egyptology, then Assyriology, showed that the art of writing in the ancient East, so far from being of modern growth, was of vast antiquity, and that the two great powers which divided the civilized world between them were each a nation of scribes and readers. Centuries before Abraham was born, Egypt and Babylonia were alike full of schools and libraries, of teachers and pupils, of poets and prose writers, and of the literary works which they had composed." (*Monument Facts and Higher Critical Fancies*, The Religious Tract Society, pp. 28-29.)

Higher critics have asserted that the stories of the patri-archs are not historically reliable. Therefore, they must have been written at a later time, projecting the social and cultural conditions of that later period back into those stories. [Again, how does the critic know these stories are unreliable? Not because of any archaeological information, but simply because his hypothesis requires it.] Julius Wellhausen stated, "From the patriarchal narratives it is impossible to obtain any historical information with regard to the patriarchs; we can only learn something about the time in which the stories about them were first told by the Israelite people. This later period, with all of its essential and superficial characteristics, was unintentionally projected back into hoary antiquity and is reflected there like a transfigured mirage" (*Prolegomena to the History of Israel*, Adam and Charles Black Pub., 1885, translated by Black and Menzies, p. 331). Wellhausen's theory is that the historical details found in these narratives do not fit so early a time period, so the stories must have been composed much later. Herman Schultz is even more blatant in his rejection of the historicity of the early Old Testament; he writes: "...Genesis is a book of sacred legend, with a mythical introduction. The first three chapters of it, in particular, present us with revelation-myths of the most important kind, and the following present us with mythical elements that have been recast more in the form of legend. From Abraham to Moses we have national legend pure and simple, mixed with a variety of mythical elements which have become almost unrecognizable. From Moses to David we have history still mixed with a great deal of legendary, and even partly with mythical elements that are no longer distinguishable. From David onwards we have history, with no more legendary elements in it than are everywhere present in history as written by the ancients." (*Old Testament Theology: The Religion of Revelation in its Pre-Christian Stage of Development*, T&T Clark, 1895, p. 31.)

Why are proponents of the documentary hypothesis so adamant in rejecting the historicity of the early Old Testament? The answer is simple: Belief in the Bible and belief in the God of the Bible go together; since these critics have dispensed with God, it is only natural that they would seek to dispense with the Bible. It should be pointed out that we know more now about the cultural, social, and religious history of the ancient Near East than at any other time in modern history. Archaeological discoveries in the last hundred and fifty years have confirmed time and again the historical validity of the early Old Testament. Radical criticism's baseless assertion of the historical unreliability of the early Old Testament is demonstrably false. The discovery of the Mari Tablets, the Ugaritic (Ras Shamra) texts, the Nuzi Tablets, and numerous Egyptian letters, have provided abundant validation of early Old Testament customs, civil and ceremonial practices, laws, and the names of people and places. The scholar who asserts that the early Old Testament is without historical validity demonstrates a deplorable level of ignorance in regard to the advancements made in ancient near eastern studies and archaeology. How did all this begin?

George Mendenhall, a professor of near eastern languages and literature at the University of Michigan, summarized how radical critical thinking got its start down the slippery slope when he said: "Wellhausen's theory of the history of Israelite religion was very largely based on a Hegelian philosophy of history, not upon his literary analysis. It was an 'a priori' evolutionary scheme which guided him in the utilization of his sources." (*Biblical History in Transition,* Eisenbrauns, 1979, p. 36.) In other words, according to Mendenhall, Wellhausen did not base his views on a careful analysis of the facts, but rather being committed to an evolutionary and antisupernatural view of history, Wellhausen assumed that Israel's religion, as well as the record of it, was simply the product of social, cultural, and religious evolution.

Conclusion

For those who may be wondering why this theory is still being taught since it has been so thoroughly discredited, the answer is simple: Proponents of the documentary hypothesis are antisupernaturalists, (many are atheists, agnostics, or deists). Just like their scientific counterparts, the biological evolutionists, they must deny any facts that are not consistent with naturalism. For additional information see the following works: *A Ready Defense,* by Josh McDowell; *Evidence that Demands a Verdict, Volume 2,* by Josh McDowell; *When Critics Ask,* by Norman Geisler and Ron Brooks; *A Survey of Old Testament Introduction,* by Gleason L. Archer, Jr. (for in-depth study).

Appendix: The Influence of Gnosticism on Christian Theology

As the church expanded into the Greek and Roman world Christianity was quickly transformed from a Jewish-centered religion into a Grecianized, anti-cosmic religion. However, the Bible takes a very positive view of the natural (physical) world, at least in regard to both its origin and its future. God declared his creation to be "good" (Gen. 1:31). The Old Testament is clearly *pro-cosmic*, in that it views the natural world as created for and suited to the fulfillment of the eternal promises and purposes of God for man. The New Testament does not differ from that view, though it does acknowledge the need for redemption and restoration of the physical world. Both the gospels and the book of Revelation picture Christ as returning to the earth to establish his eternal kingdom and to rule, and Revelation describes the heavenly city as descending to rest eternally upon the restored earth (Rev. 21:1-4). Unfortunately, some have failed to make a distinction between the material world and the powers that presently influence the world. According to the New Testament, the world is now under the sway, and to some degree, the dominion, of the powers of darkness (Rom. 8:18-23). Christ's atoning sacrifice has already provided the basis for the defeat of those powers and for the redemption of believing men and women, and of the material creation itself, but that redemption has yet to be applied to the physical creation; according to the Bible, it will be applied when Christ returns (Rom. 8:18-25). Hence, while the world system is evil, the natural realm itself is not intrinsically evil, but suffers from the consequences of man's sin. While the Bible recognizes that the present state of life in this world is made difficult by the presence of sin, that state is viewed as a temporary condition. The simple truth is that the Bible nowhere supports an anti-cosmic worldview.

Owing to the influence of Platonism and gnosticism in the early centuries of the church between the second and fifth centuries, Christian theology was reshaped to fit with an anti-cosmic worldview. (Anticosmic means that the physical creation is viewed as being flawed at best, and evil at worst.) This shift in worldview profoundly impacted every area of theology, especially the doctrines concerning the nature of God, Christ, original sin and salvation, and the nature of the unfolding kingdom of God (eschatology); also it directly or indirectly gave rise to virtually all of the great theological disputes of the first four centuries of the church. While the early church eventually resolved most of the difficulties with respect to the nature of God, and original sin and salvation, eschatology fell victim to anti-cosmic dualism. The interplay between Christianity, Platonism, stoicism, gnosticism, and the early doctrinal deviations from the first century apostolic faith are difficult to unravel. However, there can be no doubt that Platonism and gnosticism in their various forms had a significant and lasting effect on Christian theology—principally, the effect of displacing revealed religion (disclosed by God to man) with philosophy (reasoned by man), particularly as it relates to our understanding of the kingdom of God. Examples of the displacement of biblical revelation by philosophical theology can be seen in such figures as Basilides, Marcion, Valentinus, Clement of Alexandria, Origen, and eventually, Augustine (though these figures had sharp theological disagreements among themselves). Augustine, owing to his stature in church history, is responsible for codifying in the western church the practice of spiritualized (allegorical) interpretation of eschatological prophecy, with the aim being to provide biblical support for the view that the kingdom of God is essentially spiritual (*i.e.,* supernatural as opposed to physical) and Church-centered rather than Jewish-centered. [The replacement of Israel by the Church was an essential stepping-stone in the development of amillennialism. This scheme is generally referred to as "replacement theology." Replacement theology developed very early and can be seen in the writings of Justin Martyr in the mid-second century, even though Justin's position on the kingdom remained solidly premillennial.]

Anti-cosmic worldviews
in the early church

Gnosticism derived its cosmology from Platonism, and both Platonism and gnosticism viewed the material world as intrinsically inferior to the ideal world beyond. As such, both Platonists and gnostics conceived of the world as a place to be delivered from—through contemplation for the Platonist, and by the keys of knowledge (*gnosis*) for the gnostic. Neither worldview could conceive of the natural world as a suitable realm for an ideal existence (such as the kingdom of God). So, for both Platonists and gnostics (and increasingly for others whom they influenced), the notion of a literal, physical kingdom of God on earth seemed quite absurd. In practical terms, any anti-cosmic worldview is inherently incompatible with premillennialism; which is why gnosticism, in bloc, and eventually most of the remainder of the church came to deny the literal premillennial statements of the Bible. This must have posed a dilemma early on, since the biblical statements taken at face value unequivocally teach a premillennial return of Christ and subsequent physical (geopolitical) kingdom (Zech 14; Mt. 24-25; Rev. 19:11-20:4). However, with the increasing acceptance of allegorical interpretation, it became easier to deny premillennialism and to readjust the message of the Bible. The gnostics used allegorization in developing their particular cultic theology, and those who opposed them (Clement, Origen, and others) increasingly relied on philosophical apologetics, which often led to further allegorization of scripture such that both positions moved further away from the actual statements of the Bible and closer to a rationalized (philosophical) theology. While premillennialism can be found in some of the church fathers, the displacement of premillennialism by amillennialism was early, beginning in earnest in the early second century. [Justin Martyr's *Dialogue With Trypho* (chapters LXXX-LXXXI) provides an excellent example of premillennialism in the early to mid-second century— though Justin had come to accept replacement theology, which is a precursory step in the direction of amillennialism (see chapters CXIX-CXX and CXXXV). As such, Justin's theology is an example of the transition that took place in the early second century from biblical premillennialism, to replacement premillennialism, to replacement amillennialism (classic amillennialism).]

Basic tenets of gnosticism

Since gnosticism is less well understood than Platonism, it might be helpful to review some of its basic tenets. Early gnosticism was essentially an adaptation of Platonic metaphysics (cosmology and ontology) that integrated the dualism of Platonism with Christian themes (primarily transcendence and salvation). Unlike Platonism, gnosticism accepted the Jewish-Christian conception of a transcendent God. Thus while gnosticism shared much of Platonism's mythical cosmology and dualism, it represented a significant Christian adaptation of those ideas. While there has been much discussion on the origin of gnosticism, and whether there was a pre-Christian form of gnosticism, the earliest gnostic teachings appear to draw heavily on Old and New Testament characters, places, events, and ideas, and thus would be difficult to explain apart from Christianity. That being the case, it is best to view gnosticism as a distinctly Christian heresy. (For further discussion on the Christian origin of gnosticism, see: *A Separate God: The Christian Origins of Gnosticism*, by Simone Pétrement, HarperSanFrancisco, 1990.).

The determinative feature of gnosticism is the belief that the God of the Old Testament (Yahweh/Jehovah) is not the true (holy and eternal) God, but a powerful angelic-like creature, whom the gnostics referred to generically as the "Demiurge," or personally by the names "Ialtabaoth," or "Sakla[s]." The gnostics reasoned that since the world is flawed, the true God could not have created it. They also viewed the "God" of the Old Testament as inferior in character to the Father of Christ in the New Testament. We see in this the earliest examples of the reinterpretation (largely a dismissal) of the Old Testament in light of what was thought (by the gnostics) to be a later, superior understanding of truth—a process that, quite interestingly, remains as one of the core hermeneutical processes of amillennialism today (that is, the tendency to conform older scriptures to a particularly narrow view of later scriptures). For example, see *A Case for Amillennialism: Understanding the End Times*, by Kim Riddlebarger (Baker Books, 2003), written from the amillennial perspective. Riddlebarger provides a convenient compendium of contemporary amillennial thought; he states (p. 37): "...the Old Testament prophets and writers spoke of the glories of the coming messianic age in terms of their own pre-messianic age. They referred to the nation of Israel, the temple, the Davidic throne, and so on. These all reflect the language, history, and experience of the people to whom these promises were originally given. But eschatological themes are reinterpreted in the New Testament, where we are told that these Old Testament images are types and shadows of the glorious realities that are fulfilled in Jesus Christ. According to amillenarians, this means that Jesus Christ is the true Israel. As incredible as it might sound, Riddlebarger acknowledges that reformed theologians are "concerned about the dispensational tendency to interpret the New Testament in light of the Old..." (p. 51). What a novelty these dispensationalists (read "premillennialists") are guilty of—actually attempting to interpret the New Testament in light of the Old Testament! Amillennialists are forced to reinterpret the Old Testament in light of their particularly narrow view of the New Testament gospels, and they look with concern upon anyone who might actually attempt to understand the New Testament in the light of the Old Testament. This is, of course, a biblical theology turned upside down; and it is a process that appears to have gotten much of its initial traction from the philosophical/theological "soup" of the second century A.D. in which gnosticism developed.

Whether gnosticism produced this inversion in biblical theology or was simply a co-inheritor is unclear; but one thing is clear: Reversal of the determinative-dependent relationship between the Old and New Testaments, as seen in gnosticism and amillennialism, is highly destructive both to biblical theology and to our notion of biblical inspiration and canonicity. After all, the basis for the acceptance of the New Testament books as inspired documents was that they teach (at face value) the same doctrines as the Old Testament, but how can that be if the Old Testament must be allegorized to conform to the teachings of the New Testament? (For additional discussion of the relationship between the Old Testament and the New Testament see: *"How the Amillennial Conception of the Kingdom is Developed,"* by the author, Biblical Reader Communications, 2005.)

The gnostics believed that the true God is higher and unknown to the God of the Jews, who in his ignorance of the true God believes himself to be the highest of powers and worthy of all worship. For the most part it seems that the gnostics viewed Jehovah not as evil, but as acting ignorantly (though some sects of gnostics undoubtedly did view him as having malevolent tendencies). Perhaps the gnostics arrived at this worldview through a rejection of original sin. That is, in failing to understand, or accept the Old Testament account of the fall of man and its effects upon the world, they thus attributed the failure in creation to the Creator himself. The skids of this error were already greased by the fact that the gnostics saw what they thought was a disparity between the New Testament ideal of the Father of Christ, and what appeared to them to be the inferior deity presented in the Old Testament. Therefore, they felt justified in rejecting the theology of the Old Testament. Whatever the impetuous for the origin of gnosticism might be, it is clear that Platonism was the template for the gnostic worldview, and it is generally acknowledged that the gnostic ideas regarding creation were largely adapted from Plato's mythical account in *Timaeus*. The gnostics developed an elaborate mythology to elucidate and support their views. They were forced to do so because their doctrines obviously could not be supported through any normal understanding of the Bible. Hence, the gnostics were among the first within professed Christianity to spiritualize (allegorize) the Christian scriptures, and they eventually developed their own corpus of cultic literature to support their beliefs. They engaged in the wholesale allegorization of the New Testament, and to the extent that they used the Old Testament (which was little), they allegorized that too. (Since the gnostics viewed the Old Testament as representing the religion of the Demiurge—*i.e.*, a false religion—they mostly ignored it, except for the creation account, a few details of which they adapted to their mythical cosmology.) [For those who may be less familiar with gnosticism, documents like *The Gospel of Thomas* that are currently being popularized in modern religious fiction, such as Dan Brown's *The DaVinci Code,* are for the most part, gnostic writings that were rejected by the early church because their historical and theological content is incompatible with the Bible. In every case, these writings are pseudepigraphal, that is, they were not written by the people whose names they bear, or at the time claimed. They were forgeries written from the second century on, fabricated to support a gnostic worldview which could not be supported directly from the Bible. Unlike some other heresies, which simply misinterpreted the Bible, gnosticism's cosmology and theology were so far removed from anything biblical that they literally needed to write their own scriptures.]

Dualism is fundamental to gnosticism. Dualism proceeds naturally from an anti-cosmic worldview. If the natural realm is flawed, it is clear that the true God could neither be its creator, nor could he be joined with the physical world. Thus, gnostics not only denied that the true God made the world; they also denied the personal union of the divine and human natures in Christ (*i.e.,* that he was both God and man in one person). There were many flavors of gnosticism. Some gnostics held that Christ was not a man at all, but that he only appeared to be human (a sort of phantasm); some held that he was not God at all, that he was only a man. Still others held that Jesus was a man and that the Christ Spirit rested upon him only temporarily, but was never joined to him personally (*i.e.,* hypostatically, constituting a singular person). In all cases, however, the gnostics denied that Christ, as God in the flesh, died on the cross. Actually, the gnostics did not believe in the absolute deity of Christ as taught in the New Testament. To the gnostics, Christ was a created heavenly being, not an eternal member of the Godhead. Since the gnostics did not accept the Bible's teaching concerning original sin, they saw no need for atonement; to them, the Son was a messenger from the spiritual realm beyond and above that of the Demiurge (Jehovah). He was a messenger sent by the true God to reveal the knowledge of the truth to those capable of receiving it, that men have a spark of the divine within them that, with the proper knowledge (the *gnosis*), can return to the realm for which it was originally created. Those who do not, or cannot receive this knowledge are doomed to remain trapped in this physical realm through perpetual reincarnations. Gnostic mythology, which denies that Christ died on the cross, sometimes describes him as living out his life elsewhere, but this mythology was not based upon any historical information. It was developed only to support gnostic dualism, which could not accept the incarnation, or substitutionary atonement upon the cross.

The mythology that was developed by the gnostics was rich and varied. For instance, some gnostics taught that Jehovah (or some of his inferior powers) had relations with Eve and fathered Cain and Abel. (Some gnostic accounts present a picture of a brutal rape of Eve.) There was a widespread belief among gnostics that only Seth was the son of Adam, and they viewed only the descendants of Seth as being capable of receiving the *gnosis* (the true knowledge that provides the keys to passing from the lower realms and ascending to the higher realms at death). Of course, gnostics viewed themselves as being "Sethites." (This is, quite obviously, a form of religiously sanctioned racism.) They held that the tree of life was a trap placed in the Garden by Jehovah to keep men trapped in the material world, and that the tree of the knowledge of good and evil held the means of escaping this entrapment. Consequently, the serpent that tempted Eve to partake of the forbidden fruit was actually an agent of good, according to *The Secret Book of John*, which presents a typical gnostic account of creation. (Both Freemasonry and Mormonism incorporate elements of this theology; for additional information see: *One Nation Under Gods: A History of the Mormon Church*, by Richard Abanes, pp.23-40 and 281-310.)

One might ask why the gnostics drew upon the Old Testament at all, since their theology obviously doesn't square with the Old Testament scriptures. The answer would seem to be that while they viewed the Old Testament as having been written from the perspective of the false religion of the Demiurge, it was still the foundation of Christianity of which they viewed themselves as being a part. In other words, they were "stuck" with the Old Testament. Christianity is inseparable from the Old Testament, and the gnostics needed a connection to Christianity to validate their own religious standing. Essentially, gnosticism co-opted Christianity in its effort to forge a new religion that was incompatible with both the Old and New Testament scriptures. So rather than a complete denial of the Old Testament, they chose to reinterpret selected portions through allegorization according to their own mythology; the rest (in fact most of the Old Testament), they simply dismissed as the false religion of the Jews. Some gnostic sects did not even include the Old Testament in their canon of scriptures.

Since the gnostics viewed the God of the Old Testament as inferior, and ignorantly self-serving, they viewed the Jews as purveyors of false religion, which actually did harm by concealing the truth about the true God and the true nature of the material world. Hence, gnosticism fostered an early anti-Jewish attitude. The futuristic eschatology of the Old Testament (repeated in the book of Revelation), which was characterized as both physical and Jewish-centered, was discarded in favor of "realized personal eschatology," which the individual enters into both when he comes into possession of the *gnosis*, and at death, when he can use the *gnosis* to escape the physical realm and return to the native realm of his or her soul. In fact, as the notion of realized personal eschatology gained acceptance in the early church, we see a diminished emphasis on physical resurrection. If the goal is to escape the material realm, why would one want to be physically resurrected? The gnostics were the first within Christendom to teach that the resurrection involves not the body, but the soul—hence a spiritual resurrection. This is a theme that has been recycled and has found its way into modern liberal Christianity. It seems more than coincidental that in the history of the church the theological migration from a physical view of the resurrection to a spiritual view has been the exclusive domain of amillennialists.

Of course, before we can conclusively establish a connection between Platonism, gnosticism, and amillennialism, we must ask the question, "Was the Platonic and gnostic influence in the second and third centuries sufficient to account for the church's abandonment of premillennialism? The answer to that question is "Yes." The fingerprints of Platonism and gnosticism are on most of the theological disputation of that era. Valentinus, one of the most influential shapers of the gnostic movement, was nominated to be the Bishop of Rome (c. A.D. 143) and only narrowly missed being elected. Even after his defeat he continued to exert significant influence both locally and abroad until his death sometime around A.D. 160. Many of the early church fathers like Ignatius, Polycarp, Justin Martyr, Irenaeus, Tertullian, and Hippolytus argued powerfully against the gnostics and eventually the church rejected gnosticism in most of its forms. However, in the process of refuting the gnostics many of the apologists adopted the Greek philosophical mode of apologetics (trying to "fight fire with fire"). This is most clearly illustrated in Clement of Alexandria and Origen. While the particulars of gnostic doctrines were being refuted, the church was unwittingly buying into the same error that produced gnosticism—the supplanting of biblical revelation by philosophy. In the end gnosticism lost out, but the collision of Platonic ideas (from both philosophic and religious sources) with Christianity left a huge dent in the church—a decidedly Greek mindset which was both anti-cosmic, and sadly, anti-Jewish. That mindset, of which Augustine was the inheritor, undoubtedly affected not only the church's attitude toward the nature of the kingdom of God, but also set the stage for asceticism, the monastic movement, and the anti-Semitism of the middle ages and beyond. The original biblical conception of the kingdom developed in the Old Testament had been for a physical (geopolitical) Jewish-centered kingdom with Messiah physically present to rule. Whether the church thought that such a quaint and geopolitically local notion wouldn't sell in the sophisticated Greek world, or whether the church simply bought into the Platonic attitude toward the material world is unclear; likely it was a combination of both, along with the growth of anti-Semitism. In any case, Christianity's encounter with Greek thought redefined the faith in an indelible way that is still seen in the Roman Catholic, Greek Orthodox, Coptic, and Reformed faiths.

The influence of gnosticism on eschatology

Tracing the major movements of philosophic and gnostic thought within the early (2nd – 5th century) church, we will begin with Philo, a Jewish philosopher and interpreter of the Old Testament who lived in the 1st century A.D. (c. 20 B.C. – c. A.D. 40). Philo was one of the first Jewish interpreters to make extensive use of allegorization in Old Testament interpretation (likely this was due to stoic influence; the stoics were noted for their allegorization of Greek mythic literature). Many early Christian interpreters were heavily influenced by Philo's method of spiritualization, that is, interpreting a passage according to a supposed spiritual meaning, as opposed to the actual (normal/objective) meaning of the statements. While not holding strictly to a Platonic cosmology, Philo's cosmology was nonetheless heavily influenced by Platonism. Philo, while viewing God as the framer of ideas (and necessarily transcendent), viewed the material world as an expression of those ideas that existed more perfectly in the heavenly realm. While not strictly Platonic (the Platonists did not view God as transcendent), Philo's concept of the nature of the creation and its relationship to the realm of ideas certainly shows the influence of Platonism, and may have served as a framework for early gnosticism. Philo lived in Alexandria, Egypt, which was the epicenter of the revival of Greek philosophy in the first and second centuries A.D. It is probably not coincidental that Philo, Valentinus, Basilides, Clement, and Origin—five of the most influential figures that helped to ensconce allegorical and anti-cosmic interpretation in the church (though Philo was not a Christian) all lived in Alexandria in the second century A.D., and there undoubtedly interacted with both Platonists and stoics. It is also probably not coincidental that the individuals in this string of figures, particularly Origen, were a major influence in the development of Augustine's hermeneutics, and as we know Augustine's influence was the single greatest factor in the eventual adoption of amillennialism in the western church.

Are there other connections between Platonism, gnosticism, and the early church? Absolutely, however, it is not always easy to determine on any particular issue whether gnosticism was the principal influence, or whether the philosophical soup of the first through the fourth centuries simply affected both the church and gnosticism to varying degrees. Undoubtedly both forces were at work; that is, it is likely that both Platonism and what might be termed "Christianized Platonism" (one form of which was gnosticism) both exerted an influence on the church. Therefore rather than attempting to show causal connections, we will consider common threads between Platonism, gnosticism, and early amillennialism. Consider the following: 1) The gnostics denied any physical eschatological promises. To them eschatology was about escaping the physical realm; that is so say, they believed in a "personal realized eschatology" which was entirely spiritual; and they simply reinterpreted (*via* allegorization) any scripture that did not fit their model. Amillennialism, both historic and modern, is built on this same framework. 2) The gnostics dismissed the centrality of the Jewish people and nation, believing them to be deceived by the Demiurge and purveyors of false religion; thus they dismissed any promises made to the Jewish people and nation in the Old Testament. [This is clearly illustrated in the Gospel of Judas in which Jesus is seen to be laughing at the ignorance of the disciples, because they had been deceived by Jewish religion. In this mythic gospel Judas is the only disciple who came to understand the truth about Jesus and his mission.] The dismissal of the centrality of the Jewish people and nation in eschatology was built on replacement theology, the origin of which is unclear, though it was undoubtedly very early. (The tendency toward this error was forcefully addressed by Paul in Romans chapter 11, adding support to the notion that this was a very early deviation from apostolic Christianity.) Replacement theology undoubtedly set the stage for amillennialism and for Christian anti-Semitism from the middle ages forward. Whether gnosticism promoted anti-Semitism to the church broadly or was itself influenced by other forces that influenced the church is unclear. However, one thing is clear: Gnosticism, amillennialism, anti-cosmic theology, replacement theology, and anti-Semitism all developed in the same religious/philosophical soup at the same time (*i.e.*, the early post-apostolic era), though it took longer for amillennialism to gain popularity in the western church. 3) The gnostics reinterpreted the Old Testament (that is, the part they didn't ignore) in light of the New Testament, which they had already reinterpreted in the light of their cultic literature, some of which is ironically now being referred to as "lost gospels," implying a level of validity to these documents of which they are entirely unworthy. The reinterpretation of earlier writings on the basis of later writings has always been, and continues to be a core process in amillennial hermeneutics (which reverses the determinative/dependent relationship of the Old Testament to the New Testament), and in this aspect gnosticism and amillennialism have always been close cousins. Amillennialists have always been insistent that the Old Testament must be re-interpreted in light of the New Testament, even if the normal (and obvious) meaning of the actual statements must be denied in order to do so. 4) The decline of premillennialism in the early church matches the expansion of Platonic influence in the church, both geographically and historically. The expansion of gnosticism was from Alexandria, to Syrian Antioch, to Rome, then to the rest of the Empire. Amillennialism followed the same route, and as far as can be determined appeared at approximately the same times; thus, there is both a geographical and historical connection between the two. 5) With its emersion into the Greek world the church was under great pressure to repackage its fundamentally Jewish-centered message and to present a version of Christianity that would be palatable, even attractive to non-Jews. This pressure undoubtedly increased after the destruction of Jerusalem in A.D. 70 with the dispersal of the Jewish people. The problem for the church of the second through the fifth centuries was: How does one proclaim a Jewish-centered religion with future promises of global Jewish ascendancy, to a Greek world that viewed itself as vastly superior to anything Jewish (particularly after the Jewish state had ceased to exist)? In the end, when faced with retaining its original message or morphing its theology into something more palatable to appeal to non-Jews, the church chose the latter path. Unfortunately, the message of the Bible had to be adjusted to accommodate this change, and allegorization was the only practical alternative to denying the received canon and rewriting scripture as the gnostics had done (and which ultimately proved to be the gnostics' downfall). What happened in the early church in the second through the fifth centuries can perhaps best be explained in terms of Hegel's dialectic, with apostolic Christianity (which was premillennial) representing the thesis, Platonism and gnosticism (both anti-cosmic and anti-Semitic) representing the antithesis, and amillennialism representing the synthesis.

Anyone familiar with the kingdom promises of the Old Testament must confess that they were for a physical, earthly kingdom. The notion of a spiritual kingdom must be injected backwards from a particularly narrow understanding (or rather, misunderstanding) of the New Testament gospels. In fact, it seems to have been a particularly gnostic trait to think of the relationship of the New Testament to the Old as analogous to that of the spiritual realm to the physical realm. In other words, to the gnostics the Old Testament represented the theology of the physical realm (an inferior theology), whereas the New Testament represented the theology of the spirit realm (a superior theology). This is, of course, a low view of inspiration, and calls into question the inspiration of both the Old and New Testaments, since the inspiration of the New Testament is based on its connection to and consistency with the Old Testament. It is interesting that throughout the history of the church amillennialism has continued to ply this same error of reinterpreting (spiritualizing) the Old Testament in the light of the New Testament. [There is a reason this practice is called "spiritualizing." In spiritualization the earthbound (local, cultural, geopolitical) statements of the Old Testament are reinterpreted in a higher, superior (universal, spiritual) form.] This is fundamentally the same view of the relationship of the Old Testament to the New as seen in gnosticism. The fact is that all forms of allegorization, whether Jewish or Christian, devalue the literature allegorized by implying that it is, at face value, conceptually inferior to the higher standard against which it is being reinterpreted. One might argue that the New

Testament is superior to the Old; however, such an assessment would be difficult to sustain since virtually all of the key points of the New Testament were established by means of appeal to Old Testament authority, and logically that to which one appeals for validation cannot itself be inferior to the thing being validated (a circular fallacy). In this case, the Old Testament is clearly determinative and the New Testament is clearly dependent. By what logic does one argue that a dependent proposition redefines a prior proposition upon which it depends for its own validity? This is, of course, a classic "boot-strapping" conundrum. The reinterpretation of the Old Testament by means of the New Testament is patently absurd. Of course, owing to the progressive nature of biblical revelation the New Testament does contain a more complete picture of the divine program than that contained within the Old Testament; however, the New Testament picture merely completes the picture given in the Old Testament, it does not replace or alter that picture as amillennialists assert. While amillennialists have been intent on finding examples of allegorical interpretation of the Old Testament within the New Testament, they have been unable to point to even one example. The New Testament does make use of Old Testament material in constructing a pedagogical allegory in Galatians 4:21-31; however, the use of material to construct an allegory for illustrative purposes, and the interpretation of material allegorically, are two entirely different things. The fact is, neither Christ, nor the New Testament writers ever interpreted the Old Testament allegorically.

There can be no doubt that the development of amillennial thought, particularly in Augustine, was influenced by the dualism of Platonism and gnosticism. Augustine's Platonic frame of reference is generally acknowledged. As historian Simone Pétrement states, both Origen and Augustine were "...profoundly influenced by gnosticism and to a large extent incorporated it into their doctrines" (*A Separate God,* p. 24). The denial of the doctrine of a literal, earthly theocratic kingdom is not the result of the discovery of a superior truth in the New Testament leading to the true spiritual meaning of the kingdom theology of the Old Testament; it is largely the result of the infusion of heathen anti-cosmic and anti-Jewish worldviews that crept into the church in the early centuries of its theological development, and has now been codified in Roman Catholic, Greek Orthodox, Coptic, and Reformed theology. In the western church, this was largely due to the influence of Augustine, who adopted many of the core interpretations and key hermeneutical principles of Tichonius, a North African Donatist who was the first to present an entirely allegorical interpretation of the book of Revelation. (Tichonius' principles of hermeneutics are presented in Augustine's *De Doctrina Christiana*, book III, chaps. 30-37.)

Of course in speaking of Augustine we must keep in mind the political-religious context. Augustine's *City of God* was written as a defense of Christianity after the sacking of Rome (A.D. 410). Had Augustine then taken a premillennial stance, he would have exacerbated Roman criticism of Christianity by implying that Christ would eventually overthrow even Rome in the establishment of his kingdom. Such an idea would hardly have accomplished what Augustine desired in his attempt to conciliate Romans to a more favorable view of Christianity. While Platonism, gnosticism, and replacement theology provided the philosophical and theological soup in which amillennialism could develop, it was likely a combination of several factors that led to the codification of amillennialism in the early church: the early acceptance of replacement theology, the general acceptance of philosophical apologetics and theology, the influence of Platonism and stoicism, the desire to make the scriptures palatable to skeptical and philosophically minded Greeks, a growing acceptance of anti-cosmic dualism within the church, and concern over the negative criticism that likely would have resulted from premillennialism.

A summary of gnostic beliefs

There were many varieties of gnosticism; the following is a summary of some common themes.

The gnostic view of God

The gnostics did not believe the God of the Old Testament to be the true, eternal God. They believed that the being who is called "God" ("Jehovah," or "Yahweh") in the Old Testament is a created spirit being, whom they refer to as the Demiurge. They believed that because the Demiurge is unaware of any power above himself, he mistakenly thinks that he is the highest of all beings. According to the gnostics the religion of the Old Testament (the religion perpetuated by the Jews) was false religion, and thus the Jews worshiped a false god. (Note the anti-Semitism.) Consequently, some gnostic groups did not include the Old Testament as part of their scriptures. According to gnosticism, Jehovah is either ignorant or evil (opinions varied).

The gnostic view of the Bible

The gnostics viewed the Old Testament as the false religion of the Demiurge and the Jews whom he had deluded; accordingly they viewed the teaching of the Old Testament as the propaganda of the Demiurge; this resulted in a tendency not only to deny the truths of the Old Testament, but to the reversal of many Old Testament ideas; thus, they viewed the serpent in the Garden as good (he was trying to help Eve understand the truth about the world and the Demiurge), those who rejected the religion of the Demiurge as the righteous (the people of Sodom and Gomorrah were unjustly persecuted by the Demiurge), and the enemies of Israel as good (again, note the anti-Semitism). Some gnostics even believed that Cain and Abel were the products of Eve's rape by the Demiurge or one of his cohorts. The gnostics denied the account of man's fall, and thus saw no need of redemption.

While the gnostics adapted parts of the Old Testament to their mythology, they basically dismissed the rest. Some gnostic Bibles did not include the Old Testament; and since the gnostics viewed the apostles and early disciples as having been deceived by the religion of Jehovah, they largely dismissed the New Testament also. That being the case, they found it necessary to produce their own scripture. Many gnostic writings from the second through the fifth century are known, and incredibly, many are now being purveyed to those unaware of early church history as, "lost gospels."

The gnostic view of creation

Following Platonism, the gnostics viewed the material world as an inferior realm because it was created by an inferior being—the Demiurge. Some gnostics viewed the Demiurge and his creation as benignly inferior, others viewed them as evil. Their account of the creation was derived from Plato's creation myth. According to this myth, the true God (not Jehovah) created numerous angelic beings; one of these being, "Sophia," created or gave birth to the Demiurge, who was born into a lower realm and knows nothing of the higher realm of Sophia. Since the material world is the creation of the Demiurge, the kingdom of God cannot unfold in this realm. This view deeply impacted early Christian thinking and is likely the source of realized eschatology (amillennialism).

The gnostic view of man

There are different gnostic accounts of how man was created; the following presents only the basic ideas. The gnostics believed that when Sophia gave birth to the Demiurge, part of her spiritual essence was passed to the Demiurge, and thus became trapped in the lower realm of the Demiurge. This essence, which comprises the human soul, always wants to get back to its native realm (Sophia's realm). In an effort to recover that essence, the true God allowed the Demiurge to see a reflection of a heavenly being called "Adamas." (Adamas was the model for humanity.) The Demiurge and his cohort whom he created, set out to copy what they saw, but the man had no life. By this the true God tricked the Demiurge into breathing the essence of Sophia into the man he had created, to bring him to life. Thus, the essence that had passed to the Demiurge was passed to the human Adam. (According to gnostic myth, Adam later passed this essence to Eve; this and other gnostic doctrines are the basis for some of the modern feminist theology.) According to gnosticism man is not a fallen creature in need of redemption, he is a trapped and deluded creature in need of light and knowledge to escape the clutches of the Demiurge. The gnostics believed that Christ came to deliver this light and knowledge.

The gnostic view of Christ and salvation

The gnostics did not believe in original sin, and consequently, they saw no need for redemption. They did not believe Christ to be God, but an angelic being who was sent into this realm to tell men the truth about the Demiurge, the material world, and the true God, and how they could escape the perpetual cycle of reincarnation in which man is trapped. The gnostics did not believe Christ died on the cross; some believed that he miraculously switched identities with Simon who carried the cross, and so it was actually Simon who died on the cross; others believed that the spirit being left the human Jesus before he died. Others simply dismissed the New Testament account of the crucifixion entirely. In any case, the gnostics did not believe in the Trinity, the hypostatic union of Christ's two natures, or substitutionary atonement. Since the gnostics believed that men possess a spiritual essence that is trapped in a perpetual cycle of reincarnation, salvation entails gaining freedom from that cycle and ascending to Sophia's realm. How does one get out of the cycle of reincarnation? The gnostics believed that when a person dies the powers of the Demiurge turn the soul back and do not allow it to pass out of the Demiurge's realm, and thus those souls are reincarnated. (Note the doctrine of the pre-existence of the soul.) For the gnostics, the way of salvation was to discover the knowledge that would allow one to pass out of this realm and into the higher realms beyond until they finally reach Sophia's realm. It is this knowledge that Christ came to deliver, and which the gnostics (whose name means "to know") claimed to possess.

Conclusions regarding gnosticism

As the church expanded into the Greek and Roman world, Christianity was transformed from a Jewish-centered religion into a Grecianized, anti-cosmic, and to some degree anti-Semitic religion. Contrary to this, the Bible takes a very positive view of the physical world, at least in regard to both its origin and its future. God declared his creation to be "good" (Gen. 1:31). The Old Testament is clearly pro-cosmic, in that it views the natural world as created for and suited to the fulfillment of the eternal promises and purposes of God for man. The New Testament does not differ from this view, though it does acknowledge the need for redemption and restoration of the physical world. Both the gospels and the book of Revelation picture Christ as returning to the earth to establish his eternal kingdom and to rule, and Revelation describes the heavenly city as descending to rest eternally upon the restored earth (Rev. 21:1-4). According to the New Testament, the world is now under the sway, and to some degree the dominion of the powers of darkness (Rom. 8:18-23). Christ's atoning sacrifice has already provided the basis for the defeat of these powers and for the redemption of believing men and women, and of the material creation itself, but that redemption has yet to be applied to the physical creation. According to the Bible, that redemption will be applied when Christ returns (Rom. 8:18-25). Hence, while the world system is evil, due to the fall of man, the natural realm is not intrinsically evil, it simply suffers from the effects of man's sin. While the Bible recognizes that the present state of life in this world is made difficult by the presence of sin, that state is viewed as a temporary condition. How such views could have arisen in the early church must be understood as a product of religious and philosophical syncretism. Regrettably, many gnostic heresies from the past have reappeared in modern times. Most of the Christian cults (most particularly Mormonism and Christian Science) are based largely on gnostic theology and cosmology; and today there is a resurgence of interest in gnostic teaching through the rediscovery of gnostic documents (such as "The Judas Gospel") and popular quasi-religious fiction.

Bibliography

Abanes, Richard. *One Nation Under Gods: A History of the Mormon Church.* New York: Four Walls Eight Windows, 2003.

Albright, William F. *Archaeology and the History of Israel.* Baltimore: The John's Hopkins Press, 1942.

Barackman, Floyd H. *Practical Christian Theology.* Old Tappan: Fleming H. Revell Company, 1984.

Beisner, E. Calvin. *Answers for Atheists, Agnostics, and Other Thoughtful Skeptics: Dialogs About Christian Faith and Life.* Wheaton: Crossway Books, 1993.

Berkhof, Louis. *Systematic Theology.* Grand Rapids: William B. Eerdmans Publishing Company, 1996.

Brown, Walt. *In the Beginning: Compelling Evidence for Creation and the Flood.* 8th ed. Phoenix: Center for Scientific Creation, 2008.

Burrows, Millar, *What Mean These Stones: The Significance of Archaeology for Biblical Studies.* New York: Meridian Books, 1957.

Buswell, J. Oliver. *A Systematic Theology of the Christian Religion.* 2 vols. Grand Rapids: Zondervan Publishing House, 1972.

Calvin, John. *Institutes of the Christian Religion.* (trans. by Henry Beveridge), Peabody: Hendrickson Publishers, Inc., 2008

Chafer, Lewis Sperry. *Systematic Theology.* 8 vols. Grand Rapids: Kregal Publications, 1993 reprint.

Chafer, Lewis Sperry, and John F. Walvoord. *Major Bible Themes.* Grand Rapids: Zondervan Publishing House, 1978.

Elwell, Walter A. ed. *Evangelical Dictionary of Theology*. Grand Rapids: Baker Book House, 1990.

Erickson, Millard J. *Christian Theology*. Grand Rapids: Baker Book House, 1986.

Free, Joseph P. *Archaeology and Bible History*. Wheaton: Scripture Press Publications, Inc., 1972.

Geisler, Norman L. *In Defense of the Resurrection*. Clayton: Witness, Inc., 1993

_____. *The Battle For the Resurrection*. Nashville: Thomas Nelson Publishers, 1989.

_____ and Thomas Howe. *When Critics Ask*. Wheaton: Victor Books, 1992.

_____ and Ron Brooks. *When Skeptics Ask*. Wheaton: Victor Books, 1990.

Hacket, Stuart C. *The Reconstruction of the Christian Revelation Claim: A Philosophical and Critical Apologetic*. Grand Rapids: Baker Book House, 1984.

Habermas, Gary and Anthony Flew (with Terry L. Miethe, ed.). *Did Jesus Rise From the Dead? The Resurrection Debate*. San Francisco: Harper & Row, 1987.

Hawking, Stephen. *The Universe in a Nutshell*. New York: Bantum-Dell, 2005.

Hengel, Martin. *Judaism and Hellenism*. 2 vols. Philadelphia: Fortress Press, 1981.

Hodge, Charles. *Systematic Theology*. 3 vols. Peabody: Hendrickson Publishers, Inc. Fourth printing, 2008.

Humphreys, D. Russell. *Starlight and Time: Solving the Puzzle of Distant Starlight in a Young Universe*. Green Forest: Master Books, 1995.

Kaiser, Walter C. *Toward an Old Testament Theology*. Grand Rapids: Academie Books, 1978.

Lindsell, Harold. *The New Paganism*. San Francisco: Harper and Row Publishers, 1987.

Mc Donald, H.D. *The Death and Atonement of Christ: In Faith Revelation, and History*. Grand Rapids: Baker Book House, 1985.

McDowell, Josh. *A Ready Defense*. Nashville: Thomas Nelson, 1993.

_____. *Evidence that Demands a Verdict*. Campus Crusade for Christ, 1972.

_____ and Bill Wilson. *He Walked Among Us: Evidence for the Historical Jesus*. Nashville: Thomas Nelson Publishers, 1993.

_____ and Bart Larson. *Jesus: A Biblical Defense of His Deity*. San Bernardino: Here's Life Publishers, Inc., 1988.

_____. *More Evidence that Demands a Verdict: Historical Evidences for the Christian Scriptures*. Campus Crusade For Christ, 1975.

Mendenhall, George E. *Biblical History in Transition*, Winnona Lake: Eisenbrauns, 1979.

Moreland, J.P. and Kai Nielsen. *Does God Exist: The Great Debate*. Nashville: Thomas Nelson Publishers, 1990.

Morris, Thomas V. *Our Idea of God: An Introduction to Philosophical Theology*. Downers Grove: InterVarsity Press, 1991.

Murphey, Cecil B. (compiler) *The Dictionary of Biblical Literacy*. Nashville: Thomas Nelson Publishers, 1989.

Nickelsburg, George W.E., and Michael E. Stone, *Faith and Piety in Early Judaism: Texts and Documents*. Philadelphia: Fortress Press, 1983.

Packer, J.I. *Knowing God*. Downers Grove: InterVarsity Press, 1973.

Pentecost, J. Dwight. *Things to Come: A Study in Biblical Eschatology*. Grand Rapids: Zondervan Publishing House, 1976.

Pétrement, Simone. *A Separate God: The Christian Origins of Gnosticism.* San Francisco: HarperSanFrancisco, 1984.

Pritchard, James B. *The Ancient Near East: An Anthology of Texts and Pictures.* 2 vols., Princeton: Princeton University Press, 1973.

Riddlebarger, Kim. *A Case for Amillennialism: Understanding the End Times.* Grand Rapids: Baker Books, 2003.

Ross, Hugh. *The Creator and the Cosmos: How the Greatest Scientific Discoveries of the Century Reveal God.* Colorado Springs: NavPress Publishing Group, 1993.

_____. *The Fingerprint of God.* Orange: Promise Publishing Co., second edition 1991.

Ryrie, Charles C. *Basic Theology.* Wheaton: Victor Books, 1986.

_____. *Dispensationalism Today.* Chicago: Moody Press, 1976.

Sayce, A.H. *Monument Facts and Higher Critical Fancies,* London: The Religious Tract Society, 1904.

Schroeder, Gerald L. *The Science of God: The Convergence of Science and Biblical Wisdom.* New York: Simon Schuster, 1998.

Shedd, William G.T. *Dogmatic Theology.* 3 vols. Grand Rapids: Zondervan Publishing House, 1997 reprint of 1888 edition.

Shultz, Herman. *Old Testament Theology: The Religion of Revelation in its Pre-Christian Stage of Development.* 2 vols. Edinburgh: T&T Clark, 1895.

Smith, A.E. Wilder, *The Natural Sciences Know Nothing of Evolution.* San Diego: Master Books, 1981.

Smith, Sam A. "Daniel 9:24-27—The Prophecy of Daniel's 70 Weeks," Internet paper: Biblical Reader Communications, 2009.

_____. "How the Amillennial Conception of the Kingdom is Developed," Internet paper: Biblical Reader Communications, 2005.

_____. "Regeneration and Indwelling in the Old Testament," Internet paper: Biblical Reader Communications, 2009.

_____. "The Biblical Basis of Premillennialism," Internet paper: Biblical Reader Communications, 2004.

_____. *The Olivet Discourse: A Reconstruction of the Text From Matthew, Mark, and Luke, with Commentary,* Raleigh: Biblical Reader Communications, 2010.

_____. *What the Bible Says About the Future.* Raleigh: Biblical Reader Communications, 2010.

Stoner, Don. *A New Look at an Old Earth: What the Creation Institutes are Not Telling You About Genesis.* Paramount: Schroeder Publishing, 1992.

Strong, Augustus Hopkins. *Systematic Theology.* 3 vols. Valley Forge: The Judson Press, 1967.

Thiessen, Henry C. *Lectures in Systematic Theology.* (Revised by Vernon D. Doerksen) Grand Rapids: William B. Eerdmans Publishing Co., 1990 reprint.

Unger, Merrill F. *Biblical Demonology: A Study of Spiritual Forces at Work Today.* Wheaton: Scripture Press, 1963.

_____. "Rethinking the Genesis Account of Creation." *Bibliotheca Sacra,* January 1958.

Walvoord, John F. *Jesus Christ Our Lord.* Chicago: Moody Press, 1969.

_____. *The Millennial Kingdom.* Grand Rapids: Zondervan Publishing House, 1959.

_____. *The Return of the Lord.* Grand Rapids: Zondervan Publishing House, 1955.

Wellhausen, Julius. *Prolegomena to the History of Israel.* Edinburgh: Adam and Charles Black, 1885.

Subject Index

Accident theory of the
atonement, 132

Adoption (by God), 210

Adoptionism, 61

Amillennialism

reinterpretation of the OT,
370

Angels, 315

classes, number,
organization, 316
demons and demon
possession, 318
function, 317
moral character, 316
nature and appearance, 315
Satan, 317

Anthropological argument, 41

Apollinarianism, 125

Apostasy (personal), 253

characteristics, 277
defined, 253
described, 253
major passages, 254
the path to, 275

Arianism, 61, 108, 124, 185

Atheism, 32

arugment from failure of
theistic arguments, 34
failure of religion, 35
linquistic argument, 34
naturalism, 33
problem of universal
negative, 36
summary, 37, 42
the problem of evil, 32

Atonement, 130, 131

extent of, 197
theories of, 131, 197

Augustine, 343, 381

Baptism (by the Holy Spirit),
144

Bible

a revelation from God, 83
allegorical interpretation, 341
canonicity, 90
compatible with scientific
fact, 75
history of, 98
how obtained, 83
its message, 76
reliability of MSS, 96
self-authenticating, 80
singularity of purpose, 75
textual criticism, 95
the Textus Receptus, 99
translation, 100
uniqueness, 73
validity of its claims, 78

the necessity of obedience
(submission), 206
the necessity of truth, 206

Fall (of man). *See* "Man, fall of

Fellowship, 270

definition, 209
the doctrine frequently
misunderstood, 270

Fidism, 37

Filling (by the Holy Spirit), 146

Finite godism, 47

Forgiveness, 207

Forgiveness of sin by God, 130

Free will. *See* total depravity

effects of the fall, 183
in Pelagianism, 184
in semi-Pelagianism, 185
limited by prior choices, 62

Future, the (eschatology), 339

allegorical interpretation, 341
Christ's future work, 135
eternity, 353
Heaven, 353
Hell, 353
historic connection between
amillennialism and
gnosticism, 341
interlude between
millennium and eternity,
352
interlude between tribulation
and millennium, 350
replacement theology, 341

the eternal kingdom, 353
the future regathering of
Israel, 345
the millennium, 350
the rapture of the Church,
346
the tribulation, 347

Gap theory, the, 292

General redemption, 132

Gifts (spiritual), 146

Glorification. *See* Sanctification,
final

Gnostic view of Christ, 124

Gnosticism

a distinctly Christian heresy,
370
anticosmic, dualistic, 368,
369, 373
beliefs, 370
determinative feature, 370
early theological influence,
367
historic connection to
amillennialism, 375
influence on eschatology, 377
mythology, 374
pseudopigraphal writings, 91
use of the OT, 374
view of creation, 384
view of God, 372, 382
view of man, 384
view of salvation, 385
view of the OT and NT, 383

God

arguments against his
    existence, 32
attributes, 51
categorization of attributes,
    51
Christ's deity, 108
eternality, 52
existence, 31, 38
goodness, 63
Holy Spirit, 141
immutability, 53
Judaic and Christian
    conception, 45
justice, 64
moral attributes, 61
moral holiness, 61
non-Christian conceptions, 45
non-moral attributes, 51
omnipotence, 54
omniscience, 53
open theism, 48
personal, 55
prayer to, 56
purposiveness, 57
righteousness, 63
spirit, 52
trinity, 57
truth, 64
will of, 65

Gospel

meaning, 252

Governmental theory of the
    atonement, 132

Grace, 224

as the means of salvation, 224
does not mean that believers
    should give in to sin, 250

law and grace mutually
    exclusive, 251

Guidance (in the will of God),
    66

Guilt before God, 130

Hawking, Stephen, 167

Heaven, 353

Hell, 353

Holiness of God (metaphysical),
    51

Holiness of God (moral):, 61

Holy Spirit, 141

a person, 141
baptism, 210
deity, 141
works, 142

Illumination, 102

Immaculate conception (of
    Mary), 127

Impeccability (of Christ), 122

Imputation

federal view, 189
headship view, 189
immediate, 188
mediate, 188
radical effect, 190
seminal view, 189
substantive view, 189
theories, 188

teleological argument, 41

Theology
  importance, 24
  importance of organization, 24
  nature of, 23
  possibility of, 23
  use of induction and deduction, 25

Tichonius (Tychonius), 382

Tongues, the gift of, 150
  cessation, 161
  desirability, 157
  earthly, not heavenly languages, 150
  extent of in the NT, 157
  misconceptions regarding, 159
  nature of gift in NT, 150
  purpose, 158
  use in the church, 158

Total depravity, 183

Traducian theory (of soul), 187

Translation (of the Bible), 100

Transmission (of the scriptures), 94

Transmission of sin, 186

Tribulation period, the, 347

Trichotomy, 177

Trinity, 57
  biblical support, 58
  incorrect views, 60
  logical support, 57

Truth
  incomplete, 25
  interrelatedness, 27

Ubiquity of Christ's human body not orthodox, 124

Unconditional election, 201. See election

Union with Christ, 209

Unlimited atonement, 132

Virgin conception and birth of Christ, 128
  no parallel in mythology, 129
  objections, 128

Will (of God), 65
  decreed, 66
  discovering, 66
  expressed, 66
  sovereign, 66

85643267R00222

Made in the USA
Columbia, SC
04 January 2018